Marketing

Made Simple

Marketing

Made Simple

Geoff Lancaster

Paul Reynolds

OXFORD AMSTERDAM BOSTON LONDON NEW YORK PARIS
SAN DIEGO SAN FRANCISCO SINGAPORE SYDNEY TOKYO

Made Simple
An imprint of Elsevier Science
Linacre House, Jordan Hill, Oxford OX2 8DP
225 Wildwood Avenue, Woburn, MA 01801-2041

First published 2002

British Library Cataloguing in Publication Data
A catalogue record for this book is available from the British Library

Library of Congress Cataloguing in Publication Data
A catalogue record for this book is available from the Library of Congress

ISBN 0 7506 4771 X

For information on all Butterworth-Heinemann publications
visit our website at: www.bh.com

 Designed and typeset by Elle and P.K. McBride, Southampton

Printed and bound in Great Britain

Contents

Foreword

One of the most challenging commissions for authors is to take a complex subject like marketing and explain it simply and comprehensively. Nevertheless, I am pleased to confirm that this is precisely what this book does. Marketing is all around us and plays a significant part in our lives whether we be consumers, business executives or students or even all three! Furthermore, the application of marketing concepts and techniques can also enhance our personal lives and ambitions, for marketing is not only an important core business function and an organization's business philosophy (consisting of putting the customer first), it can also be translated into a personal life skill, for we all have to 'market' ourselves and our ideas to others during our life in order to fulfill career ambitions and achieve our goals. With all of us living busy lives, any book that can provide an overall insight into such a subject as marketing which draws from so many disciplines is to be applauded.

It is an accepted fact that everyone can contribute to the marketing effort of their company or organization, as it is not just the preserve of the marketing department. Therefore everyone should read this book. There are chapters on every specialist area covering advertising, sales, pricing, buyer behaviour, supply channels and marketing strategy with additional chapters to cover the more contemporary areas such as customer relationship marketing. Many real-life mini case study are also included to illustrate successes and failure but above all I would like to commend this book on the basis that its user-friendly layout is a great aid to understanding. You can learn more from this book than from many of the more weightier tomes that are four times the length and three times the price! No businessman's or business student's bookshelf should be without a copy. There is no other convenient sized book of which I know that can summarize this subject so well. I guarantee that you will be regularly making reference to it and benefiting from its comprehensive contents.

Norman Waite

Formally Director of Education, Chartered Institute of Marketing and currently Director of Education, Institute of Sales and Marketing Management

1 Marketing explained

1.1 Introduction

Marketing is neither complex nor original. Personal dialogue has always existed between customers and producers. At one time craftsmen knew their customers personally and to gain repeat business they had to provide satisfactory service and 'care' for customers. The Industrial Revolution brought about mass production and mass distribution so dialogue became more impersonal. Once the link between producers and customers had been broken the problem facing manufacturers was to estimate demand for goods and this was done through distributive intermediaries including wholesalers and retailers.

Based on the principle of consumer sovereignty, marketing has developed as a management discipline. The way in which marketing is understood conditions people's perceptions of its value and the contribution it can make, to the success of an organisation and the competitive health of the economy.

Marketing is based on the premise that the customer is the most important person to the organisation. Most people think of the term 'customer' in the context of making profits. It is true that the marketing concept is more widely adopted and practised in profit-making sectors of the economy, but its principles are equally applicable in the not-for-profit sectors.

Marketing is not confined to a particular department, and a problem that companies have is the vision by other departments (and sometimes marketing itself) that somebody 'does' marketing in the process sense. Marketing is an attitude of mind or an approach to business problems that should be adopted by the whole organisation. It is only when it is understood in this wider context that marketing's role can be properly appreciated.

1.2 The customer or consumer

In 1776 Adam Smith, wrote in his classic work *The Wealth of Nations*:

'Consumption is the sole end and purpose of all production and the interests of the producer ought to be attended to only so far as it may be necessary for promoting that of the consumer.'

In this statement Smith provided the guiding theme for marketing. The key word is 'consumer' as it is the identification and satisfaction of consumer requirements that forms the basis of modern marketing. Smith's statement went on to say:

> 'The maxim is so perfectly self-evident that it would be absurd to attempt to prove it. But in the mercantile system, the interest of the consumer is almost constantly sacrificed to that of producers who seem to consider production, and not consumption, as the ultimate end and object of all industry and commerce.'

Here he said that producers made what they deemed the market needed. It is from his statement that we now define two business orientations: the first describes 'marketing orientation' and the second 'production orientation'.

To survive and prosper, a company must be aware of changes in consumer tastes to satisfy existing customers and secure new ones. Not-for-profit organisations have to justify their existence by answering to interested parties who might withdraw financial support if their goods or services do not match the requirements of the community. Satisfying consumer requirements, means it is the central focus of an organisation's activities.

People who work in specific areas of marketing, like advertising, selling, brand management or marketing research, often regard their speciality as the most important facet of marketing. Some see marketing as a collection of techniques, which, when combined, constitute a functional area of the organisation's management operations. More enlightened people see the subject as an overriding business philosophy that guides the organisation in everything it does. There is confusion because it lacks a unified definition depending on the way the subject is approached. Marketing is often viewed as:

1   A *social process* by which individuals and groups obtain what they need and want by creating and exchanging things of value.

2   A *distributive system* where there evolves a system of distribution that facilitates transactions resulting in exchange and consumption.

3   A *functional area of management* based in a specific location, which uses a collection of techniques, e.g. advertising, public relations, sales promotion and packaging, to achieve specific objectives.

4   An *overall business philosophy* in which marketing is a profit-orientated approach to business that permeates not just marketing but the entire business. The organisation's central mission is seen as the satisfaction of customer requirements at a profit (or, in not-for-profit sectors, at a maximum level of efficiency or minimum level of cost). This is achieved by focusing the attention of the entire organisation on the importance of the needs of the market-place.

5   A *targeting system* in which an organisation matches its capabilities to the needs and wants of customers. Its objective is to provide a product or service to consumers or users to achieve optimum profit or cost efficiency in the case of a not-for-profit organisation.

1.3   Definitions of marketing

The Chartered Institute of Marketing (CIM) defines marketing:

> 'Marketing is the management process responsible for identifying, antici-pating and satisfying customer requirements profitably.'

Some writers use the terms 'needs', 'wants' and 'demands' rather than customer 'requirements'. Kotler (1997) defines a 'need' as a basic requirement (e.g. food, shelter and self esteem). He defines a 'want' as a particular way of satisfying a 'need' (e.g. a person may need food, but perhaps in a curry rather than Chinese style). He defines a 'demand' as a requirement for a specific item plus an ability to purchase that item.

A more technical definition is given by the American Marketing Association (AMA):

> 'Marketing is the process of planning and executing the conception, pricing, promotion and distribution of ideas, goods and services to create exchanges that satisfy individual and organisational objectives.'

Although this second definition is not as succinct, it is more correct. The first definition highlights 'profitability', whereas marketing principles are equally applica-ble in not-for-profit organisations.

1.4   Historical development

Marketing is concerned with exchange or trade, which has existed ever since humankind was capable of producing a surplus. Historically, surplus was agricultural produce that was traded for manufactured goods like textiles. Exchange brought into existence places that facilitated trade, like fairs and markets, which allowed people to specialise in producing particular goods and services.

1.4.1   Industrial Revolution

Pre-Industrial Revolution, distribution tended to be small scale. Craft industries were based on the division of labour, resulting in specialisation and greater productivity.

1760–1830 saw the UK economy transformed, losing its dependence on agriculture with a dramatic increase in industrial production. Industrialisation took specialisation and division of labour a stage further. Enterprises became larger, production runs longer and products more standardised which resulted in the 'factory system'. Production became geographically concentrated in purpose-built mills or factories causing a migration of the population from the countryside to rapidly expanding industrial towns. Specialisation resulted in greater productivity that, in turn, reduced costs and prices.

However, the rise in job specialisation increased the need for trade. Firms could produce more than the local economy could absorb, so consumption became dispersed nationally and internationally. Producers no longer had immediate contact with their markets. Larger-scale production meant that marketing channels had to be created to facilitate distribution, enabling demand from the larger market to be met. To make goods that would appeal and sell in widely dispersed markets, it became necessary for entrepreneurs to carefully analyse and interpret the needs and wants of customers and to manufacture products that would fit their needs. This development laid the foundations of the modern industrial economy that is based on the concept of trade or exchange.

1.4.2 Types of production

We can define the main types of production in the context of this historical discussion:

❏   Project or job production is 'one off' production where every aspect of construction (project) or manufacture (job) is done as a separate activity from design to completion. Skilled personnel are needed during the design and manufacturing processes. An example of a project is the construction of a hospital and for job production it is the construction of a ship. The distinctions are unimportant. The implication is that the manufacturing process is a relatively skilled and expensive procedure.

❏   Batch production is where the numbers produced are more than one, but the skills required, and the means of production, are similar to job production and the reality is that batches produced are usually in single figures. Such production is more appropriate to manufacturing than construction.

The two types of production just described applied in manufacturing until 1913. This is when Henry Ford set up the first flow-line assembly plant in Detroit, USA. The Model 'T' Ford was developed in 1908 and was initially manufactured using batch production principles. In 1913 Ford's production line was established on the principles of the division of labour. Workers no longer assembled large components of the car, but did a single task repeatedly so it was completed better and faster. Another principle he established was that all components should be interchangeable and precisely identical. The result was that he was able to produce and sell Model 'T' cars at US$550 each, or 35% less than when they were initially introduced in 1908. Moreover, the car remained in production for 19 years and by 1925 production line refinements brought the price down to US$260.

❏   Flow (or flow-line) production (sometimes termed 'mass production') as just described is where all aspects of the manufacturing process are broken down into their simplest components of assembly. Less skilled, relatively inexpensive labour can be used so it is more cost effective. The process is quicker and end costs and prices are lower, but the marketing implication is that all products are basically the same so there is a need for a mass market. Another type of production that is similar to this, but does not involve physical manufacture is process (or continuous) production. This describes procedures that are used in extraction industries like oil production or a chemical plant, where the objective is to keep the process functioning continuously.

1.4.3 Marketing implications following developments in manufacturing

Flow line production did not receive widespread acclaim or application in the UK following Ford's revolutionary idea in the USA in 1913. This was because the UK was divided into a small number of 'haves' who owned most of the wealth and huge numbers of 'have nots' who could only afford the basic necessities of life, plus relatively small numbers of middle classes. The USA was a more equal society, so socio-economic circumstances meant that they could expand car production in the knowledge that there was a huge middle class ready to purchase these cheaper mass produced automobiles.

In the UK, the upper classes would certainly not have considered a mass-produced vehicle and the middle class market was small. The large working class population could not have afforded to run a car even if it was free. Ford did produce a number of Model 'T' cars at Trafford Park, Manchester, but these were not primarily for UK consumption.

The Second World War in 1939 was the reason for the widespread adoption of flow production in the UK. Men were conscripted for war service and women were drafted into factories, which had switched over to the manufacture of war products. As women were then largely unskilled, and war products were needed desperately, flow line technology provided the solution. Much of this expertise was provided by the Americans including switching factories from civilian to munitions production and training women in flow line production techniques.

The war ended in 1945, but rationing did not end until 1954 and it was not until the late 1950s that shortages declined, so flow production was seen as an effective way to fulfil demand. A radical post-war Labour Government under Atlee established a programme designed to remove the inequality between rich and poor. The government nationalised much of the country's infrastructure and increased Death Duties (now called Inheritance Tax). Personal taxation started at a base rate of 33% which moved up in 5% bands to 83%. Investment income commanded an extra slice of 15% on top of the top slice of tax, so effectively some people paid tax at 98%. This high personal taxation policy continued under Labour and Conservative Governments. It was not until 1979 when Margaret Thatcher, leading a radical Conservative Government committed to switching the tax burden from direct to indirect taxation, came to power that this top band of 83% was reduced to 60% in 1979, and to 40% in 1988.

The effect was a redistribution of wealth from the upper classes to the lower classes. Its effect on marketing was profound. The implication was that goods hitherto classed as luxury products became utility products necessary to live a modern lifestyle. An example is the telephone, which was a post-war luxury item but for today's lifestyle is a necessity (or utility product). Mobile phones have since moved into this utility goods classification. People now need greater amounts of goods to lead a modern lifestyle and the number of individual products needed is greater. After the war, in working class households, it was unusual to possess more than two pairs of shoes. This is unlike today where multiple pairs of shoes are the rule. Consumers not only need a greater range of products to live a modern lifestyle, they also need more individual products.

1.4.4 Expansion of trade

Entrepreneurship means matching the resources of a firm to the needs and wants of the market place. Josiah Wedgwood (1730–95) came to epitomise the traditional entrepreneur in the pottery industry with an ability to 'sense' what the market wanted in terms of design, quality and price, and then organising production and distribution to satisfy this demand at a profit. Early entrepreneurs were practising a form of marketing.

During the first half of the 19th century Britain was the dominant force in the world economy. The main factor underlying industrial growth was the development of international trade. Britain was principally a trading nation that had secured supplies of raw materials and held a virtual monopoly in the supply of manufactured goods to, and the receipt of produce from, underdeveloped countries that collectively made up the British Empire.

The first half of the 20th century saw the emergence of Germany and the United States as competing industrial powers. Although Britain faced competition from emerging nations in textiles, coal and steel, its economy continued to expand in the period to the First World War. Incomes generated in other countries resulted in a worldwide increase in total effective demand for goods and services. The value of Britain's trade increased even though its share of international trade had started to decline.

Now we have a situation where large numbers of producers compete for a share of a finite world market. In order for sophisticated products (e.g. home computers and washing machines) to be commercially successful they must be produced in volumes sufficient to bring down unit costs to a competitive level. It is no longer a case of producing good products as was the situation in time of shortages or rationing, when producers enjoyed a 'sellers' market'.

1.4.5 Modern developments

It is only since the end of the Second World War that marketing has developed as a formal business concept with a philosophy and set of techniques. Marketing was on the curriculum of major American business schools such as Harvard, Stanford and the Wharton School at the University of Pennsylvania, from the early part of this century. Consequently, many techniques of marketing were developed and first applied in the USA. It was not until the early 1960s that marketing was taken seriously by leading UK and European companies. The subject of teaching business management at degree level in the UK was generally left to the non-University sector, principally the ex-Polytechnics. In 1969 the first joint honours degree in marketing was introduced in the UK through Huddersfield Polytechnic's BA (Honours) Textile Marketing course.

For producers to achieve a sufficient level of demand, they must produce goods and services that customers will purchase in sufficient volume. The final customer's needs and wants not only have to be taken into account, but identifying and satisfying them is necessary for long-term survival. This entrepreneurial thinking has developed into the function and business philosophy that we call 'marketing'.

1.5 Different types of business orientation

There are three types of business orientation: production orientation, sales orientation and marketing orientation. Marketing maturity is a developmental process and many firms who achieve marketing orientation have done so by evolving through secondary stages of development. Many production-orientated firms develop greater sales awareness and begin to place greater importance on moving products to the consumer through the use of sales push techniques. Eventually they realise that selling plays but a single part in the operation of moving goods from the factory to the consumer. The customer becomes more than someone who is there merely to place orders. The satisfaction of consumer needs and wants becomes the rationale for everything the company does. Such companies have progressed to marketing orientation. Of all the stakeholders in a business, the customer is the most important.

An understanding of these levels of business orientation is necessary to appreciate how marketing works and each type of orientation is now discussed.

1.5.1 Production orientation

For most of the 18th, 19th and 20th centuries the primary purpose of business and industrial activity was production. The production manager was a key figure within the organisation, and it was from there that most managers reached senior positions.

Manufacturers were in a 'supplier's market', faced with insatiable demand to produce more. Firms concentrated on improving productive efficiency and bringing down costs. They produced quality products in the expectation that repeat business would be automatic. Understanding customer requirements was not important. A classic statement reflecting this thinking was:

'Build a better mousetrap and the world will beat a path to your door.'

Henry Ford also made a memorable production orientated statement that is often repeated today in relation to his mass produced Model 'T' Ford:

'You can have any colour you want; as long as it is black!'

This production-orientated philosophy was feasible as long as a sellers' market pertained. The recession that hit the USA and the UK in the 1920s and 1930s concentrated the minds of business people. To simply produce was no longer good enough as lots of goods were unsold and many businesses became bankrupt. Firms that focused attention on existing products and markets without paying attention to changing market needs ran the risk of facing obsolescence.

Some firms still have this outdated attitude and put forward reasons like: 'the consumer does not appreciate good quality'. Many firms produce excellent products, but not necessarily of the type or design that customers want to buy. The British motor cycle industry produced exceptional machines in the 1950s and early 1960s, but lost their markets to the Japanese on points of styling, design and choice.

Under production orientation the role of selling is minor and emphases are on production, finance and research and development. The sales function exists primarily to process orders.

CASE 1.1

Marks and Spencer took their eyes off the ball and are paying a heavy price.

Marks and Spencer PLC is regarded as a High street legend within British retailing. In the past they have epitomised the truly marketing orientated firm and have been seen as an example to other retailers throughout the world. Retail organisations in other countries have tried to copy the Marks and Spencer way of doing business. Perhaps the greatest accolade of all for the firm is the fact that the Harvard University Business School has, over the years, published three Marks and Spencer PLC teaching case studies which teach MBA graduates the best of retailing practice. Even today Marks and Spencer is one of the UK's leading retailers of clothing, foods, homeware and financial services. Serving 10 million customers a week in over 300 UK stores, the Company also trades in 38 countries worldwide and has a group turnover of £8 billion as of October 2001. The company was started in 1884 by Michael Marks and Tom Spencer. From humble beginnings the company went from strength to strength. Today the firm prides itself on its vision and aims to be the standard by which other retailers are measured. It prides itself on its values, which offer customers quality, value, service, innovation and trust, and on its mission, which is to make aspirational quality accessible to all.

However over the last few years Marks and Spencer has been experiencing a few problems, especially on the clothing side of the business. Customers have been shopping elsewhere. The firm no longer epitomises value and quality in the minds of its customer that it once did. Designs are lacklustre and many of the stores seem dull and shabby. Management has brought in George Davis of NEXT and ASDA fame to introduce an innovative range of new designs to stem the tide of dissatisfied customers. The company has also embarked on a programme of refurbishment to make their stores a more pleasant place to shop. Management has decided to close some of their European stores and get back to the basic business of British high street retailing. The management of Marks and Spencer, which has now been replaced by a new team, took its eye off what customers really wanted. They became product orientated and expected customer to remain loyal. They made a big mistake and have paid a big price.

1.5.2 Sales orientation

Management began to appreciate that in a competitive environment when more goods available than purchasers, it is not enough to produce quality goods as efficiently as possible. The sales concept states that effective demand must be created through persuasion using sales techniques. The sales department was seen to hold the key to economic prosperity and survival. Scant regard was taken of the needs and requirements of final consumers, but at least it was recognised that goods and services did not simply 'sell themselves'.

Peter Drucker (1954, 1973) explained the relationship between selling and marketing when he stated:

> 'There will always, one can assume, be a need for some selling. But the aim of marketing is to make selling superfluous. The aim of marketing is to know and understand the customer so well that the product or service fits him and sells itself. Ideally, marketing should result in a customer who is ready to buy!'

In a sales-orientated firm, sales volume is the criterion for success. Planning horizons tend to be short term. How customers perceive the value of goods, is of secondary importance. The implicit principles of a sales orientation are:

1   The main task is to establish a good sales team;

2   Consumers resist purchasing and the salesperson's role is to overcome this resistance;

3   Procedures are needed to induce consumers to buy more.

In the UK sales orientation was the main business philosophy in the 1960s. In the late 1950s and early 1960s, World War II shortages started to be filled and management's reaction to a slowing down in sales was to introduce 'hard sell' methods from the USA. There was little customer protection, so many consumers fell prey to such techniques with no legal redress. Sales techniques like 'putting the customer in a position where they cannot say 'No'' flourished (e.g. putting questions so they receive affirmative answers, and after having said 'Yes' so many times it is difficult to say 'No' when asked for the order). However, this kind of activity was minor in terms of dishonest practice. Many sales and advertising techniques practised in the 1960s now come under the criminal code (e.g. pyramid selling and inertia selling). It was during the 1970s that the UK Government reacted to assist consumers and much legislation was introduced to protect buyers in this era of 'consumerism'. The 1960s era of sales orientation gave marketing a bad public image, and this negative image still persists.

There is nothing immoral in production orientation as it gives customers an opportunity of saying 'No', but in sales orientation they are tricked into saying 'Yes'.

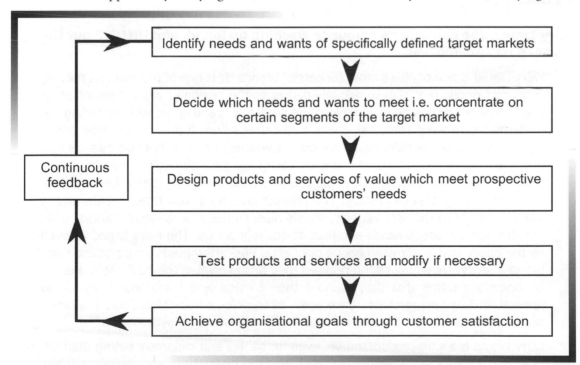

Figure 1.1 The marketing concept

1.5.3   Marketing orientation

Marketing orientation is a development from sales orientation. The marketing concept assumes that to survive in the long term, an organisation must ascertain the needs and wants of its target markets. It must then produce goods or services that satisfy these target customer requirements at a profit. The customer becomes the centre of attention and production or sales are no longer the key to prosperity, growth and survival; they are simply tools of business. The marketing concept is shown schematically in Figure 1.1:

The main difference between production and marketing orientation is that production orientated firms focus on existing products, paying little attention to the changing needs of the market. The marketing orientated firm produces goods and services it has established prospective customers will purchase.

The difference between sales and marketing orientation is summed up by Theodore Levitt (1960):

'Selling focuses on the needs of the seller; marketing on the needs of the buyer. Selling is preoccupied with the seller's need to convert his product into cash; marketing with the idea of satisfying the needs of the customer by means of the product and the whole cluster of things associated with creating, delivering and finally consuming it.'

CASE 1.2

Fairy Liquid, the consumer's favourite washing up liquid, and UNICEF put the squeeze on tuberculosis.

Fairy Liquid is one of P&G's most successful brands. It is one of the few fast moving consumer goods (FMCG's) to actually deliver to the customer what it promises. It claims to wash dishes clean and overcome grease, dirt and grime without fading the patterns on crockery, while being kind to the user's skin. It does all of these things and more. People use Fairy Liquid not only as washing up liquid but also as a general purpose cleaner. Some people use it to wash their car, although it may be a little too strong for such use. Some people use it to clean the floor, clean the toilet, the bath and even greasy machinery. The product lasts for a long time, usually cleans more dishes than the user expects, smells nice, comes in a range of colours, does not damage the user's hands and is competitively priced. The Fairy brand is loved by the public and is a trusted badge of quality. P&G attempted to change the Fairy brand a few years ago but soon realised their mistake when the public told them in no uncertain terms that they wanted their trusted and traditional Fairy brand reinstated. It is now marketed once again as traditional Fairy Liquid but in a range of attractive colours and a see-through modern-designed plastic bottle.

Fairy Liquid is a safe product to use, even for babies and children's eating utensils. It is also safe for the environment and fully bio degradable and harmless. Fairy Liquid has enhanced its reputation as a kind, 'green' product by sponsoring a programme run by UNICEF. UNICEF and Proctor and Gamble (P&G) PLC joined forces in a unique partnership to make a real difference to the lives of children all over the world. For nearly two months in 2000, P&G donated the cost of a tuberculosis vaccine to UNICEF's immunisation programme, for every two bottles of the product purchased by the public. P&G's aim was to supply four million vaccines. The general public rallied behind the company and overall the programme was a great success.

Sales orientated firms have short production runs and are preoccupied with achieving sales targets. This philosophy extends to members of the field sales force because of the way their commission and earnings are structured through the sales quota and target system. In such companies, dealing with customers is often restricted to the sales department. In a marketing orientated company, everyone appreciates the fundamental importance of customers, for without satisfied customers there is no business. To be able to progress from a 'sales' to a 'marketing' orientation, management must work to cultivate a company-wide approach to the satisfaction of customer requirements.

The main problem facing a move from sales to marketing orientation is managing organisational change. Marketing is likely to require more influence and authority over other departments to bring about an integrated organisation in which all units consistently strive to achieve customer satisfaction.

The main departmental differences and organisational conflicts this might cause are summarised in Figure 1.2.

Other department	Other departmental priorities	Marketing department priorities
Finance	'Cost plus' pricing; rigid budgetary control; standard commercial transactions.	Market orientated pricing; flexible budgets; special terms and discounts.
Purchasing	Standard purchasing procedures; bulk orders; narrow product line; standard parts.	Flexible purchasing procedures; smaller orders if necessary; wide product line; non-standard products.
Production	Long production lead times; long runs; limited range of models; supplier specified products.	Short production lead times; short runs; extensive range of models; customised orders.
Sales	Time horizon – short term; success criterion – sales; 'one-department' orientated; short-term sales.	Time horizon – long term; success criterion – customer satisfaction; whole-organisation-orientated; long-term profits.

Figure 1.2 Organisational Differences

The adoption of a proper organisational structure is a condition for marketing orientation, but is not the sole condition. A change of management titles is purely cosmetic. Such changes will not bring about the necessary shift in company attitudes. A marketing orientated firm might be organised as in Figure 1.3.

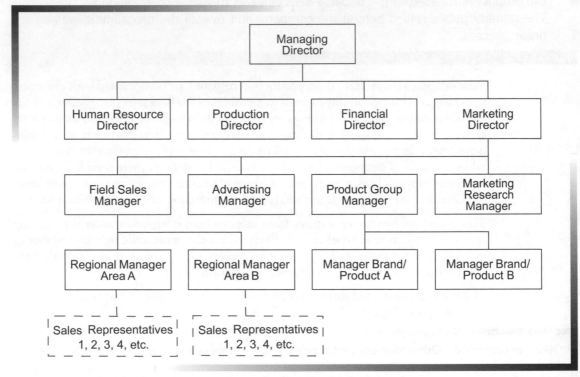

Figure 1.3 Typical organisation of a marketing-orientated firm

It is the adoption of the marketing concept as a business philosophy, rather than the organisation structure, that is important. A business philosophy that puts customer satisfaction at the centre of management thinking throughout the organisation is what characterises a marketing orientated firm.

1.6 Marketing as a business philosophy

Marketing combines the philosophy of business and its practice. These separate, yet interrelated, areas concern a basic way of thinking about business that focuses on customers' needs and wants; and a functional area of management that uses a set of techniques. Peter Doyle (1994) explains:

'The Marketing Concept is not a theory of marketing but a philosophy of business. It affirms that the key to meeting the objectives of stakeholders is to satisfy customers. In competitive markets this means that success goes to those firms that are best at meeting the needs of customers.'

To look at the subject of marketing as an overall business philosophy takes a holistic view of the discipline. Drucker (1973) explains:

'Marketing is not only much broader than selling, it is _not_ a specialised activity at all. It encompasses the entire business. It is the whole business seen from the point of view of its final result, that is from the customer's point of view. Concern and responsibility for marketing must, therefore, permeate all areas of the enterprise.'

Marketing cannot exist in a void. An integrated approach is needed. This approach drives the marketing orientated firm away from a preoccupation with selling existing products to existing customers, towards embracing new opportunities. Because of the problem of integrating the various aspects of marketing into a cohesive definition we now look at the distinctive features of marketing in summary form:

1. Marketing is dynamic and operational, requiring action as well as planning and control.

2. Marketing requires an improved form of business organisation, but on its own this is not enough.

3. Marketing is an important functional area of management, often based in a single location.

4. It is an overall business philosophy that should be adopted by everybody in the entire organisation.

5. The marketing concept states that the identification, satisfaction and retention of customers is the key to long-term survival and prosperity.

6. Business decisions should be made after considering customer requirements.

7. Marketing focuses attention from production towards the needs and wants of the market place.

8. Marketing is concerned with obtaining value from the market by offering items of value to the market.

9. It does this by producing goods and services that satisfy the needs and wants of specifically defined target markets.

10. A marketing orientated organisation is distinguished by the way it tries to provide customer satisfaction as a way of achieving its business objectives.

CASE 1.3

The Kwik-Fit Group PLC goes from strength to strength by giving the motoring public what they want and exceeding expectations.

Sir Tom Farmer opened the first Kwik-Fit Centre in McDonald Road in Edinburgh in 1971. Today the Kwik-Fit Group is one of the world's largest automotive parts repair and replacement specialists. It achieved this dramatic growth by employing the marketing concept throughout the entire organisation. Every member of staff is regarded as valuable and all have training to enable them to contribute to the satisfaction of customer needs and wants. To Tom Farmer, marketing is more than a functional area of management mainly concerned with communications. It is a business philosophy that puts customer satisfaction at the very centre of the company's mission statement. Unlike many other firms, whose mission statement is often regarded as a joke, Sir Tom takes theirs very seriously and actually delivers what it says. In January 2001 he said, 'We have tremendous opportunity at the start of the new millennium to drive the business forward again and become even more successful on a global scale. Now our aim is to double in size over the next five years – and I am confident that we have the people in place to achieve our target.' The group's vision of 5,000 service points by 2005 will be realised by an ongoing expansion programme in all the countries in which the group operates. Today more than 10,000 Kwik-Fit people service the needs of more than eight million motorists a year. Sir Tom Farmer's initiative has become a company of many initiatives and after almost 30 years of continuous growth and success, the Kwik-Fit Group remains committed to setting standards to which others can only aspire and to creating opportunities and rewards for Kwik-Fit people that remain second to none.

1.7   The marketing environment

Companies operate in a complex and dynamic external environment. A marketing orientated company has to link the resources of the organisation to the requirements of customers. This is done within the framework of opportunities and threats in the external environment. Change is a fact of life, and organisations have to adapt to this ever-changing environment. To survive they need to take account of, and adapt to, changing economic and technological conditions and monitor changing needs and wants of their target markets.

The marketing environment is made up of elements that affect the marketing function. These include inter-departmental relationships and external factors.

The marketing company's 'immediate environment' is the marketing function that ensures smooth running of marketing operations. This leads to the 'intra-firm environment', consisting of other departments like finance, production, human resource management and research, design and development. The next layer is the 'micro-environment' and consists of suppliers, customers, competitors, distributors, advertising agencies and marketing research companies.

The wider external environment is termed the 'macro-environment' and includes political, economic, socio-cultural and technological factors ('PEST'). Recently, 'legal' factors have been isolated from 'political' factors, making the acronym 'SLEPT'. Even more recently, the acronym has become 'PESTLE' with the extra 'E' standing for 'environmental'. Its latest incarnation is now 'STEEPLE' with another 'E' standing for 'ecological'. By identifying environmental trends in good time, management can anticipate their likely effect on the organisation and react quickly. Otherwise, management runs the risk of becoming a 'market follower', rather than playing a part in change and influencing events and being a 'market leader'. Companies have been divided into three categories:

1. *Companies that make things happen* identify and understand forces and conditions that bring about change. They continually adapt, and stay 'ahead of the game'. To a certain extent, they play some part in influencing the rate and direction of change.

2. *Companies that watch things happen* fail to adapt early enough to become part of that change. They have little opportunity to influence events, but usually make changes to survive. Such changes are 'reactive' rather than planned, and form a defensive 'crisis management' programme.

3. *Companies that wonder what happened* are impervious to change and fail to realise that circumstances have altered. Even when change is acknowledged, management refuses to adapt to an ever-changing environment. Such firms are unlikely to survive in the long term.

In mixed economies like those in Europe and North America, companies are allowed a great deal of autonomy when managing their business affairs. Company management has control over how they organise and integrate functions and responsibilities within the organisation. Generally, it decides what to produce, methods of manufacture and details of distribution, pricing, packaging and communications.

The business variables that are the responsibility of marketing like price, advertising, new product development, packaging and customers, to whom the product is marketed, are collectively termed the 'marketing mix'. These are discussed more fully in the next chapter.

Although marketing orientated firms have direct control over their marketing mix elements they do not formulate plans in a vacuum. Organisations are influenced by many environmental factors largely outside their control that pose both opportunities and threats to the marketing firm. Success in meeting the challenge of change depends on the ability of management in carrying out these tasks:

1 Monitoring the external environment and anticipating significant changes.

2 Evaluating likely effects of change.

3 Drawing up short, medium and long-term plans to deal with the new environmental situation.

4 Using controllable variables at management's disposal (the marketing mix elements) to successfully adapt to changes in the external environment.

5 Monitoring the plans and strategies to successfully cope with and capitalise on changed conditions and undertake corrective action where necessary.

1.7.1 The general marketing environment

The general marketing environment is made up of a number of separate but interrelated elements that are termed 'sub-environments'. Marketing management is concerned with anticipating and reacting to changes occurring outside the organisation. This external environment is termed the 'macro-environment'. The 'general marketing environment' refers to factors that impinge upon marketing management's ability to conduct its affairs successfully. A distinction is made between marketing as an overall concept or philosophy and the more narrowly held view of marketing as a functional area of management.

As a functional area of management, marketing invariably has to both compete and co-operate with other departments within the firm. We term this 'micro' area of the general marketing environment the 'intra-firm environment' and this is all part of the company's 'micro-environment'.

1.7.2   The intra-firm environment

Companies have finite resources. Marketing competes with other management functions to secure the share of budget it needs to carry out its tasks effectively. Marketing spends on advertising, exhibitions, direct mail, sales personnel, marketing research and other activities that win orders. Other departments such as production, finance and human resource management provide important services and compete for a share of the company's budget. The marketing department has to work in co-operation with these other functions, as marketing tasks cannot be achieved in isolation. Marketing managers make decisions that affect other functional areas. Likewise, decisions made elsewhere affect marketing's ability to carry out its task effectively, so it is important to appreciate the degree of conflict and co-operation in the interaction between marketing and other functions.

1.7.3   The macro-environment

Departmental rivalries and conflicts in the company's intra-firm environment can be a problem, but are within the control of management. It is uncontrollable forces in the external macro-environment that pose opportunities and threats to the company.

The term 'macro-environment' denotes forces external to the firm. Some will be closer to a company's operation than others, e.g. their suppliers, agents, distributors and competing firms. These 'closer' external factors are referred to as the firm's 'proximate macro-environment' to distinguish them from wider external forces, for example, in legal, cultural, economic and technological sub-environments.

1.7.4   The proximate macro-environment

The 'proximate macro-environment' consists of people, organisations and forces within the firm's immediate external environment. Of particular importance to marketing firms are the sub-environments of suppliers, competitors and distributors (intermediaries). These sub-environments can have significant effects on the marketing firm.

1.7.5   The supplier environment

Suppliers provide the marketing firm with raw materials, components, services or finished goods. Companies depend on suppliers who, in turn, depend on the future prosperity of the buying firm for future orders. The buyer/supplier relationship is one of mutual economic interdependence; each relies on the other for commercial well-being. Changes in the terms of the relationship can have significant effects on both parties. Any changes are usually the result of negotiation rather than unilateral action. Each party seeks security and stability from the commercial relationship that is increasingly long term.

This trend started with the development of 'just-in-time' manufacturing (now termed 'lean production') developed by the Japanese Toyota Company, but now being universally adopted in flow-line production situations. This management philosophy demands total reliability from suppliers to deliver goods that are never sub-standard ('zero defects'). Inspection for defects at the customer's works is eliminated. Components are delivered exactly when they are required so the ordering company holds virtually zero stock.

Parties to a commercial contract seek stability and security, but factors in the supplier environment are subject to change. Suppliers may be affected by industrial disputes that can affect deliveries, or a sudden increase in raw material prices may cause suppliers to raise prices. Through collection of market intelligence, the company should monitor changes in the supplier environment.

1.7.6 The competitive environment

The 'competitive environment' affects the commercial prosperity of a company. Many UK manufacturers in industries like steel and textiles have experienced intense competition from foreign products. Management must be alert to potential threats from cheaper imports or substitute products and establish exactly who their competitors are and the benefits they offer to the marketplace so they can compete more effectively.

1.7.7 The distributive environment

Many firms rely on intermediaries to ensure their products reach the end consumer. Some firms supply directly to retailers, whilst others use a more complex chain including wholesalers, factors, agents and distributors. This is more common in the distribution of consumer goods that are usually targeted at a mass market. Firms manufacturing industrial products, particularly custom made, or buyer specified rather than supplier specified, normally deliver direct to the end customer.

Because changes in the distributive environment occur slowly, marketing firms may fail to appreciate the significance of cumulative change. Existing channels decline in popularity over time, whilst new channels may develop unnoticed by the marketing firm of which a current example concerns advances in the field of e-commerce.

1.7.8 The wider macro-environment

So far we have considered the 'proximate macro-environment' which are those forces closest to the marketing firm (i.e. suppliers, competitors and marketing intermediaries). Changes in the wider macro-environment may not be as immediate to day-to-day operations, but they are equally important. The main factors comprising these wider macro-environmental elements are:

Political (and legal) factors

Economic factors

Social (and cultural) factors

Technological factors

We have mentioned that these are remembered through the acronym 'PEST'. As stated, this definition has expanded to include additional factors that make up the acronym 'STEEPLE'. However, this excessive sub-division makes for too much complexity. For our purposes, the sub-divisions under the acronym 'PEST' is appropriate. Changes in these sub-environments affect not only the marketing firm, but also those organisations that make up the proximate macro-environment. The two parts of the overall macro-environment (the proximate and wider macro-environments) are closely related. A change in the supplier or competitive environment may, for example, have its basic cause in wider changes taking place in the technological or political arenas.

Figure 1.4 shows the organisation's inner proximate marketing environment surrounded by its wider macro-environmental influences.

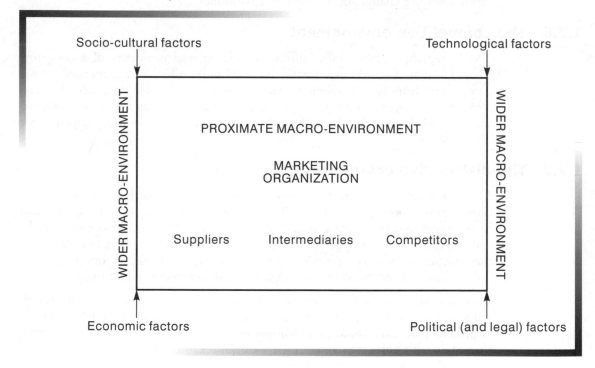

Figure 1.4 Macro-environmental factors influencing the marketing organisation

We now examine each of these wider macro-environmental influences.

Economic environment

Economic factors concern marketing firms, as they are likely to influence demand, costs, prices and profits. These factors are largely outside the control of the firm, but their effects on individual enterprises can be profound.

Changes in world economic forces can be significant to firms engaged in international marketing. Rates of inflation as well as levels of domestic interest rates are influenced by world economic factors. High levels of inflation, and high interest rates to combat inflation, affect potential returns from new investments and can inhibit the adoption of new technologies. Governments attempt to encourage economic growth through policy measures including tax concessions, grants, employment subsidies and capital depreciation allowances.

The complex interaction of economic forces and political responses made by governments in attempting to influence and manage their national economies, can have dramatic effects on individual businesses. Economic changes pose a set of opportunities and threats to the marketing organisation.

Technological environment

Technology is a variable that affects not only the marketing firm, but all elements in the company's proximate macro-environment including customers. Technology has influenced the development of many products now taken for granted. In advanced industrial nations, more mature 'smoke stack' industries such as steel making are in decline. New 'sunrise' industries like biotechnology, electronics and information technology (IT) have developed and these have had wide reaching effects on marketing organisations.

IT has revolutionised the collection, processing and dissemination of information, which has affected the whole spectrum of marketing activity. Marketing research is an illustration of how changes in practice have resulted from the adoption of new technology. Questionnaires can now be designed and coded by computer. Data collected from respondents can go directly back to the computer via optical readers. 'Computed-aided telephone interviewing' (CATI) provides sophisticated screen presentations and enormous capacity in terms of the complexity, scope and sample size of the respondents to be surveyed. Fast data processing turnaround time is the principal advantage of this system.

The impact of IT on marketing can be seen in retailing. Electronic point of sale (EPOS) data capture is now applied by retailers. A laser checkout reads a bar code on the product being purchased and stores this information. It is then used to analyse sales and reorder stock, as well as giving customers a printed readout of what has been purchased and the price charged.

Political and legal environment

Although we have examined factors in the firm's macro-environment in isolation they are interrelated. This is especially true when considering political factors. The outcomes of political decisions are seen in government legislation. Changes in the legal environment are preceded by political debate and decisions. This is why political and legal forces are grouped together, because in the context of 'PEST' the 'legal' part of 'P' is often subsumed under 'political'.

Many of the legal, economic and social developments in society are the result of political decisions put into practice. The UK Government, for instance, has followed a basically 'free market' philosophy since the late 1970s. This started with the privatisation of many previously nationalised state industries in 1979. There is now a universal belief amongst major UK political parties that business enterprise should be in the hands of private shareholders rather than being controlled by the state.

A guiding objective of economic strategy is to control inflation. Great significance is attached to controlling monetary supply, reducing Public Sector Borrowing Requirements (PSBR) and keeping public expenditure to levels commensurate with a balanced budget. Entrepreneurship, self-help, private ownership and a reasonable level of profit with the lowest possible level of taxation are viewed by government as being vital to the country's prosperity.

Many aspects of the economy are directly influenced by the political climate and, whatever industry the firm is involved in, changes in political and legal environments at domestic and international levels can affect the company.

The socio-cultural environment

Social and cultural change is concerned with changing tastes, purchasing behaviour and changing priorities. The type of goods and services demanded by consumers is a result of social conditioning and subsequent attitudes and beliefs.

A society's culture is a distinctive way of life that is not biologically transmitted, but a learned behaviour that is evolving and changing over time. Cultural influences give each society its particular attributes. Although the norms and values within a society are the result of many years of cultural conditioning, they are not static. It is the cause and effects of cultural change and the resulting revised values within a society that are of interest to marketing firms.

The UK culture was greatly influenced during the late 19th century by the Victorian Protestant work ethic that prescribed hard work, self-help and the accumulation of material wealth. Cultural values change over time, and this is particularly evident amongst the young. Evidence suggests that young people today question the desirability of a culture with core values based upon materialism.

Core cultural values are those established within a society and difficult to change. Such beliefs and values are perpetuated through the family, religion, education, government and other institutions. Core cultural values act as relatively fixed limits within which marketing firms operate.

Secondary cultural values are less strong and are more likely to undergo change. Social and cultural influences are so interrelated that it is difficult to measure the effects of each in isolation. Generally, social change is preceded by changes over time in a society's secondary cultural values.

The following are examples of changes in the secondary cultural values of UK society that have caused social changes in the UK.

❑ Changes in social attitudes towards credit

As recently as the 1960s credit/hire purchase was generally disapproved of, and shame was attached to buying goods on credit. Credit was referred to in derisory terms such as 'on tick' or the 'never-never'. It gradually became more acceptable to finance major purchases like homes and cars on credit. Today, offering credit is an integral part of marketing activity. Credit transactions are conducted openly without any hint of social stigma, and are so prevalent nowadays that the person who never finances purchases on credit is unusual. Marketing's response to this change in attitudes is seen in the large numbers of credit arrangements now on offer.

❑ Changes in attitude towards health

People are more concerned about their health than they were a few decades ago and question the desirability of including artificial preservatives, colourings and other chemicals in food. In the early 1980s, people who ate 'health' foods and took regular exercise like jogging were considered to be odd. Today, eating wholesome foods and taking sensible, regular exercise is an important part of many people's lives. Marketing firms have responded to this increase in health awareness. Many foods are promoted as 'natural' or 'additive-free' and food producers have to specify ingredients on the package. Sports equipment and sportswear marketing is now aimed at all sectors in society. The concern of what were the 'eccentric few' has grown into a huge industry. This has resulted in increased business opportunities for firms who can provide goods and services that satisfy the requirements of a new, health conscious population.

Smoking, thought to be the height of sophistication a few decades ago, is now accepted as being detrimental to health, and somewhat anti-social. Many people never start smoking, and many who do, attempt to stop. It is now the norm to look for smoking sections in public places rather than for non-smoking sections. This is an example of how changes in social attitudes have posed a significant threat, in this case, to the tobacco industry. Tobacco manufacturers are diversifying into new growth areas to counteract this decline in traditional markets.

❑ Changes in attitudes towards working women

The cliché that 'a woman's place is in the home' reflects the chauvinistic attitude held by many people a few decades ago. In the UK today, social attitudes are more enlightened and a high proportion of economically active people are women. Approximately 60% of all working women are married, combining running a home with the demands of a job or career.

Marketing firms have reacted to these changes. The fact that many women have less time for traditional 'housekeeping' has contributed to the acceptance of convenience foods as a part of everyday life. The development of convenience foods raised conflict between this development and health awareness, which has been resolved by food manufacturers producing ranges of 'healthy' additive free convenience foods.

Large numbers of working women has contributed to the development of 'one-stop shopping'. When both partners are working, leisure time is at a premium. Superstores allow people to do most of their shopping under one roof and we are now witnessing developments in home deliveries through the internet. Today it is common for couples to make a major shopping expedition to a superstore, travelling by car to purchase a week's or even a month's major supplies. Freezers and timesaving devices such as food processors and microwave ovens have all increased in popularity. Meals can be pre-cooked, stored in the freezer and rapidly defrosted and cooked when required.

❑ Changes in moral attitudes

The period of the 1960s and early 1970s has been described as being the era of the 'social revolution'. The 1960s is recognised to have seen the birth of the 'permissive society'. Throughout the 1960s, society's values went through a period of change. Attitudes towards marriage, divorce, sexual relationships, drugs, religion, family, economic and social institutions and authority in general, underwent considerable change. Many members of the 'older generation' were shocked to see how values that had been held for generations were ignored by younger people. This was a period of 'individualism' where behaviour that was previously unacceptable became tolerated and even accepted as typical.

Since the 1990s, society has experienced a reversal in moral attitudes among the young. Young people have witnessed periods of economic recession, unemployment, a dramatic increase in the divorce rate and single parent families and have seen the consequences of drug abuse, sexual permissiveness and the advent of AIDS. Today, there is a tendency amongst younger people to place a greater emphasis on health, economic security and more stable relationships.

1.7.9   Other macro-environmental factors

Factors discussed so far demonstrate the main areas of environmental change. Other sub-environments may be important to marketing management. For example, in a number of countries the religious environment may pose a source of opportunities and threats for firms.

The UK population has been stable at under 60 million for many years, but the birth rate is falling whilst people are living longer. Companies that produce goods and services suitable for babies and children (e.g. Mothercare) have seen their traditional markets remain static or decline slightly. Many such companies have diversified, offering products targeted at older age groups. A larger older sector of the population offers opportunities to produce goods and services to satisfy their needs. Services like holidays and pension related financial services are being marketed to meet the needs of this relatively affluent over 55 years old sector that has spare disposable income, even amongst those who have retired who often have occupational pensions as well as a state pension. A company called SAGA specifically set itself up to target this age group with a range of products including holidays and insurance provision.

Questions

1. What characteristics distinguish a truly marketing orientated organisation from a production- or sales-orientated organisation?

2. Why should customers be the most important persons an organisation has to deal with?

3. What is meant by the idea that marketing should be seen as an 'overall business philosophy'?

4. Discuss the idea that successful marketing stems from a sound organisational philosophy rather than the application of functional skills.

5. How is the marketing concept relevant to 'not-for-profit' organisations?

6. What do you understand by the term 'macro-environment'? Show its importance to marketing management.

References

Doyle, P (1994) *Marketing Management and Strategy* (Prentice-Hall, International, (UK) Ltd, Hemel Hempstead, UK) p 57.

Drucker, P E, (1954) *The Practice of Management* (Harper and Row, New York) p 65.

Drucker, P E (1973) *Management: Tasks, Responsibilities, Practices* (Heinemann, London)

Kotler, P (1997) *Marketing Management: Analysis, Planning, Implementation and Control*, 9th edition (Prentice Hall: Englewood Cliffs, New Jersey, USA) p 9

Levitt, T (1960) 'Marketing Myopia' *Harvard Business Review*, July–August, pp 45-46

Smith, A (1776) *An Enquiry into the Nature and Causes of the Wealth of Nations*

2 Functions of marketing

2.1 Introduction

Marketing is a business philosophy whose primary objective is the realisation of profit through customer satisfaction. This philosophy is implemented through the various functions that make up marketing. It is wrong to think of marketing as a set of activities, notably advertising, selling and marketing research. The marketing concept should be paramount in the actions of every department.

Marketing specialists are directly concerned with implementing the marketing concept and are most closely associated with the customer. Specialist activities within marketing are known as marketing's functions whose role is to identify needs of the market, interpret these, and bring products and services to the market in a manner that is appealing and that will ensure lasting customer satisfaction.

2.2 The marketing mix

Marketing strategy can be likened to a recipe. The ingredients are the marketing functions. Just as recipes vary according to the dish, so different marketing strategies require differing blends of functional ingredients. If a minor ingredient is miscalculated or forgotten, a recipe may not be successful. The same is true of marketing strategy where all functional ingredients depend on each other for success.

PRICE Level Discrimination Discount	**PROMOTION** Advertising Sales promotion Personal selling
PRODUCT Design Packaging Display Brand	**PLACE** Warehousing Transportation Service Stockholding

Figure 2.1 The marketing mix – available marketing tools to target customers

E. Jerome McCarthy suggested the idea of the 'Four Ps': product, price, promotion and place (distribution). These are the key elements of marketing. Each element possesses a number of variables (see Figure 2.1) whose emphasis can be varied to a chosen strategy. Inherent in any marketing strategy is a series of inter-mix variables as well as several intra-functional variables. These functional aspects of the marketing mix include the 'Four Ps' as well as customer segmentation, targeting and positioning which Neil Borden (1964) collectively referred to as the 'marketing mix'. The company reaches its target segments by manipulating the 4Ps.

Figure 2.2 shows how the marketing mix can be utilised. A marketing strategy takes the tools of the marketing mix and ascribes to them varying degrees of emphasis that marketing considers appropriate to a given situation. This placing of emphasis on each of the boxed items is called marketing effort which has human resource allocation as one of its components. The marketing mix concept permits management to arrive at a budget for marketing strategy and allows for this budget to be allocated across the mix and within each element of the mix.

PRICE	**PROMOTION**
Level	Advertising
Discrimination	Sales promotion
Discount	Personal selling
PRODUCT	**PLACE**
Design	Warehousing
Packaging	Transportation
Display	Service
Brand	Stockholding

Figure 2.2 A marketing strategy

As the marketing mix comprises closely interrelated elements, it is necessary to examine each to be clear about their respective roles. Each function has at least a chapter devoted to it so the purpose here is to examine each at an introductory level and to put them in perspective relative to one another.

Markets are dynamic and can be affected by a range of uncontrollable environmental variables. Marketing has to devise strategies that take account of these variables using available marketing tools. These tools of the marketing mix are controllable variables that can be creatively applied in given situations. The main constraint is the level of financial support that can be given.

2.3 Product (or service)

The marketing mix combines many factors, but consumers view marketing effort in more tangible terms of the product (or service). It is important for marketers to recognise that much of the 'want-satisfying' nature of the product is derived from consumer perceptions. The true nature of the product is how the consumer perceives it, and not what the company thinks it is or would like it to be. Marketing management must find out what perceptions contribute to consumer satisfaction, and through manipulating the marketing mix ensure that the product embodies these.

The product (or service) is the cornerstone of the marketing mix and it should be considered as the starting point for marketing strategy, because without it there is nothing to promote, or to price, or to distribute. Marketing strategies have a variety of options available for their implementation. These vary in levels of sophistication and long-term impact. Figure 3.3 illustrates the popular strategy bases that can be derived from a simple matrix, whatever individual strategic path is taken by the company.

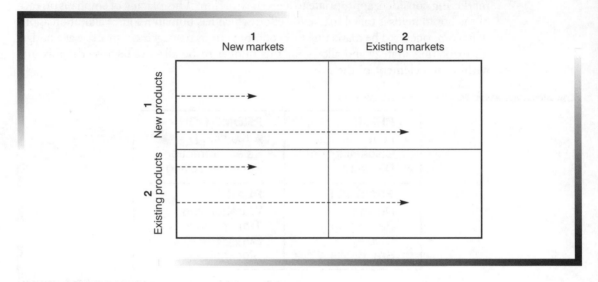

Figure 2.3 Strategic options (Ansoff's matrix)
(Originally proposed by Igor Ansoff 'Strategies for Diversification' Harvard Business Review, September 1957)

Companies who make 2/2 decisions (existing products into existing markets) lack imagination and run the risk of becoming outdated. 2/1 decision makers (existing products into new markets) represent attempts to extend the life of the product. 1/1 and 1/2 decisions are more adventurous and risky. In the long term new product (or service) development is the means of survival for the company.

CASE 2.1

Further product development on Bob the Builder character makes it acceptable to the North American market place.

UK toy characters do not always travel to other parts of the world well. Characters that are popular to a UK children's audience are not always so well received in other countries, even those countries that speak English as a first language and have a similar culture. However, dear old Bob has gone down well in the United States and the company intends to make the Bob character a worldwide brand. Bob the Builder, the children's character owned by Hit Entertainment, has itself become a big hit on the other side of the Atlantic and dramatically improved the profits of the company. The popularity of the toy character in the US was not, however, down to chance but to careful product development and positioning to make Bob attractive to American children.

Hit Entertainment is a licensing and merchandising company and holds a 70-year copyright on Bob. The character appeals more to pre school age children who are less changeable in their liking and loyalty towards toys and characters such as Bob. The company thinks Bob has a long-term future and that the Bob brand will support a growing portfolio of Bob products from dolls, videos, books, cloths and even rugs. Sales of Bob's products continue to grow in the US, and if this growth continues then there are further possibilities to expand the Bob network to other markets such as Canada, Australia, New Zealand and Japan. Bob was developed primarily for the UK market and appeals to the tastes of pre school UK children. The company is very fortunate that USA children have also taken Bob to their hearts.

Key aspects of the product as a marketing function can be summarised:

1   **Product planning**

Product/market decisions – to whom, where and in what quantity?
New product decisions, research and development programmes, marketing research studies.

2   **Product management**

Organisational decisions relating to human accountability for the success of the product.
Marketing decisions relating to the numbers and types of product on offer. These are product line and product mix elements.

3   **The physical product**

Design decisions.
Quality/image decisions.
Packaging decisions.

In service industries, the service is the product, and practitioners often refer to their individual services as 'products' (e.g. banking and insurance).

2.4   Price

Price is a potent element of the marketing mix because of its direct impact on customers, the company and the economy. To the consumer, price is a major indication of quality and an important factor in the decision-making process. For the company, the price at which a product or service is sold represents the means of recouping costs and making a profit.

The price customers are prepared to pay determines the level of demand for a product which affects the prosperity of the marketing company and the company's competitive position in the market place. Price levels have far reaching implications for the national economy. They influence wages, interest rates and government policy.

Price is not the only factor that affects demand, although in some situations companies have achieved similar levels of service, product quality and promotional support and it has become the major element of product differentiation. However, such companies have usually made major marketing efforts to reach such a state of similarity. Equally, if one company is able to differentiate its products on a non-price basis, or if a company fails to maintain the standards of its competitors, then price will decrease in importance as a determinant of product choice.

CASE 2.2

Dell Computers uses the price sensitivity of consumers to increase demand.

During 2001 all high technology sectors of the world economy experienced pressure on the demand for their products. Dell Computers were no exception. The company decided to protect its market share and improve the demand for its products by sacrificing margins and reducing prices. As a strategic response to the worrying demand figures, especially in the US consumer sector, Dell cut its prices dramatically. The global PC market was already highly competitive, with Dell's competitors such as Compaq and Gateway fighting for a share of the same market segments. Industry analysts were worried that Dell's strategic response to the demand slowdown might precipitate a huge price war in a market where margins were already slim. Dell was fortunate in enjoying a fall in its component prices and the firm was able to pass these on in the form of lower PC prices to the customer. The PC market is highly price sensitive although there is a perceived relationship between quality and price. Dell had to be careful not to damage the value of its brand in the minds of consumers through the use of aggressive price reductions.

Whilst we think of price as the monetary value, this definition is simplistic if we wish to consider price in relation to the other elements of the marketing mix. The buyer and seller have different views of price. Whatever the buyer's motive for purchasing, the economic consideration of price as an opportunity cost cannot be ignored. The decision to spend a certain amount of money on one product leaves the purchaser with less to spend on other goods or services. Whilst price is often thought of as an indicator of quality and prestige in the minds of consumers, it also has negative aspects. If the quality of two products is perceived to be equal, buyers will choose the one that is cheapest. Whilst there is ample scope for product differentiation by the seller, price remains a vital yardstick that buyers use in reaching a purchase decision.

The seller considers price as the mechanism for making profit. There is often a close relationship between selling price and the cost of production. The marketer does not, however, view price as being something that is 'attached' to the product after all the other components (tangible and intangible) have been assembled. Rather, the marketing orientated seller hopes that price will be considered as a product feature, viewed by the buyer in conjunction with other product attributes. In this way, the marketer views price as one very important element of overall marketing effort.

The pricing decision is further complicated by the fact that it can create conflict within the firm, within marketing channels and within the competitive environment. Marketing management may arrive at a price that fits in with total marketing effort and that may be considered to be optimal by the customer. The decision might be blocked by other departments who consider it to be incorrect in terms of an immediate rate of return. Distributive intermediaries may consider it to be unfair or disagree with the manufacturer's pricing policy. It might be disrupted by competitive action.

The effects of price misjudgement are quickly apparent in terms of their influence on the financial well-being of an organisation. It is economic reality that companies cannot survive unless the value of sales is in excess of costs. A price that is pitched too high may destroy the effectiveness of an otherwise well-conceived marketing mix strategy. If it is set too low and sales volumes cannot offset this disparity, it is unlikely that subsequent price increases will be readily acceptable to the marketplace.

2.5   Promotion

Promotion is perhaps the element of the marketing mix that is most subject to variation. For some products it may play a minimal role, but, for others, marketing strategy may be almost entirely based on promotion. In consumer markets, promotion often has the highest budget allocation of all mix elements. For this reason it receives much attention as a marketing function.

The effects of promotional expenditure are difficult to measure. Lord Leverhulme of washing detergent fame is quoted as saying: 'Half the money I spend on advertising is wasted. The problem is I don't know which half!'

One reason why it is difficult to evaluate is that expenditure does not create immediate tangible success. Promotion is an investment, but problems arise when fixing the promotional budget. Unlike the purchase of machinery or improved warehousing facilities, the promotional budget provides nothing that can be easily perceived as 'value for money'. This is often a source of dispute when allocating budgets. Accountants require precise outcomes, and convincing them of its value is sometimes difficult. This can be overcome by ensuring that clear, well-defined objectives are set so judgements can be made about a strategy's potential effectiveness.

Promotion covers four areas: advertising, personal selling, public relations and sales promotion. There is overlap, but these definitions help to clarify their roles:

1.   Advertising is concerned with communicating messages to selected segments of the public to inform and influence them in a manner to perceive favourably those items that the advertising features.

2.   Whilst advertising tends to be aimed at a group, personal selling tends to be tailored towards individuals. The seller may convey the same basic messages that

are included in advertising, but the presentation can be modified to suit specific situations and potential customers.

3. Public relations are a broad set of communicational activities through which an organisation creates or maintains a favourable image with its various 'publics'. These publics range from customers, company employees, shareholders and even Government. Public relations has marketing activity as its major role, but it extends to other aspects of an organisation.

4. Sales promotion involves those activities and elements of promotion not already mentioned. Temporary price reductions, displays, coupons and free sample distributions are some of the many techniques available.

The purpose of promotion is to create and stimulate demand. Most promotional strategies are likely to involve all four activities. How they are 'blended' is referred to as the 'promotional mix' or, more correctly, the 'communications mix'. Just as marketing functions go to make up the marketing mix, communications functions can be employed to form an intra-functional mix. Integration is important, as sales are easier when consumers are informed and made interested by advertising. The effectiveness of advertising is in turn increased when it is co-ordinated with specific sales promotional techniques.

CASE 2.3

Pizza Hut supplies the international space station with pizza in a publicity campaign costing $1 million.

The American fast food company Pizza Hut Inc. spent $1 million in fees, paid to the joint Russian and American international space project, for a publicity opportunity for its products. Basically the company has paid for some of its pizza products to be shipped to the international space station on a supply rocket. A video has been taken of astronauts and cosmonauts eating the pizza in a weightless space environment. The footage is likely to be used in advertising and promotional campaigns around the world. The 'stunt' will give a truly global image to Pizza Hut. The company has outlets all over the world including Russia. In appealing to potential Russian customers particularly, one video shot shows cosmonaut Yuri Usachov eating the 'space pizza' aboard the space station. When Pizza Hut first opened in Russia their fast food was very popular amongst Russian customers eager to get a taste of the West. However, in recent years demand has fallen. This publicity is intended to increase interest in Pizza Hut's fast food in Russia.

Whilst the assessment of advertising effectiveness can be difficult, it is also true that a good product, an efficient distributive system and an appropriate price are insufficient to provide overall success without the aid of promotion. A marketing mix without advertising and sales promotion might appear dull when compared to the efforts of competitors. The task of promotion is to stimulate demand by constant communication that, if effective, should convince buyers that the featured products are 'right' for their particular needs. Even when the purchase has been made, communication is necessary to reinforce to the buyer that the buying decision was correct, so positive attitudes are reinforced and repeat purchases are made. Promotion is a communication process whose objectives are to modify behaviour, to inform, to persuade and to remind.

2.6 Place

This is concerned with activities needed to move the product or service from the seller to the buyer and its origin is in the word 'placement'. To understand 'place' (or 'distribution') as a function and part of the marketing mix we divide it into two categories:

1. A structure or network through which transactions can be made so that the product is made available to the final user. This is referred to as the 'distribution channel'.

2. Once the channel of distribution has been established, the company must determine how its products can be physically moved through the distributive system. This is called 'physical distribution management' (PDM) or logistics.

2.6.1 Distribution channels

Although changes in retailing during the past 30 years have increased the number of goods that flow directly from manufacturers to retailers (in the form of hypermarkets and superstores) the use of intermediaries is still significant. Manufacturers also feature in the channel system as they receive goods (raw materials and components) from their suppliers.

The use of intermediaries in a channel system has a number of advantages:

❑ The sheer number of transactions that must be made is dramatically reduced when sales are made through intermediaries or middlemen. Instead of a manufacturer selling to numerous retail outlets or other manufacturers, distributors or wholesalers can assume this task, reducing the manufacturer's transactions to more easily manageable proportions.

❑ Middlemen relieve some of the financial burden that manufacturers need to bear when marketing directly to the end user.

❑ The manufacturer's costs of transport, storage and stock levels are reduced (the wholesaler's function is known as 'breaking bulk') and shared throughout the channel network.

❑ Channel members possess skills and knowledge of their local markets that would be impractical for the producer to possess.

The advantages of a channel system can be summarised by describing its utilities:

❑ *Time utility*: Distribution is coordinated so products reach the user or consumer when they are demanded.

❑   *Place utility*: The physical movement of goods from one place to another.

❑   *Possession utility*: Intermediaries ensure that possession is facilitated. The financial risks and burdens are reduced with the changes of 'title' (ownership) that occur as goods move down the channel towards the ultimate consumer.

❑   *Form utility*: Goods are progressively changed into a more usable form as they proceed downwards along the chain of distribution.

While the benefits of channel systems are clear these carry a cost. When responsibilities are shared or passed on, the cost to the company is loss of control. Ideally, the channel structure should operate to the mutual satisfaction of all members. In reality, there is a tendency for the behavioural dimensions of the channel to cause power struggles and conflict. Channel members may attempt to disrupt the status quo if they perceive that the actions of others are working to the detriment of their own interests. To protect themselves from such action, channel members might attempt to establish positions of power to regain control over their products that was lost when responsibility was delegated.

CASE 2.4

Vending machines are an important distribution channel in Coca-Cola's world-wide mass distribution strategy.

The Coca-Cola Corporation runs a mass distribution policy for its products and aims to get the product to the consumer no matter where they are or what they are doing. They operate an intensive channel strategy, which makes use of every conceivable channel option. Central to their policy of being able to find a Coca-Cola to drink wherever the consumer looks for one is the use of vending technology. You find vending machines offering Coca-Cola and other drinks in every 'nook and cranny' possible. On the floors of hotels next to the ice machine, in university halls of residence and teaching areas, at schools, sports centres, garages, railways stations, airports, subways, art galleries, museums and a host of similar locations. Vending machines fill the 'gap' left by the more conventional channels for this beverage. The vending machine itself is often designed in Cola-Cola livery and acts as a further advertising source for the product. The company will continue to use innovative channel strategies and new developments in vending technology will further strengthen the firm's intensive coverage of the world market.

Coca-Cola Inc. is determined this demand will be met by making the product widely available in all of the areas you expect someone to want to purchase the product. This is achieved through a policy of intensive distribution using supermarkets, smaller stores, bakeries and sandwich shops, delicatessens, public houses, cafés, sport centres, and cinemas plus a plethora of other less conventional channels.

Coca-Cola is a world icon of the twentieth century and beyond. Its distinctive name, taste, shape of bottle and design of label and can graphics make it easily recognisable by virtually everyone. Coca-Cola is truly a 'world brand' and is in great demand, particularly from the young, all over the world. In developing countries with their emerging markets Coca-Cola is seen as a symbol of Western affluence and capitalist culture. The young aspire to purchase western goods, whether in Russia or Taiwan, where Coca-Cola is almost viewed as a fashion accessory and a 'designer drink'.

The main sources of power are financial strength and strong brand leadership. For example, Kellogg Company has retained power over the supermarket chains by refusing to supply 'own label' products. Kellogg brands are strong enough for the company to control its distribution and production as indicated by their consistent advertising theme: 'We don't make cereals for anyone else'.

2.6.2 Physical distribution management

Physical distribution management (PDM) is concerned with transporting finished goods to customers, stock control, warehouse management and order processing. It is also referred to as 'logistics'. The key task of this 'place' function is to ascertain the level of service that the customer requires and to ensure that this is adhered to and the product arrives with the customer in an acceptable condition. Physical distribution, like promotion, represents a financial cost to the company. PDM attempts to achieve a preordained level of service at a cost that is acceptable to the profit objectives of the company. This is a critical area of marketing because failure to deliver on time not only negates marketing effort, but it can lose customers. PDM is important in two other ways:

1. Depending on the nature of the product, physical distribution costs can represent as much as 30% of the cost of sales (mostly transportation).

2. If a company is able to offer a particularly efficient service to its customers, this can reduce the customer's sensitivity to price.

Distribution is, therefore, an effective tool for companies pursuing a 'non-price competition' strategy.

A measure of a company's distribution efficiency is the order cycle or lead-time, i.e. the length of time that elapses between receipt of an order and delivery of the goods. Although this is significant, this lead-time has increased in importance over the past 25 years as economic pressures have compelled companies to reduce stock levels to save the working capital that helps to finance stockholding. In most industries responsibility for stockholding is placed on the supplier. Automotive manufacturers have now taken this practice to such an extreme that in some cases they only take receipt of goods hours before they are required. Such manufacturers operate a production technique known as 'just-in-time' manufacturing (JIT), more correctly termed 'lean manufacturing'. Components are offloaded from transport and directly marshalled to the production line. Sophisticated statistical techniques are employed to arrive at optimum order quantities and to ensure logistical coordination between raw material supply, production and distribution.

Management is faced with two issues when dealing with physical distribution:

1. Effort and efficiency should be judged on end results and not upon the individual efforts of separate departments.

2. The total cost approach to distribution must be considered. If a lead-time of five days is the distributive objective, this might involve maintaining high stock levels or using an expensive transport mode.

It is sufficient at this stage to suggest the following guidelines for PDM:

❑ Managers must decide the level of service a company wishes to achieve, using the overall distribution mix strategy.

❑ When a service level has been decided, the company can examine the most economic method of achieving this.

❑ The costs involved must be realistic, but the service objective should not be sacrificed in the interest of cost saving.

We conclude that it is not possible to both maximise service and minimise costs.

2.7 Personal selling

Personal selling has been discussed in Section 2.5 as a function of the communications mix. It is, however, so important that it is now considered as a function of marketing in its own right, even though it is not included separately as one of the 'Four Ps' of the marketing mix. In its promotional role, selling contributes to the overall effectiveness of marketing effort, but it has a more fundamental role to play, in that the act of selling is the end result of all marketing activity.

Sales personnel are frequently (and quite properly) requested to perform marketing tasks in addition to those of selling. These may include gathering marketing information or carrying out public relations activity. These are valuable duties, but they should never detract from their primary role of selling the company's products or services.

Selling is a process of communication. Companies promote a particular image. This may be one of a small family firm whose strong point is personal service. Others may wish to emphasise their size and ability to provide expert service. A company's philosophy of business and its particular merits combine to form a company message. It is the job of the salesperson to communicate this message to customers. Buyers usually require more than the physical product when they consider potential suppliers. As well as selling skills, it is important that companies take into account how well a potential salesperson 'fits in' with the desired company image and how well the company image will be transmitted.

The salesperson must utilise communication as a means to 'persuade' customers that the company's products can offer something that is superior to competitive products. Buyers orchestrate their needs and requirements according to a scale of preference that is linked to a budget. The selling task requires that a competitive preference scale is not merely one of financial negotiation.

Sales personnel are employed to further the communications process, but the level of direct persuasion required varies according to the particular sales task. During the process leading up to a sale (which can vary from minutes to months) the salesperson is required to adopt different approaches according to the stage the buying process has reached or to the type of customer being canvassed.

The typical caricature of a 'salesman' usually refers to the 'cold canvass' seller. The prominence of such salespersons has declined because of changing retail structures, but has re-emerged with the advent of products and services such as double glazing, cavity-wall insulation, prefabricated home extensions and life insurance policies that are 'one-off' purchases. The seller often has little prior knowledge of customers and relies heavily on persuasion. This mode of selling is unsuitable in industrial situations. 'Lead selling' is similar, but in this case the seller is supplied with lists of customers who have expressed a potential interest in the product. Such lists might be compiled from replies to advertisements or names that have been gathered as a result of a 'survey' purporting to be a market research survey. The intention of many such 'surveys' is to gain names and addresses as 'leads' for potential canvassing (this is known as 'sugging' which is short for 'selling under the guise of market research').

'Canned selling' is a method by which the salesperson is allowed little deviation from an 'approved presentation' that has been based on careful research of customer reactions, needs and objections and is a method of presentation that has been proved to be effective in certain situations. Whenever a customer objection is voiced, the 'canned sales' approach attempts to overcome this by a 'rote learned' presentation of an answer to the objection. In addition, salespersons are trained to ask question that will produce assenting answers, so it becomes more difficult for the customer to say 'No'. This method is often used when selling goods direct to the public. The level of creativity required of the salesperson is low, and sheer determination to sell is important in ensuring success, which is why such arrangements tend to be commission based.

The types of selling discussed reflect a negative image of selling that has done much to diminish the standing of selling as a profession. Most salespersons are employed selling on a business-to-business or development sales basis. They are involved in competitive selling. A high degree of product knowledge is required as well as skill in sales techniques. The salesperson attempts to achieve a sale in the face of direct competition from other offerings. Emphasis is placed on building trust. The persuasion element is concerned with convincing the buyer that the correct company has been chosen with which to do business.

2.8   Marketing information

This is the least visible of marketing functions, but it is fundamental to marketing activity. If the product or service is the foundation of marketing, it must accurately reflect the needs and wants of customers, and this can only be ascertained by gathering information.

Figure 2.4 illustrates how the information process works. To be of value, it should be a constant process. Firstly, market requirements are established and then translated into products and action. The reaction of the market is then assessed. This provides feedback and guidance as to whether customer needs have been correctly interpreted and suggests any remedial action that may be required.

In Figure 2.4, 'market' should be interpreted in a wider sense than 'customers'. It should include the macro-environment, competitive and public environments. The

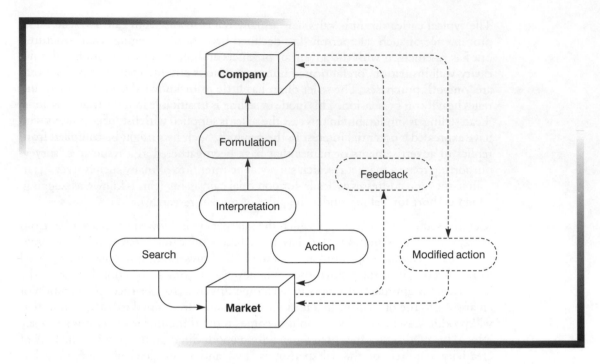

Figure 2.4 The Information Process

company should also address itself to information that can be made available from its internal management systems. The sum of all such information and activity is grouped together in a formal system designed to collect, process and report. This is known as a 'marketing information system' (MkIS), shown in Figure 2.5. The diagram shows that information sources are fed into an analytical process that guides decision making and provides feedback that can suggest modifications to the original course of action.

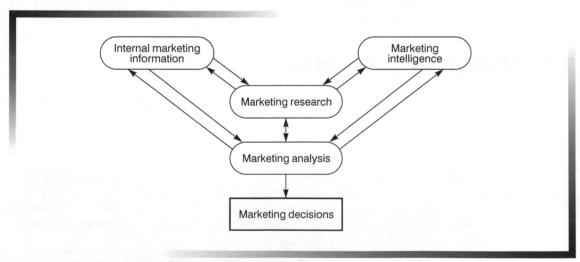

Figure 2.5 The marketing information system (MkIS)

'Marketing research' is a function of the information process. It is concerned with discovering customer needs and testing to ensure these needs have been correctly interpreted. Techniques exist for pre- and post-testing elements of the marketing mix such as advertising research and sales research. Pre-testing products and predicting their penetration into the market come under these headings. The activities mentioned relate to consumer research, in contrast to market research that focuses on the market place, including market size and market share analysis. These are some elements that come under the broader description of marketing research. Research is a continuous activity that involves fact finding, monitoring and problem solving.

Market intelligence is concerned with wider issues that affect the company as well as monitoring the market. Its role is to provide information that precedes action.

Marketing information exists within the organisation. Utilising such information depends on liaison between departments so that information is presented in a useful form for marketing analysis. Financial and sales data form the basis for customer and profit analysis. Analysis of the performance of individual products builds up a picture of company performance and provides an indication of market trends.

The various information functions have been described separately, but marketing management places reliance on them all in the decision making process. Information does not make decisions; it provides the basis for making them.

Questions

1. (a) 'Marketing is satisfying customer needs at a profit.'

   (b) 'Marketing is the process of creating unnecessary needs and wants.'

   Discuss the issues to which the above two statements give rise.

2. Consider which of the marketing mix variables is most important in:

   (a) Consumer goods marketing.

   (b) Industrial goods marketing.

3. Product is regarded as being the most important of the 'Four Ps'. Why is this?

4. Does the fact that selling is included as part of the promotional mix weaken its role as a sub-element of marketing?

5. Do you feel that channels of distribution and physical distribution management are sufficiently linked to warrant their combined grouping under 'place'?

6. Why are companies increasingly seeking to establish marketing information systems, when in the past marketing research has been sufficient for a company's information needs?

References

Borden, NH (1964), 'The concept of the Marketing Mix' *Journal of Advertising Research, June,* pp. 2–7

McCarthy, EJ (1996), *Basic Marketing: A Managerial Approach,* 12th edition, (Prentice-Hall, Homewood, Ill)

3 Consumer and organisational buyer behaviour

3.1 Introduction

This chapter examines customers in terms of their purchasing behaviour and how we can most effectively divide them into distinct purchasing groups.

Market segmentation is defined as:

> The process of breaking down the total market for a product or service into distinct sub-groups or segments, where each segment might represent a distinct target market to be reached with a distinctive marketing mix.

To improve opportunities for success in a competitive marketplace, marketers must focus their efforts on clearly defined market targets. The intention is to select those groups of customers that the company is best able to serve so that competitive pressure is minimised. The sequential steps in this process are segmentation, targeting and positioning. In this chapter we examine each of these steps, showing how they can be used to improve the effectiveness of marketing decision making. We then examine why consumers and people purchasing on behalf of their organisations make purchasing decisions.

3.2 The need for segmentation and targeting

The marketing concept puts customer needs at the centre of the organisation's decision making. Increased competition, better informed and educated consumers and changing patterns of demand have given rise to the need for effective segmentation. Market segmentation and strategies of targeting and positioning recognise that within the total market for a product, demand will differ to cater for specific tastes, needs and quantities of customers.

A market that is characterised by differing preferences is termed 'heterogeneous'. Segmentation attempts to break down this heterogeneous market into distinct subsets or segments, with customers who share similar demand preferences. Effective segmentation is achieved when customers sharing similar patterns of demand are grouped together giving rise to 'homogeneous' demand. The fact that most markets are made up of heterogeneous demand segments means that companies have to decide which segments to serve.

Varied patterns of demand require that marketers develop specific marketing mixes (i.e. product, price, promotional and channels appeals) aimed or targeted at specific market segments. Marketing writers liken this targeting versus mass marketing approach to using a 'rifle approach' as opposed to using a 'shotgun approach'.

The advantages of target marketing are:

❑ Marketing opportunities and 'gaps' (i.e sectors of unfulfilled demand) in a market may be more accurately identified and appraised.

❑ Product and market appeals (through the marketing mix) can be more finely tuned to the needs of the potential customer.

❑ Marketing effort can be focused on the market segment(s) that offer the greatest potential for the company to achieve its objectives.

3.3   Effective segmentation

The base(s) used for segmentation should lead to segments that are:

Measurable/identifiable and lead to ease of identification (who is in each segment?) and measurement (how many potential customers are in each segment?).

Accessible and lead to the marketer being able to reach selected market targets through marketing efforts.

Substantial segments that are sufficiently large to be worthwhile serving as distinct market targets.

Meaningful segments that have different preferences/needs, and show clear variations in market behaviour/response to specialised marketing efforts.

In segmentation and targeting we are seeking to identify distinct subsets of customers in the total market for a product where any subset might eventually be selected as a market target and for which a distinctive marketing mix will be developed.

It makes sense to subdivide markets as long as the resulting segments are worthwhile serving as distinct market targets with distinct marketing mixes. There are situations where complete segmentation (i.e. tailoring the marketing mix to individual customers) is essential. In office construction each customer may be treated as a separate market, but for most consumer product markets such customising would not be practical.

The following represents the sequential steps in conducting a segmentation, targeting and positioning exercise for any given product market:

1.   Select bases(s) for segmentation and identify segments.
2.   Evaluate and appraise the market segments resulting from step 1.
3.   Select an overall targeting strategy.
4.   Select specific target segments in line with step 3.
5.   Develop 'product positioning' strategies for each target segment.

6.   Develop appropriate marketing mixes for each target segment to support positioning strategies.

There is no prescribed way to segment a market. Different segmentation bases should be sought by the marketer. There are, however, a number of relatively common bases used by marketers that are now examined.

3.4 Segmentation bases in consumer product markets

3.4.1 Geographic segmentation

In international marketing, different countries may be deemed to constitute different market segments. Within a country a market may be segmented into regions that might represent individual salesperson's territories.

3.4.2 Demographic segmentation

This approach consists of a wide variety of bases, of which the more common are: age, income, sex, education, nationality, family size, family life cycle, social class/occupation and type of neighbourhood (ACORN). Demographic bases constitute the most popular for segmentation in consumer product markets, as they are often associated with differences in consumer demand and they are meaningful to marketers.

Family life cycle segmentation is based on the idea that consumers pass through a series of phases in their lives. Each phase gives rise to, or is associated with different purchasing patterns and needs. For example, the unmarried person living at home will probably have different purchasing patterns to someone of the same age who has left home and recently married. Similarly, it is recognised that purchasing patterns of adults often change as they move into retirement. The stages are defined as:

1.   **Unmarried**

This carries with it the 'young, free and single' label. Financial and other responsibilities are low, whilst disposable income is high. Young, unmarried consumers tend to be leisure orientated and are opinion leaders in fashion.

2.   **Newlymarried couples – no children**

This group does not have responsibilities of children. They concentrate expenditure on those items considered necessary for setting up a home and have been labelled 'DINKIES' meaning 'double income, no kids'.

3.   **Young married couples with youngest child under six (Full nest I)**

Here, expenditure is children-orientated. Although spending is high there is little 'spare' money for luxury items. Much recreational activity takes place in the home. Such consumers are eager for information and are receptive to new product ideas, but are particularly economy-minded.

4.   **Married couples with youngest child six or over (Full nest II)**

Children are still dependent, but expenditure has switched to more durable items for children like bicycles and computers. Fashion clothes purchases for children become important and much recreational activity takes place away from the home.

5. **Older married couples still with children at home (Full nest III)**

   Disposable income may have increased. Often both parents are working and children are relatively independent and perhaps working. Parents are likely to be more independent, with more time for their own leisure activities. Often consumer durables are replaced at this stage. Furniture purchases may have an aesthetic, rather than a functional orientation.

6. **Older married couples with no children living with them (Empty nest I)**

   At this stage the family unit has been transformed. Income is likely to be at a peak. Such consumers are, however, likely to be conservative in their purchasing patterns. Although spending power is high, marketers may experience difficulty in changing existing attitudes and preferences. These have been dubbed 'WOOPIES' meaning 'well off older persons'.

7. **Older retired couples (Empty nest II)**

   The family has made most of their major purchases of consumer durables. The thrust of fast moving consumer goods (FMCG) marketing is not directly aimed at this group as their consumption is relatively low and buying patterns are firmly established. In demographic terms, the number of older and retired consumers is increasing rapidly. Although income is probably significantly lower, many retire with occupational pensions, which allows them to lead full and active lives. The tourist industry specifically addresses these consumers.

8. **Older alone (in work)**

   Solitary survivors used to be typified by the pensioner whose spouse had died, but increasingly this category includes divorced people. This is a group to whom marketing appeals can be made on the basis of their particular circumstances. Many have come to terms with their new 'single' status and seek a more fulfilling life through the pursuit of educational, social and leisure activities. They often like to entertain at home and be entertained.

9. **Older alone (retired)**

   This category typifies the pensioner whose spouse has died. In terms of purchasing, especially if there is no occupational pension, budgeting for basic items is the main problem.

Within the family unit the marketer needs to identify the principal decision-maker and to ascertain the level of influence exerted on him or her by family members. Traditional thinking suggests that the male takes responsibility for car, garden and DIY purchases, and the female makes decisions on furnishing and kitchen-related purchases. Social changes over recent years have affected such precepts. Marketers should not approach a market with preconceptions; strategies should be based on enquiry and research into purchasing motivations.

In most developed economies socio-economic group (*social class*) categorisations are based on occupation. Of all the demographic bases for segmenting markets, social class is the most widely used because it is easily identifiable and accessible.

The social class grading system used in the UK, together with a broad indication of the type of occupation associated with each is shown in Figure 3.1.

Social Class Grading	Type of Occupation	Approx UK %
A	Higher managerial	4
B	Intermediate management	11
C1	Supervisory, clerical, administrative	27
C2	Skilled manual	30
D	Semi-skilled/unskilled	24
E	Pensioner (no supplementary income)	4
	Casual and lowest grade workers	

Figure 3.1 Social Class Categories

Doubt is sometimes expressed about social class still being a meaningful basis for segmenting markets. For example, it is often the case that the skilled manual group (C2) earn higher incomes than their counterparts in supervisory or even intermediate management (C1 or B). C2s are often able to purchase products and services that were traditionally the prerogative of the higher social grades.

Education is related to social class because the better educated tend to get higher paid jobs. Education is expressed as terminal education age (TEA). This classification is open to criticism because of an increase in the provision of part-time and distance education, meaning that although the TEA might be low, education might have been enhanced through later part-time qualifications.

Type of neighbourhood/dwelling (ACORN). New forms of classification have emerged that take account of a wider range of factors than occupation. An example is the ACORN system (that stands for '*A Classification Of Residential Neighbourhoods*'). This system takes dwellings, rather than individuals, as a basis for segmentation. It is based upon the 10 yearly return made by the householder in the census, where householders must complete their return by law. In the UK, there are around 125,000 such census districts. The ACORN system has classified each of these into one of 11 major groups. Each major group is further subdivided to yield 36 specific neighbourhood types. The 11 major groups, and some examples of how Group A is further subdivided into neighbourhood types, are given in Figure 3.2:

A	agricultural areas
A1	agricultural villages
A2	areas of farms and small holdings
B	modern family housing, higher incomes
C	older housing of intermediate status
D	poor quality, older terraced housing
E	better off council estates
F	less well off council estates
G	poorest council estates
H	multi-racial areas
I	high-status non-family areas
J	affluent suburban housing
K	better of retirement areas
U	unclassified

Figure 3.2 ACORN

The *ACORN* system is based on the idea that the area and housing in which people live is a good indicator of purchasing patterns, including the types of products and brands that might be purchased. The ACORN system goes some way to fulfilling the 'meaningfulness' criterion for segmentation.

The effectiveness of census data in providing segmentation bases has been further refined. *Pinpoint (PIN)* is based on census data and it claims 104 census variables to delineate 60 neighbourhood types clustered into 12 main types.

MOSAIC is also based on census data. It has added data on the financial circumstances of target customers living within each district by relating it to Royal Mail postcodes. Each postcode represents on average between 8–12 individual homes of a similar type and each is ascribed an individual 'Mosaic' categorisation. For example, M1 is 'High status retirement areas with many single pensioners', M17 is 'Older terraces, young families in very crowded conditions', M34 is 'Better council estates but with financial problems' and M55 is 'Pretty rural villages with wealthy long distance commuters'. This classification is a powerful database for direct mail, because individual house-holders can be personally targeted according to the type of MOSAIC categorisation of their home, and in the specific geographical area in which their home is situated. For instance it is possible to specify that a personal letter goes out to all residents in South-East Huddersfield (HD8) who fall in the M46 'Post 1981 housing in areas of highest income and status' MOSAIC category.

3.4.3   Life-style segmentation

This is referred to as *psychographic segmentation*. It is based on the idea that individuals have modes and patterns of living that may be reflected in the products and brands they purchase. For example, some individuals prefer a 'homely' lifestyle, whereas others may have a 'sophisticated' lifestyle.

Young and Rubicam, the advertising agency, put forward a lifestyle classification called '4Cs' where 'C' stands for 'Customer Type'. Consumers are put into one of the following categories:

❑   Mainstreamers (the largest group)
❑   Aspirers
❑   Succeeders
❑   Reformers

3.4.4   Direct or behavioural segmentation

The approaches to consumer segmentation described so far have been examples of *associative segmentation*. They are used where it is felt that differences in customer needs and purchasing behaviour may be associated with them. For example, if we use age to segment a market, we assume that purchasing behaviour in respect of a certain product is a function of age. Most problems which arise from using associative bases are concerned with the extent to which the bases are truly associated with a reflection of actual purchasing behaviour.

Because of the problems of associative segmentation, marketers believe that it is better to use direct bases. Such bases take consumer behaviour as the starting point for identifying different segments, and hence they are referred to as behavioural segmentation bases. These divide into three categories:

1. *Occasions for purchase* – where segments are identified on the basis of differences in the occasions for purchasing the product. In the market for men's ties, the 'occasion for purchase' might include gift-giving, subscription to clubs or societies, and purchasing a new shirt or suit.

2. *User/usage status* – where a distinction may be made between 'heavy', 'light' and 'non-user' segments for a product.

3. *Benefits sought* – is where the total market for a product or service is broken down into segments that are distinguished by the benefit(s) sought by that segment. The household liquid detergent market might include the following benefit segments: economy, mildness to hands, cleansing power and germ protection.

3.4.5   Loyalty status

A direct approach to segmenting is the extent to which different customers are loyal to certain brands (brand loyalty). Identifying segments with different degrees of loyalty enables a company to determine which of its prospective customers may be brand loyalty prone. Such a market segment is clearly attractive. Once convinced of the relative merits of a brand/supplier, such customers are less likely to switch brands.

Consumers fall into one of four categories as far as loyalty status is concerned:

1. *Hard core loyals* have loyalty to a single brand (e.g brands AAAAAA).

2. *Soft core loyals* divide their loyalty between two or more brands (e.g brands AABABBA).

3. *Shifting loyals* brand-switch, spending some time on one brand and then move to another (e.g brands AAABBCCCAA).

4. *Switchers* show no brand loyalty, often purchasing products that are lowest in price or have a special offer (e.g brands BCBAACD).

3.5   Segmentation in organisational product markets

Segmenting industrial, or 'organisational' markets suggests a number of additional bases. The most frequently encountered bases:

Geographic e.g. Northeast and Southwest, Holland and France.

Type of application/end use e.g. cotton for clothing or that used for bed linen.

Product/technology e.g. plastic bottles and glass bottles.

Type of customer e.g. retailing sector or manufacturing.

Customer size e.g. by customer turnover or by the average value of orders.

Loyalty of customer

Usage rate e.g. heavy or light.

Purchasing procedures e.g. centralised or decentralised, the extent of specification buying, quotation/tender procedures.

Benefits sought is based on the product needs that customers require from their purchase e.g. a car may be needed for the company's representatives, or for hiring out or as the chief executive's personal car.

Shapiro and Bonoma have suggested a 'nested' approach to industrial market segmentation. They identified five general segmentation bases arranged in a nested hierarchy as shown in Figure 3.3:

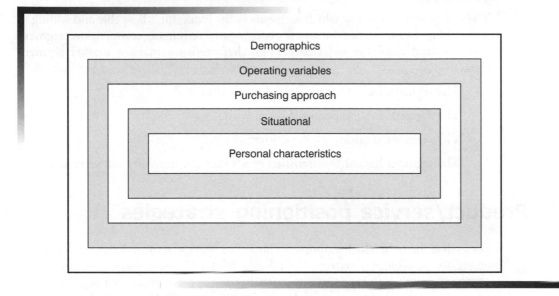

Figure 3.3 'Nested' approach to industrial segmentation

Demographic variables give a broad description of the segments that relate to general customer needs and usage patterns.

Operating variables enable a more precise identification of existing and potential customers within demographic categories.

Purchasing approaches looks at purchasing practices (e.g centralised or decentralised purchasing). It also includes purchasing policies/criteria and the nature of the buyer/seller relationship.

Situational factors consider the tactical role of the purchasing situation, which requires knowledge of the individual buyer.

Personal characteristics relate to people who make purchasing decisions.

As with consumer markets, industrial market segmentation may be on an indirect (associative) or a direct (behavioural) basis. The criteria for consumer market segmentation – being identifiable, accessible, substantial and, most important, meaningful, are also applicable to industrial market segmentation.

3.6   Assessing and selecting market segments

The marketer has to evaluate the various market segments. They should be appraised with respect to sales and profit potential or, for 'not-for-profit' organisations, the potential to contribute to organisational objectives. This requires that each segment be appraised with respect to: overall size, projected growth, extent of competition, nature of competitive strategies and customer requirements.

The company must decide which segments in the market it is best able and willing to serve. This decision must be based on company resources, competition, segment potential and company objectives. Four characteristics make a market segment attractive:

The segment has enough sales and profit potential.

The segment has the potential for growth.

The segment is not over competitive.

The segment has some unsatisfied needs that the company can serve well.

3.7   Product/service positioning strategies

For each segment in which a company chooses to operate, it must determine a product or service positioning strategy. Positioning relates to the task of ensuring that a company's market offerings occupy a predetermined place in selected target markets, relative to competition in that market. This process is called 'perceptual mapping' or 'brand mapping'.

Positioning is applicable to both industrial and consumer markets. The key aspects of this approach are based on a number of assumptions:

1.   All products and brands have both objective and subjective attributes that they possess to a greater or lesser extent.

Examples of objective attributes include:

Size:	**Large**	⇦⇨	**Small**
Weight:	**Heavy**	⇦⇨	**Light**
Strength:	**Strong**	⇦⇨	**Weak**

Examples of subjective attributes include:

Value for money	**Good value**	⇦⇨	**Poor value**
Fashion	**Very fashionable**	⇦⇨	**Old fashioned**
Reliability	**Very reliable**	⇦⇨	**Very unreliable**

2.   Customers consider one or more of these attributes in choosing between products and/or brands in a given segment.

3. Customers have their own ideas about how the various competitive offerings of products or brands rate for each of these attributes, i.e positioning takes place in the mind of the customer.

Using these criteria it is possible to establish:

1. Important attributes in choosing between competitive offerings.
2. Customer perceptions of the position of competitive market offerings with respect to these attributes.
3. The most advantageous position for the company within this segment.

CASE 3.1

Re-positioned store chain J. Sainsbury's are regarded as the best UK supermarket in the imaginative use of in store sales promotions.

J. Sainsbury plc, the UK based grocery multiple, has come to be regarded as a creative expert and pioneer in the field of retail sales promotions. Sainsbury's used to be positioned further towards the 'higher end' of the UK grocery market and tended to leave the use of sales promotions to other more 'down market' chains such as Asda and Tesco. However Tesco in particular actively repositioned its store image back in the late 1980s to attempt to attract the Sainsbury type of shopper. Sainsbury's realised it was going to lose market share and that the British public had become more 'economic' in their shopping habits for grocery items. Management repositioned the firm to compete head on with Tesco and other grocery chains. Sales promotions have been one of the tools Sainsbury's have used to achieve this successful repositioning. Over the last ten years in particular, the quality of Sainsbury's in store promotions have dramatically improved. They have become much more creative, imaginative and more interesting to the customer.

A particularly successful promotional initiative has been the use of 'buy-one-get-one-free' (BOGOF) offers. This gives the customer extra value and such offers are difficult to resist. The customer gains immediate value when purchasing the product, unlike competitions or vouchers.

Sainsbury's practices a customer retention strategy. The main tool they use is the loyalty card. Customers can apply for a Sainsbury's loyalty card that enables them to earn points. Customers save up the points and have the amount saved subtracted from their grocery bill. Sometimes different products earn extra points or BOGOF offers are combined with extra loyalty points to make the perceived value of the purchase even better.

Figure 3.4 illustrates a company proposing to enter the market for a new washing powder in which there are two major competitors. They have six brands between them: A, B, C, D, E and F. The company should first establish what customers believe to be the salient attributes in choosing between brands. In addition, the perceived position of existing brands with respect to these attributes should be investigated. If the important attributes have been found to be 'price' and 'strength' a positioning map might be drawn as shown in Figure 3.4:

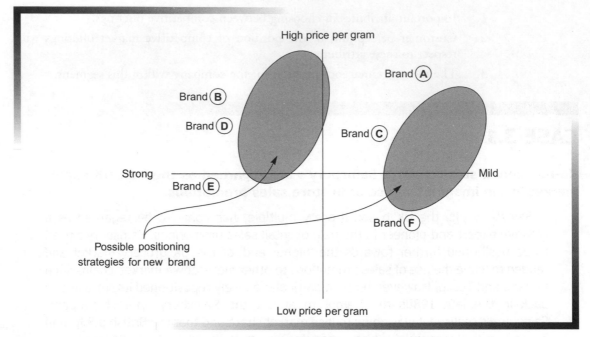

Figure 3.4 A product-positioning map for the washing powder market

Using this information, the company must decide where to position its product. A possibility is to position the new brand in the high-to-medium-price, medium-strength part of the market; another, to position it at the medium-price, milder area, both of which constitute market 'gaps' as there are no other occupants. Both strategies would give the new brand distinctiveness, as opposed to positioning the brand next to an established brand.

The final step in segmentation, targeting and positioning is to design marketing programmes that will support the chosen positional strategy in selected target markets. The organisation must determine how to apply the '4Ps' of its marketing mix, i.e what price, product, distribution (place) and promotional strategies will be necessary to achieve the desired position in the market.

3.8   Consumer buyer behaviour

As consumers, we are exposed to various experiences and influences. Some of us are more susceptible to change and influences than others. Some of our responses to our environment are the results of our psychological make-up. As our situations change, opportunities emerge and we are subjected to a wider range of influences to which we may consciously or subconsciously respond, in a positive or negative manner. Changes in circumstances may arouse inherent needs or promote new needs and wants in our consumption patterns.

The task of marketing is to identify these needs and wants and develop products and services that will satisfy them. The role of marketing is not to 'create' wants, but to fulfil them. It is more valuable to find out why something is required. Only by gaining a deep and comprehensive understanding of buyer behaviour can marketing's goals be realised in terms of becoming better equipped to satisfy customer needs effectively. This should lead to the establishment of a loyal group of customers with positive attitudes towards the company's products.

Consumer buyer behaviour is defined as:

> 'The acts of individuals directly involved in obtaining and using goods and services, including the decision processes that precede and determine these acts.'

The underlying concept of consumer buyer behaviour relates to a system in which the consumer is the core, surrounded by immediate and wider environments that influence individual goals. Such goals are satisfied by consumers passing through problem-solving stages leading to purchase decisions.

CASE 3.2

Many United States consumers reduce spending because of uncertainty about the future.

Evidence suggested that many areas of the US economy were beginning to slow during 2001. This was particularly evident in high technology sectors where growth slowed considerably and share prices plummeted. However retail sales seemed to be reasonably buoyant as consumers relied on a little 'retail therapy' to get over the economic gloom. The US economy was slowing, President Bush expressed concern for jobs and Allen Greenspan, Head Of the US Federal Reserve, cut interest rates to try and increase business confidence and get businesses investing and consumers spending. Large tax rebates also put more money in people's pockets and thus pumped spending power into the economy. However this was before the September 2001 atrocities in New York and Washington D.C. In September 2001 retail sales within the US fell at the greatest rate since 1992 prompting economic commentators to say with some confidence that the US economy is officially in a recession. Amongst those sectors hardest hit was clothing stores (5.9% down), restaurants and bars (5.1% down) and car dealers (4.6% down). Generally consumers feel very uncertain about the future and the prospect of war and further attacks on the US have not exactly put consumers in a spending mood.

3.8.1   Cultural and social influences

Marketers attempt to recognise how culture shapes and influences behaviour. Culture is a group of complex codes and passed down through generations as determinants and regulators of human behaviour in society. These codes include attitudes, beliefs, values, language, religion, art, music, food, housing and product preferences. Culture is 'learned' behaviour that is passed down over time. It is reinforced in our daily lives through the family unit and educational and religious institutions. Cultural influences concern unwritten laws about what is socially acceptable or appropriate in a given society. A comparison of Far Eastern culture with that of Western Europe provides an example of two opposing cultures. Even within Western Europe, distinct cultures exist like differences in social etiquette and sense of humour. Such general norms of behaviour are called 'social mores'.

Much of our life is directed by 'customs'. Similar to 'mores' in how they have developed, customs can be deeply rooted in society. Many customs are so deeply rooted that they have not changed or evolved to reflect the existing cultural climate.

Laws relating to Sunday trading and the licensing of alcohol consumption in the UK are examples of laws that have been changed to catch up with the liberalising demands of changing attitudes within UK society. Marriage remains an important custom, but this has been challenged in the UK over the past 25 years. When couples began to set up home and raise families outside of marriage, society adopted an attitude of condemnation. Today, society has adopted a more relaxed attitude to those who ignore the convention. The belief that work is 'good for the soul' has faded since the beginning of the last century. It is no longer accepted that work should be viewed as toil. Most employers attempt to ensure that the workplace is a pleasant environment, realising that this might increase productivity.

A major cultural change in the twentieth century that accelerated since the 1950s and 1960s, is the changing role of women in society. Working women in particular, have helped to change traditional stereotypes that society applied to women. Increased independence and economic power have not only changed the lives of women, but have also influenced society's and women's own perception of their socio-economic role.

Society has witnessed profound changes in family structure. We have moved away from the extended family towards the 'nuclear family'. Increased mobility of labour has produced a migrant attitude with family units moving from their native regions and close relatives. Average family size is smaller and couples wait longer before having children.

We must also consider subcultures. Immigrant communities have become large enough in many countries to form a significant proportion of the population. Marketers must consider these because of their interactive influence on society and because, in some cases, they constitute sufficiently large market segments for certain products. Subcultures are often identified on a racial basis, but this is a limited view. Subcultures can exist within the same racial group sharing common nationality and such bases may be geographical, religious or linguistic.

3.8.2 Social class

Social class is an easily recognised social influence. Marketing research uses social class as the main criterion in identifying market segments because such a classification reveals a lot about likely behaviour. Social class is an indicator of lifestyle and its existence exerts a strong influence on individual consumers. Whatever income level a consumer, evidence suggests that basic attitudes and preferences do not change radically. It is reasonable to expect the 'level of consumption' to rise in line with income.

As consumers, we usually identify with a particular class or group. Often it is not the social class that is revealing, but that to which the consumer aspires. People who 'cross' social class barriers usually begin when they are young. Income and/or education allow younger people to adopt different lifestyles to their parents. The young consumer tends to absorb the influences of the group to which they aspire, and gradually reject the lifestyles of their parents and relatives. For this reason, occupation is a useful pointer to social class.

'Eating out' and drinking wine were once pleasures only enjoyed regularly by upper class members of society. Today, wine marketers target a wide variety of consumers, with a different marketing mix strategy being designed for each identifiable group of consumers.

In studying social class (like all marketing topics) this must be approached without preconceptions. Marketers should not associate social class or social stratification with any derogatory interpretations. Marketing should not make value judgements in its distinctions of social class; a 'lower' or 'higher' social grouping does not imply inferiority or superiority. Such a classification is simply an aid to the identification of market segments and how they should be approached. The marketer makes decisions on the basis of information revealed by objectively designed research as this is the way that changes in behaviour can be identified.

3.8.3 Reference groups

A reference group plays a more intimate role in influencing consumers. This is a group of people whose standards of behaviour influence a person's attitudes, opinions and values. In general, people tend to imitate and seek advice from those closest to them. Reference groups can be small, for instance, the family group. The frame of reference can be large, for instance, a person in a certain occupation is likely to behave in the manner expected and accepted by the wider occupational group. Reference groups are also found in a person's social life, for instance, membership of a club or organisation concerned with a particular hobby or interest. Members are unlikely to deviate far from the behavioural norms laid down by the group, whether these are formal or informal norms.

One only needs to consider school children to see how reference groups influence the individual. Although children are strongly influenced by their family group, they are also keen to 'fit in' with their peers, and it is never long before a new fashion or fad has spread through classrooms.

The smaller and more intimate a reference group, the stronger its influence is likely to be. Within a small social circle like the family, advice and opinion of those who are regarded as knowledgeable will be highly influential. Such people are termed 'opinion leaders'. There can also be influences from outside the group. 'Snob appeal' is often initiated by the existence of opinion leaders outside the immediate reference group who are emulated by 'opinion followers'. Some companies make a direct appeal to this 'snob' instinct where marketing strategy is based on the assumption that if a company can make its products acceptable to social leaders and high-income groups, then other sectors of the population will follow. Credit and charge cards are frequently marketed in this manner. The strategy is to create an aura of exclusivity around the target group, whilst effectively intimidating and isolating those not targeted. For a number of charge cards, this strategy is reinforced by income requirements set down for applicants. American Express is such an example, and the company also makes appeals within reference groups (i.e cardholders) encouraging them to enlist new members.

Of all the different reference groups, the family is very important, as it is the most intimate. The nature of the family can be identified by considering the 'family life cycle', of which nine stages have been identified in section 3.4.2.

3.8.4 The consumer as an individual

We have considered consumers in the context of a wider environment where behaviour is influenced by cultural and social structures. We now consider the individual from an 'inner' or psychological point of view.

As the consumer is a physical being, it is not difficult to define characteristics that may provide explanations for some of those actions described collectively as 'behaviour'. Consumers are male or female; some live in towns, some in the country; they are tall, small, young or old. The psychological state of the consumer, on the other hand, is more difficult to determine. The consumer as an individual absorbs information and develops attitudes and perceptions. A personality also develops that affects the needs that person has as well as the methods chosen to satisfy them. Any need-satisfying action is preceded by a motive. Although each person is physically and psychologically unique, marketing must attempt to identify patterns of behaviour that are predictable under given conditions. This increases the marketer's ability to satisfy human needs, which is an essential aim of marketing.

CASE 3.3

Hope for British agriculture as demand for organic produce starts to take off.

Consumer behaviour in relation to the purchase of agricultural produce has changed over the last ten years. It does not seem long ago that people who preached the 'organic gospel' such as HRH The Prince of Wales were seen by many as 'cranks'. Today things are different. The British public has faced an almost unbelievable series of serious public health scares concerning the food they eat. Most of this has been concerned with meat, particularly BSE and the foot and mouth epidemic.

Worries about the effect of chemicals on human heath and on the natural environment has also led consumers to look for more healthily produced food. Today organic farming is about the only area of growth within the UK agricultural sector. Many supermarket chains now offer a full range of organic produce. Margins for producers of these tend to be more realistic and consumers are less price sensitive when purchasing such products. More and more farmers are moving to fully organic production and to some the shift in consumer tastes has been a lifesaver.

The psychology of human behaviour is highly complex. We now focus on five psychological concepts that are recognised as being most important in understanding buyer behaviour:

1. The *self-concept* or *self-image* is an important determinant of individual behaviour because it is concerned with how we see ourselves and how we think other people see us. Individuals attempt to create a picture of themselves that will project an image that is acceptable to their reference groups. This inner picture of the self is communicated to the outside world by behaviour. The behaviour that interests marketers is that relating to the consumption of goods e.g the choice of clothes, type of house, choice of furniture and the type of car. The sum of this behaviour is a statement about self and lifestyle. Consumption is a non-verbal form of communication about the self.

   The individual will reinforce his or her image through verbal statements that express attitudes, feelings and opinions. Individuals express their self-image in a way that relates to their inner ideal and this promotes acceptance within a group. The self-statement can also be an expression of rejection. For example, the music, fashion and values adopted by the punk movement of the early 1980s showed a reference group process in action. The punk movement rejected much within society that was considered to be 'normal' amongst other reference groups.

   Marketing makes direct appeals to self-image through advertising. Many car advertisements appeal to the executive whose self-image is one of confidence, success and sophistication. Self-image is influenced by social interaction and people make purchases that are consistent with their self-concept. We know that we are subjected to a changing environment and changing personal situations, so individuals are involved in a constant process of evaluating and modifying their self-concept.

   Personality has a strong influence on buyer behaviour. It is a component of self-concept. This is universally accepted, but attempts to further define personality are less clear and more difficult to bring together. It is too simplistic to define personality merely as 'an expression of the self-concept', but we do know that certain purchase decisions are likely to reflect personality.

   Marketers can learn from psychoanalytical theories of personality, which suggest that we are born with instinctive desires that cannot be gratified in a socially acceptable manner and are repressed. Indirect methods of satisfying such desires are sought by individuals attempting to find an outlet for repressed urges. The implication for marketing is that a consumer's true motive for buying certain products may be hidden in the subconscious. The stated motive may be an acceptable translation or substitution of the inner desire. The task of marketing is to appeal to inner needs, whilst providing products that enable these needs to be satisfied in a socially acceptable way.

2. *Motivation* can be defined as goal-related behaviour. Marketers are interested in motives when goals are related to purchasing activity. For a motive to exist there must be a corresponding need. Motives and needs can be generated and classified in a variety of ways. Some motives like hunger, thirst, warmth and shelter are physiological; others, such as approval, success and prestige are psychological.

Having made this distinction, we can distinguish between instinctive motives such as survival and learned motives that include cleanliness, tidiness and efficiency. Still further, we can distinguish between rational economic motives and emotional ones. However, this last distinction is imprecise, as many purchase decisions are compromises due to economic restrictions.

Motivation is a complex psychological issue. Marketing accepts a classification of motives, based on a 'hierarchy of needs'. Although this classification has been refined, the model developed by A H Maslow in 1943 (Figure 3.4) serves us best.

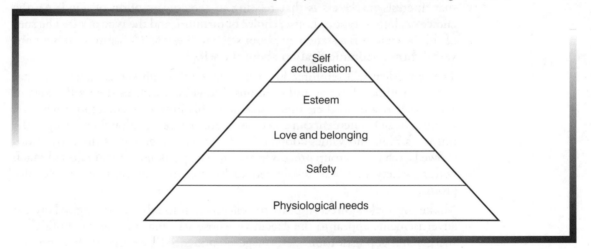

Figure 3.4 Maslow's hierarchy of needs
(*Source*: Maslow A H, 'A theory of human motivation' Psychological Review, 1943, 50.)

He suggests that an individual's basic (or lower-order) needs must be satisfied before higher needs can begin to influence behaviour. As lower-order needs are satisfied to an increasing degree, so the individual will have time and interest to devote to higher needs. Once the basic physiological needs (e.g hunger, thirst) are satisfied the individual will concentrate on acquiring products and services that increase social acceptability (e.g love, sense of belonging) and status (e.g esteem, recognition). Maslow describes the ultimate need as one of 'self actualisation'. When somebody has reached a stage in life when basic needs, love and status have been achieved, then the overriding motivation is one of acquiring products and carrying out activities that permit self expression. This may take the form of hobbies or new purchases that have been desired for a long time, but have been put off until lower order needs have been satisfied.

Within this hierarchy, marketers should appreciate that enormous differences exist between individuals. Furthermore, a product that represents self actualisation for one person may only satisfy a lesser need for another. 'Motivation research' has developed considerably in recent years, although this is more directly related to specific consumer and product problems. The hierarchy of needs has general value in that it suggests that marketers of consumer products should understand and direct their effort at the higher needs of their customers. The theory also provides a useful starting point when attempting to explain the basic nature of consumer behaviour.

3.   Whilst motivation is an indication of willingness to act or respond to a stimulus, *perception* concerns the meaning that the individual attaches to that stimulus. Marketers are concerned with influencing a buyer's perception of their products in relation to factors like price, quality and risk. The product image is only as good as the consumer's perception. The product can only exist commercially if the consumer perceives that it is capable of satisfying a need.

Any stimulus is received through the five senses (sight, hearing, smell, taste and touch). The perception of the stimulus is, therefore, affected by its physical nature, by the environment of the individual and by the buyer's psychological condition. Before any kind of perception can take place, it is necessary that the stimulus (in this case the product) receives attention.

An individual is exposed to many stimuli most of which receive little attention. Advertisers face a challenge in attempting to ensure that their particular stimuli receives the consumer's attention. Having gained that attention, the marketer must then attempt to ensure that it is retained. At this point the task becomes difficult because perception is selective. Consumers are only exposed to a limited proportion of all marketing stimuli (we do not read all newspapers and magazines or visit every part of a store). Even when a medium of communication has our attention (e.g a magazine or television) we do not read or watch every advertisement that appears. Individuals have many sources of stimuli competing for their attention. An advertisement may only be partially read and easily forgotten and consumers only act on information that is retained in the mind. Marketers cannot provide 'blanket' exposure for their products, so they attempt to place their stimuli where they think they are most likely to be well received.

Although marketers might succeed in gaining maximum attention, perhaps because the consumer has a need and is involved in the search process, there is no guarantee that the consumer's perception of a particular product will be the interpretation that the marketer desires. Previous experience of a similar product might influence perception, either favourably or unfavourably. Experience, environment, immediate circumstances, aspirations and many other psychological factors combine to shape, alter and reshape consumer perceptions.

4.   *Attitudes* can be defined as a set of perceptions that an individual has of an object. In this context, the 'object' could be a person, product or brand. For example, our attitude towards imported goods might be influenced by our feelings about the country of origin. Similarly, our attitudes towards a particular store are likely to be favourable if the staff are helpful. The influence of reference groups on the individual tends to be strongly emphasised. Social interaction plays a major part

in attitude formation. These may be learned from others, particularly from the family group, and attitudes that are developed in our formative years tend to remain with us throughout our lives.

Attitudes can be positive, negative or neutral and are often firmly held. This is not to say that they never change. A bad experience can rapidly alter an attitude from positive to negative. Marketers must be aware of the importance of generating favourable attitudes because once established, they are hard to alter.

5.   *Learned behaviour* results from experience. This is important when studying behaviour because it has the power to change attitudes and perceptions. Learning not only provokes change, but can reinforce a change in behaviour. A consumer may 'learn' that certain products are more acceptable than others to their family or reference group. In an attempt to promote this acceptability, the purchaser might reinforce this with similar repeat purchases. A prime objective of marketing is to influence consumers so they make a first purchase. The ultimate success of marketing effort depends on a succession of repeat purchases.

Such learning is referred to as *conditioned learning*. Each time a satisfactory purchase is made, the consumer becomes less and less likely to deviate from this behaviour. This results in brand loyalty.

Learning also occurs as a result of information received. The information source may be a reference group or a direct approach to the consumer through advertising, publicity or sales promotion. For learning to have an affect on motives or attitudes, a company's marketing effort should attempt to direct these changes towards products or services that are offered for sale.

The consumer is subjected to the combined and continuous influences of the socio-economic and socio-cultural environments as well as to closer social interaction and psychological influences. Having examined the more complex issues that make up consumer behaviour, we reflect on the consumer's fundamental goal. When consumers buy products, their aim is to achieve satisfaction. This might seem obvious, but it has two important implications:

(i)   Those companies who provide most satisfaction will enjoy the greatest success. (The basis of the marketing concept.)

(ii) Because consumers are constantly engaged in a search for satisfaction, competition will always have potential appeal.

It is not, therefore, sufficient to simply provide satisfaction. Companies must strive to maintain and improve the level of satisfaction they provide.

For most consumers, it is unlikely that total satisfaction will ever be achieved. Consumers are subject to a variety of competing demands that are made on limited financial resources. Satisfaction may only be partial and is a compromise. Satisfaction is not simply a function of spending power, although it is suggested that freedom from financial worries helps us to achieve material satisfaction that, in turn, contributes to satisfaction. Consumer goals also have an aesthetic component that concerns quality of life rather than simply quantities of products or services that money can buy.

CASE 3.4

British Airways and other airlines face a huge fall in demand, as people are more worried about flying.

Since the terrorist attacks in the USA on September 11th 2001, many people have become nervous about flying. Airlines world-wide have seen a tremendous drop in demand for their services. Some, like Swiss Air are close to bankruptcy, and the first bankruptcy was Sabena, the Belgian airline. Fear of flying has always been a problem and airlines have done everything they can in the past to reassure the public that flying is safe. Statistics show that people have more chance of being injured or dying in a car crash, by being hit by lightning, or being involved in an accident simply crossing the road, than being involved in an air crash. However this was before the terrorist attacks in the USA on September 11th 2001. Things are different now and many people are simply refusing to fly. British Airway (BA) was losing cash at around £125 million per month in the months after the terrorist attacks in the US. The collapse in consumer confidence has sent costs spiraling. BA has greater resources than most other European airlines and experts are predicting it will be able to survive in the long term if it can control costs. There are likely to be three European airline survivors; these are BA, Air France and Lufthansa. Other European airlines are financially vulnerable and could easily go the way of Swiss Air. BA has announced huge price incentives to get people back on their aircraft. These incentives include 'kids go free' offers and big reductions on the seat price for European flights. However, it is not price that is the problem for many people but fear. All the world's airlines must find a way to convince the international and domestic flying public that flying is safe. This is the only way to restore consumer confidence and alter the behaviour of potential customers.

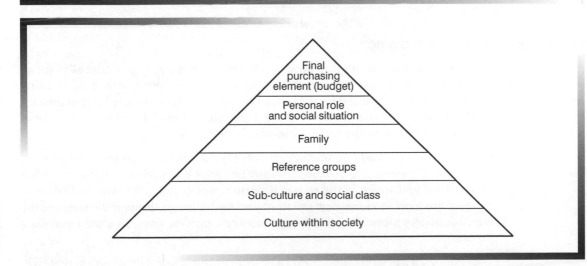

Figure 3.5 Purchasing Influences on Individual Consumers

To summarise the various elements that affect consumer choice, a hierarchy is proposed in Figure 3.5 that shows how purchasing behaviour is affected from a general cultural level to an individual purchasing level. It is suggested that each subsequent stage in the hierarchy might have a more direct effect on the purchase decision than the preceding stage.

3.8.5 Models of consumer buying behaviour

Psychological influences and wider forces that influence consumer behaviour exert themselves continually on the consumer and are explained as models of consumer behaviour. They relate to the buyer/decision process and new product adoption. Consumer behaviour is complicated and behavioural models attempt to reduce this complexity. Our aim is to bring together a series of simple models that attempt to explain buying or decision processes.

The purchase of washing powder is simpler for consumers than purchasing a home. Whatever the buying task and associated degree of complexity, it is important to consider the steps leading to a purchase as a problem-solving process. Figure 3.6 is a simple model of the mental states that the buyer passes through during the buyer/decision process (referred to as AIDA):

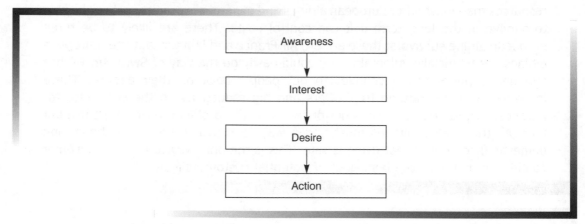

Figure 3.6 Mental states of buying

The consumer is aware of many products, but does not desire to purchase all of them. This state of awareness becomes important when a product is perceived as being capable of solving a problem for the consumer. For this reason, Figure 3.7, put forward by Robinson, Jarvis and Wind (1967), is a more useful model of the buyer/decision process, as it describes the activities involved.

Our daily lives are made up of constant processes of problem recognition and need satisfaction. e.g we need to buy food to satisfy hunger. Our problem is in deciding what kind of food and which brand to purchase from which store. We may be invited to a special function to view a new model of car. Again, we go through the stages of the buyer/decision process. By identifying or feeling a need or want, we then recognise a problem.

For example, if a person moves from an apartment to a house with a garden, there will be a need to mow the lawn. He or she will be aware that lawnmowers exist, but this

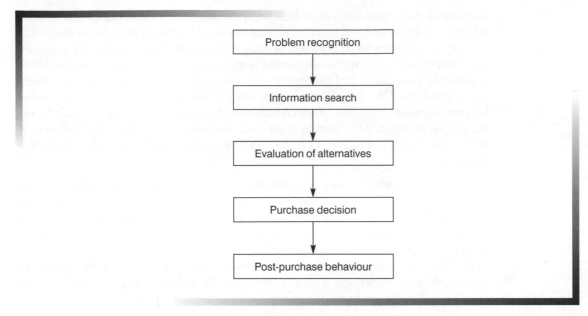

Figure 3.7 Steps in the buyer/decision process

basic knowledge may constitute the full extent of awareness at that time. The next move towards purchase involves information search.

A lawnmower might be an expensive purchase and the potential consumer knows little about the product, so the search process will be extensive (in contrast to the routine search carried out for everyday shopping items). Information sources may include family, neighbours, colleagues and the promotional material provided by lawnmower manufacturers. The degree of influence each source has on the consumer will depend on the nature of the product and on the individual making the purchase. We know that reference groups, in particular the family, exert a powerful influence. In this lawnmower example, the consumer might turn to parents or friends for advice. Marketing provides information through advertising and promotion. Magazines and newspapers may feature articles and advertisements for selected products. By the time that the search nears completion, the consumer will already have rejected certain lawnmowers as being unsuitable in some way, perhaps being too expensive or too large. A mental short-list of possible alternatives will remain.

This 'short-list' allows the consumer to move to the next stage of alternative evaluation. The merits of each potential product must be assessed so the chosen product maximises (or optimises) satisfaction. Often an ideal choice is arrived at relatively easily, but financial limitations may oblige another alternative to be the product finally chosen.

In the information search period, the short-list is usually easy to establish and basic product features bring about attraction or rejection in the consumer's mind. When the range of choices has been narrowed down, evaluating alternatives is more difficult. This is especially true when the potential purchase has involved an extensive search process. Here, the differences in product features or attributes are likely to be subtle, and more difficult to evaluate. For fast moving consumer goods (FMCG) brand image is a major influence.

Looking at the buyer/decision process from the marketer's viewpoint, segmentation strategy can be considered most influential during the information search stage. The consumer eliminates some products because they are clearly unsuitable. By segmenting the market a company is eliminating some consumers from the total population of potential purchasers, and concentrates its efforts on segments more likely to 'short-list' its products. As well as segmenting the market, the marketer's task is to ensure that because of certain attributes, products receive high ratings in consumers' minds during the evaluation stage. The creation of product attributes is, therefore, the 'fine tuning' of a segmentation strategy. This can only be achieved after detailed marketing research.

Finally, the 'purchase' decision must be made. When making a choice, the consumer is not only seeking satisfaction, but also aiming to reduce risk as much as possible. This is especially true when a product is costly and where the purchase decision is accompanied by anxiety. Anxiety relates to making the right choice from the chosen product group, and also the wisdom of having made the purchase in the first place. In the lawnmower example, there will be a wide range of demands on the consumer's limited resources – perhaps it would have made better sense to pay a gardener and purchase a new carpet instead?

Immediately prior to purchase, the consumer is still susceptible to 'influence'. A decision not to purchase may be the result of influence from any of the motives discussed. Conflicting influences only serve to confuse and make the purchaser's task more difficult.

The salesperson can be highly influential at this stage. Forcing a sale at the final delicate stage might help the salesperson's commission, but from a marketing standpoint, it does not give lasting satisfaction that will lead to repeat business. Often a 'hard sell' will only reinforce post purchase anxiety or what is termed *cognitive dissonance*. Marketing strategies should concentrate on reducing anxiety and perceived risk.

Marketing must be aware of post-purchase behaviour, because it affects repeat sales. Consumers can be satisfied or dissatisfied with their purchase. If the consumer is satisfied then all is well. Advertising must take care not to build consumer expectations too high as this might lead to post purchase dissatisfaction. Post-purchase dissonance, or cognitive dissonance, is a feeling of dissatisfaction or unease that consumers sometimes feel following a major purchase. The product itself may be perfectly acceptable, yet the consumer feels that the purchase was not as good as it could have been. Despite these feelings of unease, consumers frequently rationalise and reinforce their purchase decision. In other words, they will not wish to voice their dissatisfaction and thus appear to be poor decision-makers in the eyes of their reference group. They prefer to feel positive in their own minds about their actions and actively seek information that justifies their purchase, and tend to ignore any doubts they might still have.

If consumers publicise dissatisfaction, marketers face a problem because of the power and influence attached to 'word of mouth' communication. Clearly, if a product is faulty, or does not perform as claimed, the marketer is at fault, but marketers should be aware of the negative effects of dissonance that can occur when there is nothing wrong with the product. Whilst actions to reduce potential dissonance can be taken before the purchase is made, marketers can do much to instil confidence and security after the sale. Companies should attach as much importance to after-sales service as to making the sale. This reduces dissonance in the case of genuine complaints. In addition, companies can follow up sales by some form of communication with customers. This builds customer confidence in having made the 'right' decision and some advertising campaigns are expressly designed with this purpose in mind. The term that relates to this kind of after sale follow-up is 'customer care'.

The importance of each stage of the buyer/decision process varies according to the type of product under consideration. For some products, the whole process is routine, whilst for others each stage involves long and careful consideration. Understanding how the buyer/decision process works is vital to the success of marketing strategy. Where purchases are routine, the task of marketing is to break that routine in favour of the company's own products. The more complicated the buying process, the more important it is that companies assist consumers in the problem-solving process, and reassure them that their choices have been made wisely.

3.8.6 The adoption process

As marketers we are interested in consumer behaviour as it relates to new products. Figure 3.7 showed a sequential model of the buyer/decision process. It referred to general situations for existing products or services and focused initially on problem solving and search. Figure 3.8 shows the adoption process for an innovatory new product. The key difference between the two models is that the adoption model begins with awareness. The marketer's task is to create awareness and then guide the consumer through subsequent stages of the process. Without awareness of the new product, consumers cannot even consider it as a solution to need-related problems.

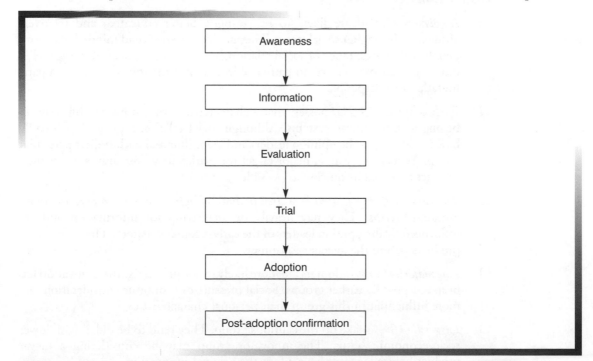

Figure 3.8 Stages in the adoption process

Awareness can come about by 'word of mouth' communication or from the company's marketing effort. The individual is exposed to the innovation and becomes aware of its existence. If the product has initial appeal, further *information* is sought. At the *evaluation* stage, the consumer weighs the relative advantages of the new product against those of existing products.

The consumer might make a temporary adoption by obtaining a sample to *trial*. Many new FMCG products are produced in a 'trial size' and companies distribute free samples. If a trial cannot be made, the likelihood of adoption decreases.

At the *adoption* stage the decision is made whether or not to *adopt* (buy or begin to use) the product. *Post-adoption confirmation* is when the product has been adopted and the consumer may be seeking reassurance (unconsciously perhaps) that the correct decision has been made. New information has been accepted and prior information rejected. Often, after an important purchase, cognitive dissonance is present and it is important that this is countered by providing a follow-up.

The rate of adoption for an innovation depends on the type of consumer to whom the product is marketed. Some adopters are receptive and readily adopt innovations, whilst others are slow to adopt. This 'diffusion of innovation' process suggests that certain groups of consumers are highly influential and this influence will 'diffuse' through to subsequent consumer groups. We should, however, be aware that consumers who exhibit particular adopter characteristics for one category of product might behave differently in the adoption of another product type. Diffusion of innovations is dealt with more fully under product related issues, but in the context of consumer buying behaviour we can see how each adopter group possess distinct characteristics:

❑   *Innovators (2.5%)* are likely to be younger, better educated, and relatively affluent with a higher social status. They are likely to be broad minded, receptive people with a wide range of social relationships. Their product knowledge relies more on their own efforts to gather objective information, than on company literature or salespeople.

❑   *Early adopters (13.5%)* possess many characteristics of innovators, but tend to belong to more 'local' systems. Although social relationships are less broadly based, they tend to be opinion leaders and are influential within their particular group. As such, they are a major target for marketers whose aim is to get their product accepted as quickly as possible.

❑   *The early majority (34%)* is a group that is slightly above average in socio-economic terms. They rely heavily on marketing for information and are influenced by the opinion leaders of the early-adopter category. They adopt new products before the average consumer.

❑   *Late majority (34%)* adopters are more likely to adopt because the innovation has been accepted by earlier groups. Social pressure or economic considerations are more influential in this group than personal characteristics.

❑   *Laggards (16%)* make up the cautious group. They tend to be older, with lower socio-economic status. The innovator group may be considering a newer product before laggards have adopt the original innovation.

3.9   Organisational buying behaviour

Industrial buying is often thought to be devoid of the emotional connotations attached to consumer behaviour. Industrial purchasers cannot afford the luxury of impulse buying. They are employed to make purchases for a specific reason. They have budgets and possess a great deal of knowledge about what they purchase. Although there are differences, parallels can be drawn between industrial and consumer buying.

First, note that the heading of this section is *organisational* buying behaviour, whereas we are now referring to *industrial* buying behaviour. *Organisational buying* is a wider term, used to cover industrial, retail and public authority (called 'institutional') purchasing. However, the principles of organisational buying are, for our purposes, the same as those for industrial buying.

The main similarity between organisational and consumer buying is that both activities represent a need-satisfying process. Although these needs may differ, they must be fully understood before any selling approach is made. Figure 3.9 is a model of the industrial buyer/decision process and it closely resembles the earlier model that was used for consumers. The approach and reaction to new products is also broadly similar. Diffusion theory can, for example, be applied with equal validity to both types of buying situation. In fact, a 'diffusion of innovations' model was originally developed by Everett Rogers for consumer markets. We should also consider that

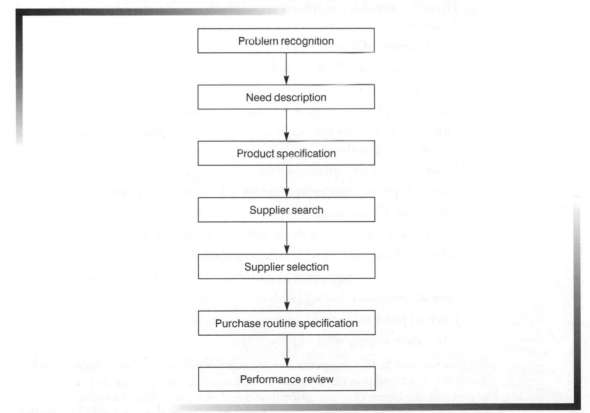

Figure 3.9 The organisational buyer/decision process

organisational buyers are subject to influences that affect purchase decisions: marketing effort from suppliers; reference groups within organisational situations; as individuals, buyers are influenced by their own psychological make-up.

An important question that organisational marketers must ask is: 'Who is the purchasing decision maker?' This does not necessarily correlate with rank within the purchasing organisation. Those with little formal power may be able to stop a purchase or hinder its completion.

Five major power bases are highlighted:

❑ *Reward*: Ability to provide monetary, social, political, or psychological rewards to others for compliance.

❑ *Coercive*: Ability to provide monetary or other punishments for non-compliance.

❑ *Attraction*: Ability to elicit compliance from others because they like you.

❑ *Expert*: Ability to elicit compliance because of technical expertise.

❑ *Status*: Compliance through a legitimate position of power in a company.

Organisational markets tend to differ from consumer markets in these respects, which should be considered when developing a sales communication strategy:

Rational buying motives.

Derived demand (i.e purchases are normally for intermediate rather than end products).

Small number of buyers.

Larger number of influences on buyers.

Often a multi-person decision making unit.

Buyers and sellers are sometimes in competition with each other.

Organisational customers can have more economic power than the companies who are selling to them.

Many products are 'buyer specified'.

Economic relationship between buyer/seller is often long term.

High value of purchases.

Distribution is most often direct, rather than through an intermediary.

Sales are often preceded by lengthy negotiation.

Company policies may act as a constraint on the buyer's decision making.

Possible 'reciprocal' buying (we buy from you and you buy from us).

Unequal purchasing power amongst customers.

Often there is geographic concentration.

We now focus on factors that pertain to organisational buying. Most evident is the fact that it is a structured process. Consumer markets attract much attention and it is easy to overlook the extent of organisational sales and purchases. When a consumer makes a purchase, a derived demand is created for a series of component parts and materials that make up the finished product. We can add to this complex chain of supply, companies who buy and sell machinery, packaging materials and maintenance equipment. To control this constant flow of goods and services, companies must organise their buying activity so that they have:

❑ Constant supply (in terms of quality and delivery).

❑ A system of control that monitors performance specifications.

❑ A review policy towards existing and potential suppliers.

A formal process should be established for each of the components that make up the organisational purchasing process as outlined in Figure 3.9.

For most consumer purchases the negative aspects of an ill-advised purchase are short-term and can be easily rectified. For a large company, perhaps operating 24 hours a day, even a small quality or delivery problem from suppliers can cause considerable loss in terms of 'down-time' on the production line. Organisational purchasing must, therefore, adopt a formal structure because of the responsibility it carries.

Just as consumer behaviour varies according to what is purchased, organisational purchases demand more or less attention according to their nature. The purchasing approach for each type of product bought can vary according to the buying situation.

Three major types of organisational buying situation are identified:

1. The *new task* is challenging. The product item may be a new machine or a new component for a new product. Although buyers have professional expertise, they will be relatively unfamiliar with the product and must engage in extensive need description, product specification and supplier search.

2. *Straight rebuy* purchases involve little effort and are routine in the prevailing purchasing structure. This routine is only possible because careful buying in the past has established a reliable supply pattern.

3. The *modified rebuy* can occur because the product specification or supplier has to be changed. Although the basic product is known, change involves risk. Often organisational buyers keep alternative sources as minor suppliers, occasionally buying a little from them to test their reliability in preparation for greater participation should the need arise.

The principal difference between consumer and organisational buying is that the latter usually involves group decision making. Here, individuals have different roles in the purchasing process, and this idea was first put forward by Frederick E Webster (Jr) as the *Buying Centre*. The categories described are now more commonly referred to as the *Decision Making Unit (DMU)*.

❑ *Users* work with or use the product and may be involved in product specification.

❑ *Buyers* have authority to sign orders and make purchases. Their main role is supplier negotiation and selection.

❑ *Deciders* are people who make the buying decision (most often the decider and the buyer is the same person).

❑ *Influencers* can affect the buying decision in different ways (e.g technical people may have helped in some way to develop the product specification).

❑ *Gatekeepers* control the flow of information to and from people who buy (e.g a purchasing assistant or the Chief Buyer's secretary).

Organisational buyers' roles vary widely according to the complexity, size and structure of the company. In technical sales situations, the salesperson may hardly meet the buyer until the technical department is satisfied with the salesperson's offering. The buyer then takes over to handle commercial aspects of the sale. Many companies employ buyers who are skilled in purchasing procedures, but who have limited technical knowledge of products being purchased. Some employ buyers for specific product areas. In some cases buying is centralised and in others it is devolved to separate manufacturing units. Whatever structure exists, the organisational salesperson should appreciate that the buyer is not necessarily the final decision-maker.

Marketers should be aware of factors that influence organisational buyers. Although many are beyond control of the seller, it is essential that problems faced by purchasers are understood and marketing and sales strategies designed accordingly. Figure 3.10 highlights the main tools available to industrial markets when targeting DMUs.

Figure 3.10 Targeting the DMU

With a move towards holding less stock because of JIT (lean) manufacturing, reliable delivery is vital. Buyers require a constant stream of quality products. Relationships tend to be long term and it is as common for buyers to visit sellers as for sellers to visit buyers (the traditional pattern). This is termed *reverse marketing* where buyers take the initiative and actively source suppliers who match up to their criteria of reliability of quality and supply. There is the notion of 'open accounting' where price does not enter the equation, as buyers are fully aware of the price make-up of components that are being marketed. In turn, suppliers also know the profit margin of their customers, and buyers and sellers agree a common mark-up. If the supplier then devises a way to make the products more cheaply without compromising quality, the savings are divided between the supplier and the customer. Needless to say, such agreements have long term implications from which has been coined the term 'relationship marketing'.

Organisational buyers are, of course, individuals as well as purchasing professionals. In many markets, the levels of service and price are such that there is little to distinguish suppliers. The personal impression that the buyer or DMU has of a supplier's image, as well as any personal rapport that the salesperson can achieve, can influence buying decisions. Just as purchasers of consumer goods are responsive to actions of sellers, organisational buyers have individual personalities that sellers must acknowledge. Some buyers may be aggressive, devious or indecisive. Human factors also extend to the buyer's relationships with colleagues within the organisation. Companies have 'personalities' in terms of attitudes and policies.

Whilst we can identify factors common to both consumer and organisational buying behaviour, the two markets should be approached differently. The needs of consumers should be ascertained and marketing response communicated through appropriate media. In organisational markets, buyers and sellers do communicate through media, but rely heavily on personal communication. Organisational buyers work to obtain satisfaction for the company's 'physical' needs, whereas consumer behaviour has a psychological basis. Although organisational buyers have a clear rationale for their actions, this is not to say that they are insensitive to psychological influences. This is especially important in a market where the products on the offer are essentially similar.

Questions

1   How far do you agree with the idea that advertising is the biggest single influence on consumer buying behaviour?

2   What do you understand by the term 'product positioning'?

3   It is common to think of the purchasing decision processes of organisational buyers as being devoid of emotion. How far would you agree with this?

4   Using two consumer and two organisational goods/services examples suggest segmentation bases for each of these.

5   (a)   *Organisational buying.* How does organisational buying relate to industrial buying?

(b)   *Targeting.* Explain each of the following types of targeting strategy:

(i)   Undifferentiated marketing

(ii)   Differentiated marketing

iii)   Concentrated marketing

6   Discuss the considerations that should be made when selecting specific target markets.

References

Maslow, AH, (1954), *Motivation and Personality,* (Harper and Row, New York), pp. 80–106

Robinson, PJ, Jarvis, CW and Wind, Y, (1967), *Industrial Buying and Creative Marketing,* (Allyn & Bacon, Boston, Mass.) p. 14

Shapiro, BP and Bonoma, TV, (1984), *How to Segment Industrial Markets,* (Harvard Business Review), May-June, pp. 104–110

4 Advertising, promotion and public relations

4.1 Introduction

Advertising, sales promotion and public relations form three elements of the 'marketing communications mix'. The fourth is 'selling' which is sufficiently important to warrant a separate Chapter 5. Sales promotion also includes the area of 'direct marketing'. This is a contemporary area of marketing that has increased in popularity because of the development of effective databases and improved information technology. This area, too, is sufficiently important to warrant a separate Chapter 6. Communications can be broadly defined as:

The process of establishing a commonality or oneness of thought between a sender and a receiver.

Two ideas are highlighted:

❑ Communication is a process that has elements and inter-relationships that can be modelled and examined in a structured manner.

❑ Oneness of thought must develop between sender and receiver for true communication to occur, which implies that a sharing relationship must exist between them.

It is incorrect to view the 'sender' (e.g. a speaker) as the active member in the relationship and the 'receiver' (a listener) as passive. Consider a person (the sender) speaking to somebody who is not really listening (the intended receiver). It might appear that communication is taking place, but thoughts are not being shared, and there is no communication. The reason for this lack of communication is the passivity of the intended receiver. Although soundwaves are being transmitted, the listener is not receiving and sharing thought. A human receiver can be likened to a television set. The television can receive signals from several stations, but it will receive only the station to which the channel selector is tuned. Human receivers likewise receive stimuli from many sources simultaneously and, like TV, a person selects one source to be 'tuned to' at any moment. Both sender and receiver must be participants in the communicative relationship for thoughts to be shared. Communication is something one does *with* another person, not *to* another person. We see the relevance of this analogy later.

4.2 Marketing communications overview

In its simplest form, the communications process can be modelled as shown in Figure 4.1. The *sender* (source) is a person or group having a thought to share with some other person or group (the *receiver* or destination). The *message* is a expression of the sender's thoughts. It may take the form of the printed or spoken word, a magazine advertisement or a television commercial.

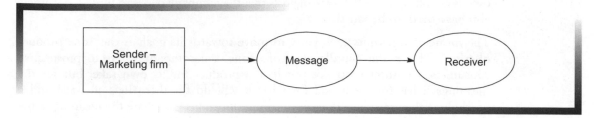

Figure 4.1 A simple communications model

Figure 4.2 shows a more sophisticated model. *Encoding* is the process of putting thought into a symbolic form controlled by the sender. *Decoding* is the process of transforming message symbols back into thought by the receiver. Both are mental processes. The message is the manifestation of the encoding process and the instrument used in sharing thought with a receiver. The *channel* is the path through which the message moves from the sender to the receiver. *Feedback* recognises the two-way nature of communications. Individuals are both senders and receivers and interact with each other. Feedback allows the sender to monitor how accurately the message is being received and gives a measure of control. In marketing, it is acknowledged that often an advertising message is not received by customers as originally intended. Based on market feedback, the message can be re-examined and corrected.

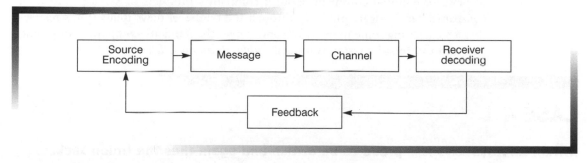

Figure 4.2 A more detailed model of the communication process

4.3 Elements of marketing communications

4.3.1 The marketing communications process

Traditionally, promotion (in its broadest sense of one of the '4Ps') has been viewed as the organisation's link with prospective buyers. Promotion is now seen as only one element of an organisation's effort to communicate with customers and to view it simply as promotion is to take too narrow a perspective. Marketing mix variables, as well as other actions, must be seen as part of the total message the company conveys to consumers about its 'offerings'.

If we consider the company and its customers as systems, we see they share certain characteristics. For example, the company may wish to increase profits and market share or enhance its reputation among competitors, the trade, and its customers. These desires are expressed in the form of goals that the company needs to fulfil. Consumers also have needs to be satisfied.

The means that permits each party to move towards its goals is the 'total product offering'. This is the 'bundle of satisfactions' the company offers to prospective consumers. Consumers do not purchase a product for its own sake, but for the meanings it has for them and for what it will do for them in a physical and a psychological sense. Thus, the role of communications is to share the meaning of the company's total product offering with its customers to help them attain their goals and move the company closer to its own goals.

4.3.2   The marketing communications mix

Advertising is a visible form of mass communications that is non-personal and paid for by an identified sponsor. *Personal selling* is communication in which a seller attempts to persuade prospective buyers to purchase the company's product or service. *Sales promotion* relates to short-term marketing activities that act as incentives to stimulate quick buyer action. e.g. discount coupons and free samples. These promotional activities (advertising, personal selling, and sales promotion) are variables over which the company has control. The company has less control over *publicity*. Like advertising, publicity is a form of non-personal communication to a large group of people, but unlike advertising, it is not paid for by the company. Publicity is usually in the form of news or editorial comment about a company's products or services. However, companies can instigate publicity through the release of news items (press releases) thereby exercising some measure of control over the publicity component of promotion and this broader vision is termed *Public Relations (PR)*.

CASE 4.1

British Airways says it is proud to be British and again flies the Union Jack.

After enormous pressure and large numbers of public complaints, the beleaguered airline British Airways is admitting it was wrong. The firm is to scrap the last of its ethnic tail-fins and repaint its remaining aircraft with a derivative of the Union Jack. The change of policy follows the decision of the then Chief Executive Robert Ayling to paint the fleet in a range of abstract designs from around the world. This new livery policy was supposed to show customers that BA was a world airline. Commentators, including Margaret Thatcher regarded the move as treachery and a signal that the airline was ashamed of its British connection. Despite huge public pressure BA's leader 'Bob' Ayling insisted he had done the right thing. He is no longer with the company. Mr. Ayling said at the time that customers perceived British values as 'aloof and stuffy' and that BA needed to change its image if it wanted to become a truly global company. The present Chief Executive, Rod Eddington has a different view. He thinks that customers around the world find British values attractive, and link them with quality, reliability and safety. Independent research also showed that both British and overseas customers want to 'fly the flag'. The 'wavy' version of the flag known as the 'Chatham Union Jack' is already used on Concorde, which started flying again in 2001. The livery makeover will also extend to all areas of the firm's marketing communications including advertising, promotions, public relations, baggage tags, business cards and even the BA uniform.

The blend of promotional activities is called the *promotional mix*, or the *communications mix*. Emphasis placed on each element in the mix varies according to:

❑ Product type.

❑ Consumer characteristics.

❑ Company resources.

❑ Competitors in the same industry who may have different communication mixes depending on size of firm, competitive strengths and weaknesses, and managerial style.

Other communications elements with which promotion must be coordinated are the product, price and distribution channels. Elements of communication include brand name, package design and colour, size, shape, trademark and the product itself. These characteristics provide the consumer with messages about the total product offering. Price also has important communications value and is often used by sellers to imply quality in the product.

Retail stores (place) have significant communications value. Stores, like people, possess 'personalities' that consumers perceive and associate with the merchandise located in the stores. Two stores selling similar products can project different product images to prospective consumers, particularly when the customer is not familiar with the product category. For example, a camera sold exclusively through specialist camera shops may project an image of higher quality than one sold in a discount department store, even though they may be comparable.

Marketing effectiveness depends on communication. The market is activated by information flows. The buyer's perception of the seller is influenced by the amount and type of information provided by the seller and the buyer's reaction to that information. According to this view, marketing relies heavily on information flows between sellers and buyers. Marketing involves decision-making, whereas marketing communication is the process of implementing marketing decisions. This requires enactment of the communications process. The company's message is a combination of product, price, place and promotional stimuli it transmits to the marketplace, and communication takes place when consumers in the market interpret these stimuli.

4.3.3 Defining marketing communications

We have described what marketing communications is to convey an idea of the breadth of the area. A practical definition defines marketing communications as:

Presenting an integrated set of stimuli to a market target with the intent of evoking a desired set of responses within that market target. Setting up channels to receive, interpret and act on messages from the market to modify current company messages and identify new communications opportunities.

This definition recognises that the company is both a sender and a receiver of market-related messages. As a sender, a firm in a competitive environment must attempt to persuade consumers to buy the company's brands to achieve profits. As a receiver, the company must attune itself to the market to realign its messages to its market targets, adapt them to changing market conditions and take advantage of new opportunities. This is in line with the marketing concept.

4.4 Message source

The nature of the source of a message in the communications process can have a great influence on receivers. Some communications are more persuasive than others, and how successful they are depends on how credible the audience perceives them to be. Credibility is the set of perceptions that receivers hold in relation to a source. If the audience believes that a communicator has underlying motives, especially ones of personal gain, he or she will be less persuasive than someone they perceive as having nothing to gain. 'Overheard conversation' has a similar effect as the receiver knows he or she was not the intended target of the message and believes that the communicator had no intent to manipulate, so increasing the source's credibility.

Some television advertisements attempt to increase credibility by using 'candid' interviews with householders. The householder is asked to explain why they purchase a particular brand or asked to 'trade' their usual brand for two of another (the answer always being 'No'). Another approach is to ask 'consumers' to compare their brand of product with another, both in disguised form. The 'consumer' acts surprised when they learn that the sponsor's brand performs better than their regular brand. In these commercials advertisers are attempting to imply a degree of objectivity to establish credibility for their message.

When a receiver likes a source, the source will be more persuasive than if disliked. There is evidence that age, sex, dress, mannerisms, dialect and voice inflection affect source credibility. These are characteristics that subtly influence an audience's evaluation of the communicator and the message. Sources high in credibility can cause opinion changes in receivers, but evidence suggests that influence of a credible source dissipates rapidly after initial exposure to a persuasive message.

4.5 Advertising

A feature of advertising is that it is paid for by a sponsor attempting to convey a message to the recipient. However, a salesperson is paid to convey an employer's (sponsor's) message to a recipient and this is not regarded as an advertisement. Another distinguishing feature is that the ad should be received by a large number of recipients through mass, paid-for communication. It is referred in the advertising industry to as '*above-the-line*' promotion. This means that it is advertising that is paid for through the advertising industry commission system. Advertising agencies must be '*recognised*' (by their professional body The Institute of Practitioners in Advertisers) to receive a commission, (a typical rate being 15% within a range from 10% to 25%), from the media for the advertising they place on their clients' behalf. The 'line' is simply the line above which they receive commission. Promotional activity that does not receive such commission is termed '*below-the-line*' promotion.

Above-the-line promotion (advertising) has three main aims:

1. To impart information.

2. To develop attitudes.

3. To induce action beneficial to the advertiser (normally the purchase of a product).

CASE 4.2

Claims of sexism in French advertising results in government enquiry.

The French Secretary of State for Women's Rights is acting on complaints from TV viewers of both sexes, that much of French advertising is sexist and depicts women in an unsuitable and degrading manner. Following an independent report issued in July 2001, Nicole Pery, a French junior minister, said that guidelines for French advertising, which have not been reviewed since 1975, should be reviewed and strengthened. What was acceptable to the majority of television viewers of both sexes 25-years ago is not necessarily acceptable today in these more 'politically correct' times. In fact an independent survey sponsored by the Government in June 2001 showed that 57% of all respondents thought that some French advertising was hurtful in some way to women. The Government Report stated: 'Going back a number of years and with an increased frequency during the last few months, advertising shows images of women that many find humiliating and degrading'. The government is taking the complaints so seriously that it plans to radically alter the law on discrimination, dating back to 1981. Organisations representing women will be able to take legal action against discriminatory advertising campaigns.

Advertising can rarely create sales by itself. Whether or not the customer buys depends on the product, price, packaging, personal selling, after-sales service, financing and other aspects of marketing. Advertising is just one element of communications, that performs certain parts of the communicating task with greater economy, speed and volume than can be achieved through other means.

The amount of communication performed by advertising varies, depending on the nature of the product, frequency of purchase and price. Where the product is sold through mail-order or direct mail almost the whole task is achieved by advertising. In contrast, in industrial markets, the salesperson normally closes a sale, but the task of selling the product is helped by the potential client's awareness of the product achieved in part through company advertising. Here, advertising's purpose is to enhance clients' responses to the firm and its products.

The contribution of advertising is likely to be greatest when:

> Buyer awareness of the company's product is low.
>
> Industry sales are rising rather than remaining stable or declining.
>
> The product has features not normally observable to the buyer.
>
> The opportunities for product differentiation are strong.
>
> Discretionary incomes are high.
>
> A new product or new service idea is being introduced.

A number of models have been developed to answer the question. 'How does advertising work?' These models have been drawn from varying disciplines, particularly psychology as well as from advertising practitioners. Early models relied on the stimulus/response formula, while later ones took into account the environment in which purchasing decisions are made.

1   Starch

One of the oldest models of advertising is that of Daniel Starch (1925) who said:

> 'For an advertisement to be successful it must be seen, must be read, must be believed, must be remembered and must be acted upon.'

This model takes little account of the state of mind of the consumer with respect to the product. The advertisement is assumed to be the main influence and no allowance is made for the combined or multiple effects of advertisements, implying that the effects of single ads on consumers are independent of each other. In reality, it is likely that the cumulative impact of repetition of ads in a campaign will have a greater effect on the consumer than a single viewing of one. Advertisers still refer to 'Starch Ratings' that have become a generic term relating to effectiveness ratings of ads.

2   The DAGMAR philosophy

This model allows for the cumulative impact of ads, although not in a quantitative way. Colley's 'DAGMAR' model (Defining Advertising Goals for Measured Advertising Results) refers to the sequential states of mind through which it is assumed consumers must pass:

1   From unawareness to awareness.
2   To comprehension.
3   To conviction.
4   To action.

These levels are the *marketing communications spectrum*. Advertising is seen as one of a number of marketing tools (the others being promotion, personal selling, publicity, price, packaging and distribution) that move consumers through the successive levels of the spectrum:

1   **Unawareness/awareness**

People who have never heard of the product are at the unawareness level.

Sometimes people buy products they do not know, but at this level advertising tries to make the customer aware of the product's existence.

2   **Comprehension**

At this level the consumer is aware of the product, recognises the brand name and trademark and has some degree of knowledge of the product – what it is and what it does. This knowledge may have been gained from the advertisement or following an information search prompted by the advertisement. For example, a potential hotel guest would recognise the names of hotels X and Y, and know that hotel X is a three-star hotel near the airport, while hotel Y is a four-star hotel in the centre of town.

3   **Conviction**

This implies a firm attitude towards the product. In the hotel example conviction is when the customer says 'Hotel A is a four-star hotel in city Z where I can get good service for a reasonable price. I intend to stay there next time I visit city Z.'

4   **Action**

At this stage the consumer has made a move toward purchase. In the hotel example this occurs when the customer tries to book a room. Inducing purchase may be beyond the power of advertising (the hotel may be fully booked, or the room rate too high) but the ad will have been 'acted upon'.

The idea that advertisements 'nudge' consumers along a spectrum that extends from complete ignorance to attempting to purchase, rather than individually achieving or failing to achieve results that owe nothing to previous exposures, leads to the concept that the purpose of advertising is to bring about a change in state of mind towards the purchase of a product. A single advertisement is rarely powerful enough to move a prospect from complete unawareness to action. Advertising effectiveness should be measured in terms of the extent to which it moves people along the spectrum. Adoption of the DAGMAR model can lead to a clearer statement of advertising objectives and to valid measurements of success in obtaining these objectives.

3   The Lavidge and Steiner model

Lavidge and Steiner proposed a hierarchical sequence of effects resulting from the perception of an ad that moves the consumer ever closer to purchase. The six levels are:

1   Awareness
2   Knowledge
3   Liking
4   Preference
5   Conviction
6   Purchase

The six steps indicate three major functions of advertising: the first two relate to information or ideas; the second pair, to attitudes or feelings toward the product; and the final stages, conviction and purchase, produce action, or the acquisition of the product. They claimed that these three functions (information, attitudes and action) are directly related to classic psychology that divides behaviour into three components: cognitive, affective, and conative (motivational).

'Hierarchy-of-effects' models have been criticised. Joyce said: '…they are put forward not on the basis of empirical evidence, but on the basis of an appeal to intuition or common sense.' Although these models differ in the number and nature of the stages in the process leading to buying action, there is agreement that buying action is the culminating stage of a sequence of persuasion events. This assumes a one-way relationship between changes in a consumer's knowledge and attitudes towards a product and changes in buying behaviour towards that product.

4   Dissonance theory

This indicates that the flow of causality is not one directional as proposed by hierarchical models. Most decisions involve the decision-maker in 'cognitive dissonance' or the idea that the chosen option will have some unattractive features, while rejected options will have attractive ones. It is predicted that, after making a decision, the decision-maker will seek information to reinforce and justify the decision and filter information to which he or she is exposed, favourable data being assimilated and unfavourable data being discarded.

The implication of dissonance theory is that for existing brands in the repeat purchase market the role of advertising is defensive. It should seek to maintain the brand, within the buyer's choice portfolio and be aimed at existing users who are aware of the brand, and have formed positive attitudes towards it. Repetitive reassurance advertising should reinforce continuation of buying in the face of competition.

5   Unique selling proposition

The models discussed have been developed by researchers drawing on research in psychology or observations in the market place. People in advertising who put forward models often have a particular view of advertising to promote. A well-known example is the theory developed by Rosser Reeves who reported the principles his agency had worked with for 30 years, embodied in the *Unique Selling Proposition (USP)*.

> 'The consumer tends to remember just one thing from the advertisement – one strong claim, or one strong concept. Each advertisement must make a proposition to the customer. The proposition must be one that competition either cannot, or does not, offer. The proposition must be so strong that it can move the masses (i.e pull them over to your product).'

Reeves is saying that an advertisement works by making a claim for the product that is clearly related to consumer needs and that will be recalled by the consumer and motivate purchasing action at the appropriate time.

6   The brand image school

The brand-image school, led by David Ogilvy. concentrated on non-verbal methods of communication, evoking moods and investing a brand with additional favourable connotations that are not necessarily specifically associated with the product's properties in use e.g. connotations of prestige and quality that Ogilvy claims 'give a brand a first-class ticket through life'. An advertisement is the carrier or channel through which the sponsor communicates a message to an audience. Aaker and Myers (1980) developed the communication process as shown in Figure 4.3.

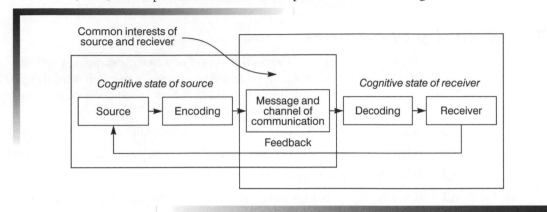

Figure 4.3 Aaker and Myers' model of communication

The sponsor's encoded message is transmitted (by advertising or salespeople) to recipients who decode and absorb it, either in whole or in part. The accuracy of communication depends on the 'exactness' with which the message is transmitted and the similarity between the meaning assigned to the symbols used by the source and by the receiver.

Good communication requires an area of overlap between the cognitive fields of the sender of a message and the receiver. Anything that distorts the quality of transmission, reducing the effectiveness of a message is called *'noise'*. Noise can occur because the receiver does not interpret the message the way the source intended. A further example of noise is *'cognitive dissonance'* that occurs when experience (receipt of the message) does not agree with what they believe.

The receiver may handle dissonance in a number of ways:

1. Rejecting the message
2. Ignoring the message
3. Altering the previous opinion
4. Searching for justifications

The first two reactions are negative effects from the source's point of view. Noise may also act as a message to the source (feedback) which may well change the behaviour of the source; to change the message or cease communication if there is evidence that the receiver is not receptive to ideas.

The view that advertising works by converting people into users of a brand can be misleading. Advertising may have a positive effect, even if sales are steady, by preventing loss of users. In some markets increasing loyalty of existing users and the amount they purchase may be a better proposition than winning over non-users.

Advertising situations are so varied, it is impossible to generalise how it works. Models can be misleading because every advertising campaign is a unique situation and should generate its own measure of effectiveness. This supports the idea that advertisers should have an advertising plan setting out what they are trying to achieve, how they intend to achieve this goal, and how they are going to measure its effectiveness – known as *'advertising-by-objectives'*.

7   Advertising by objectives

Few companies quantitatively assess the impact of a specific campaign and they give little thought to precisely what they are trying to achieve through advertising. Clear objectives assist operational decision-making when conducting advertising campaigns. Operational decisions for advertising include:

- ❑   How much should be spent on a particular campaign?
- ❑   What should comprise the content and presentation of the advertisement?
- ❑   What are the most appropriate media?
- ❑   What should be the frequency of display of advertisements or campaigns?
- ❑   Should any special geographical weighting of effort be used?
- ❑   What are the best methods of evaluating the effects of the advertising?

According to DAGMAR, the main objective of advertising is to accomplish clearly defined communication objectives. Thus, advertising succeeds or fails according to how well it communicates predetermined information and attitudes to the right people, at the right time, at the right cost.

Majaro (1970) set out a number of advantages of the *advertising-by-objectives* approach:

It helps to integrate advertising effort with other elements of the marketing mix, thus setting a consistent and logical marketing plan.

It facilitates the task of the advertising agency in preparing and evaluating creative work and recommending the most suitable media.

It assists in determining advertising budgets.

It enables marketing executives and top management to appraise the advertising plan realistically.

It permits meaningful measurement of advertising results.

It is often the case that many people in a company who influence advertising decisions do not have a common understanding of its purpose, for example:

- ❑   The Chairman may be most concerned with building corporate image.
- ❑   The Sales Manager may regard advertising solely as a means of getting larger orders from retailers.
- ❑   The Finance Director deals with advertising as an expense, chargeable to a given fiscal period.
- ❑   The Advertising Manager or the Agency Account Executive may see it as an investment directed toward building a brand image.

The difficulty is differentiating between marketing and advertising objectives. The proper sequence is to define the overall marketing objectives and then determine the contribution that advertising can make to each. An advertising objective should be one that advertising alone is expected to achieve.

The following should be considered when setting advertising objectives:

❑ Advertising objectives should be consistent with broader corporate objectives.

❑ Objectives should be realistic in terms of internal resources and external opportunities, threats and constraints.

❑ Objectives should be widely known so people understand the goals of their work and how they relate to the broader objectives of the firm as a whole.

❑ Objectives need to be flexible, acknowledging that all business decisions, including advertising, have to be made in circumstances of partial ignorance.

❑ Objectives should be periodically reconsidered, to take account of changing conditions and ensure that objectives are generally known.

Before work on setting advertising objectives can begin, information on the product, the market and consumers must be available. Of prime importance is a thorough assessment of consumer behaviour and motivation with reference to the company's target group of customers. A statement of advertising objectives should then make clear what basic message is intended to be delivered, to what audience, with what intended effects and the specific criteria that are going to be used to measure success. The main considerations in setting advertising objectives are:

❑ *WHAT* role is advertising expected to fulfil in the total marketing effort?

❑ *WHY* is it believed that advertising can achieve this role? (What evidence is there and what assumptions are necessary?)

❑ *WHO* should be involved in setting and agreeing objectives; coordinating their implementation and subsequent evaluation? Who is the intended audience?

❑ *HOW* are the advertising objectives to be put into practice?

❑ *WHEN* are various parts of the programme to be implemented? When can a response be expected to each stage of the programme?

4.6 Sales promotion

4.6.1 Scope of sales promotion

Sales promotion is a dynamic and flexible sales tool. Two related definitions are:

1. *The short-term achievement of marketing objectives by schematic means*

2. *Immediate or delayed incentives to purchase, expressed in cash or in kind*

The main elements of sales promotion normally associated with retailing are:

❑ Self-liquidating offers (e.g. where something, often bearing no relation to what is in the pack, is offered at a low price – normally at cost – and where the promoters have purchased in bulk to attain a low price. The customer is normally required to provide proofs of purchase and send money for the item offered).

- ❑ On-pack offers.
- ❑ In-pack offers.
- ❑ With-pack premiums.
- ❑ Container premiums (where the container has a secondary use e.g. a storage jar)
- ❑ Continuing premiums (e.g. a set of 'collectables' in the pack).
- ❑ Trading stamps.
- ❑ Gift coupons/vouchers.
- ❑ Premium offers (e.g. two for one).
- ❑ Competitions.
- ❑ Money-off coupons.
- ❑ Sampling (often in the retail establishment).
- ❑ Reduced price pack or increased quantity pack.
- ❑ Limpet pack (or 'banded pack') where the pack has a free one taped to it.

Other marketing elements coming under general realm of sales promotion are:

- ❑ In-store display materials (e.g. stands, header boards, shelf strips, 'wobblers').
- ❑ Packaging (e.g. pack-flashes).
- ❑ Merchandising (i.e demonstrations, auxiliary sales forces, display arrangements).
- ❑ Direct mail (e.g. coupons, competitions, premium offers).
- ❑ Exhibitions.

Organisational promotions include trade competitions, but tend to be incentives to persuade customers to buy more and are usually between manufacturers and retailers.

CASE 4.3

Mills and Boon use £1 million worth of give-aways in a promotional strategy aimed at attracting lost readers.

Mills and Boon, the romantic fiction brand of books is planning to engage in a nationwide promotion to woo back lost customers. Many readers of romantic fiction see the brand as a little staid and old-fashioned and prefer other material. However, Mills and Boon has moved on and has brought its products up to date. Not only are the contents more modern in terms of story lines but the cover, packaging and the whole presentation of the book is now much more up to date. The trouble is not all of the reading British public realises this with many still, wrongly, viewing the image of the brand as outdated. The publishers of the brand, Harlequin Mills and Boon intend to put a copy of a Mills and Boon book into every British home, either by a free book delivered through the letter box or through some other form of voucher promotion in book stalls and shops. So far the company has placed 3,500 books through letterboxes in the Birmingham area with a further 12,000 books given away free through a redeemable voucher scheme. Eventually the company is planning up to a million door drops across the UK and a furthering of its voucher promotion.

4.6.2 Sales promotion planning

As with any business task, a full plan should be prepared beforehand. A typical planning sequence of stages of sales promotion is:

Analyse the problem/task

Define objectives.

Set the budget.

Examine the types of promotion likely to be used.

Define support activities (e.g. advertising, incentives, auxiliaries).

Testing (e.g. a limited store or panel test for a short period, then report back).

How to measure success of the campaign.

Plan timetable.

Present details of the sales promotion to sales force, retailers, etc.

Implement the promotion.

Evaluate the results.

4.6.3 Importance of sales promotion

Sales promotional expenditure can easily be collected and analysed. The amount spent on sales promotion has been increasing over the past 15 years, which underlines its importance as a tool of marketing communication.

Advantages

❑   Easily measured response.

❑   Quick achievement of objectives.

❑   Flexible application.

❑   Can be relatively cheap.

❑   Direct support of sales force.

Disadvantages

❑   Price-discounting can cheapen brand image.

❑   Short-term advantages only.

❑   Retailers might not want to cooperate.

❑   Difficulty in communicating brand message.

4.7   Public relations (PR)

4.7.1   Communications and PR

The Institute of Public Relations (IPR) defines PR as:

'PR practice is the deliberate, planned and sustained effort to establish and maintain mutual understanding between an organisation and its publics.'

The definition refers to an organisation's *publics* in the plural, since PR addresses many different audiences.

Communication is central to PR, whose purpose is to establish a two-way communication to resolve conflicts of interest by seeking common ground or areas of mutual interest. A further implication is that PR exists whether an organisation wants it or not. Simply by carrying out day-to-day operations, an organisation communicates certain messages to those who interact with the organisation and they will form opinions about the organisation and its activities. The task of PR is to orchestrate those messages in order to help the organisation project a *corporate identity* or *corporate personality*.

CASE 4.4

Television chefs are asked to get public relations 'fillip' to aid lamb sales in the UK.

UK meat consumers have had a hard time of late. Virtually nothing, from beef to eggs, has been totally free of suspicion of something being wrong with it from a health point of view. Lamb sales were hit by the foot and mouth outbreak as well as the BSE epidemic in cattle. Some scientists believe BSE has crossed to sheep on a large scale. There have always been cases of sheep brain disease similar to BSE in cattle, known as 'scrapie' but not enough cases to put people off eating the meat. Television and other celebrity chefs have been asked to co-operate in a public relations campaign to try and get the British public to eat more lamb. The Meat and Livestock Commission (MLC) has asked the Ministry of Agriculture for an emergency £25 million payment to fund a publicity campaign. Recent independent research commissioned by the MLC has indicated that whilst most people are happy with the health standards of British lamb there are a significant group of meat eaters, about 30 to 40% of all meat eaters, that are not. An intensive public relations campaign is hoped to raise lamb sales within the UK by an extra £100 million per year. Celebrity chefs are regarded as 'opinion leaders' and their imaginative new recipes are likely to appeal to a large number of potential consumers. Consumers hold the view that if chefs such as Jamie Oliver or Delia Smith are using lamb in their recipes then it must be safe to eat. The message from such well-known and trusted individuals has a high level of 'source credibility'.

4.7.2   Corporate identity/personality

PR activity is carried out within the framework of a corporate personality, which can become a tangible asset if it is managed properly and consistently.

Managers do not consciously consider the role of personality when they make decisions. The PR executive should be aware of all issues, policies, attitudes and opinions that exist in the organisation, and have a bearing on how this is perceived by outsiders who form part of the organisation's 'publics'.

Corporate 'personality' rather than 'image' is a more appropriate term as 'image' is deliberate. An image is a reflection or impression that may be too polished, or too 'perfect'. True PR is more than superficial. This is important because a 'PR job' implies that the truth is hidden behind a glossy, even false, facade. Properly conducted PR emphasises the need for truth and full information. The PR executive, as manager of the 'corporate personality', can only sustain a long-term corporate identity that is based on truth and reality.

PR is difficult to evaluate because of the abstract nature of 'personality'. Measurement tends to be in terms of column centimetre coverage or TV/radio coverage that might have been achieved from a press release and PR campaign.

The next two chapters cover the remaining elements of the communications mix – Selling and Sales Management and Direct Marketing.

Questions

1.   'Evaluation of advertising effectiveness is so difficult that it is not worth the effort and cost involved'.

   Critically evaluate this statement.

2.   What advantages are there for an organisation in evaluating the effectiveness of sales promotional expenditure with reference to clearly defined communication objectives?

3.   What form would such a marketing communications evaluative procedure take? Outline a scheme for such an evaluation programme.

4.   Is PR purely a function of marketing or is its role broader than this?

References

Aaker, DA and Myers, JA, (1982) *Advertising Management*, 2nd edition, (Prentice-Hall, Inc, Englewood Cliffs, New Jersey, USA), pp 233–236.

Joyce, P, (1967) 'What Do We Know About How Advertising Works?', *Advertising Age*.

Lavidge, RJ and Steiner, GA, (1962) 'A Model of Predictive Measurement of Advertising, *Effectiveness Journal of Marketing*, October.

Majaro, S, (1970) 'Advertising by Objectives', *Management Today*, January.

Ogilvy, D, (1961) *Confessions of an Advertising Man*, (Atheneum, New York, USA).

Reeves, R, (1961) *Reality of Advertising*, (A. A. Knopf Inc, New York, USA).

5 Selling and sales management

5.1 The nature of selling

'Personal selling' involves face-to-face contact between sellers and buyers. Selling tasks differ, depending on the type of goods and services. Some salespeople are order-takers, while others employ sophisticated skills of prospecting, negotiating and demonstrating.

Personal selling is a primary communication tool in organisational (especially industrial) marketing, where up to 80% of the total marketing budget can be spent on salesforce costs. Personal selling is less important in many retail market situations (especially fast moving consumer goods (FMCG) markets). Selling to final customers increasingly uses non-personal communication such as packaging, advertising, merchandising and sales promotion. Communications mix elements are not used in isolation; they complement each other.

'Everyone lives by selling something.' Every time we engage in a discussion, we are exchanging views and ideas. When we attempt to persuade others to accept our point-of-view, we are attempting to 'sell' our ideas. Without selling, many transactions would not take place as it plays a vital role in the exchange process.

The importance of personal selling varies from situation to situation. Goods entailing low-involvement decisions like FMCGs are routinely purchased in retail stores on a 'self-service' basis. Salespeople are, however, needed to 'sell' these products in bulk to the retail trade. The degree of selling skill required here depends on the reputation of the manufacturer and the popularity of the brands involved. It is not necessary to 'sell' well-known brands to the trade, because they will stock them because of their popularity. In such situations, the salesperson's role becomes one of reordering, ensuring stock replenishment and rotation, merchandising advice and customer liaison. When selling to supermarket chains, head office buyers simply perform a negotiating role direct with manufacturers, and sales representatives have little reason to visit individual supermarkets, except for display and merchandising activities.

With goods and services requiring high-involvement decisions, the role of personal selling is clearer. Negotiating the sale of expensive consumer durables like cars usually requires a personal approach, a high degree of product knowledge and selling skills. Selling in business to business (B2B) situations presents the greatest sales challenge and requires a high degree of selling skill. Expensive capital equipment is bought only after intense negotiation, and there is a degree of perceived risk. Therefore the buyer (or DMU members who are involved in the decision process) require detailed knowledge of goods or services. The salesperson must identify prospective customers' key requirements, not only in terms of product performance, but price expectations, delivery, credit and after-sales service.

As an element of the communications mix, the importance of personal selling depends on company objectives, the type of business in which the company is involved and conditions in the market. Personal selling can be effective but expensive, and the salesperson's salary is not the only selling cost. Other 'add-on' costs like a company car, expense account, extra travelling costs, administrative support and share of general overheads, can exceed salary costs. Personal selling should be used where it can achieve results more cost-effectively than other communications mix elements like advertising or direct mail.

5.2   Situations requiring a personal approach

A personal approach is required in a number of selling situations:

Situations of high perceived risk are where purchase of products that are new, expensive or technically complex might be viewed as risky by prospective buyers. A salesperson uses professional skill to identify the customer's areas of concern and takes steps to lower the concern or eliminate the perceived problems.

Technically complex products like robotic machine tools or a new computer system are complicated and may need to be explained to customers so they can grasp the capabilities of the productsystem. The sales task can only be carried out face-to-face by salespersons with high levels of product knowledge.

Commercially complex negotiations might involve financial arrangements, maintenance contracts, spare-parts availability, staff training and other areas that make commercial details complicated. The complexity of a buying situation contributes to the degree of perceived risk on the part of potential purchasers and such situations require negotiation and explanation at a personal level.

Industrial/organisational markets where the tradition is to deal direct. Goods and services sold often differ between sales calls and are sometimes technically complex, expensive or innovative. There is now a tendency towards 'relationship marketing' where salespersons visit buyers with the purpose of keeping open lines of communication and not necessarily with the intention of making a sale.

CASE 5.1

Rudolph Giuliani brings the British back to the 'Big Apple'.

Rudolph Giuliani, the mayor of New York in 2001, is an all American hero. Not only has he demonstrated great leadership qualities in the aftermath of the tragedies afflicting New York but he has also shown himself to be an expert salesman with great persuasive ability. Mr. Giuliani has shown so much kindness and sensitivity to British families living in New York and to the families affected by the tragedy back in the UK, that he is to receive an Honorary Knighthood from the Queen. There are lots of people in the UK who just love New York, and many visit every year. However, many have thought that New Yorkers may not like it if lots of British tourists were around the city. Some tourists had been concerned about the appropriateness of visiting the city so soon after the attacks, especially as the locals might regard outsiders as voyeuristic. However Mr. Giuliani has asked tourists to return to the city. He said 'I encourage people to come here and spend money. Go to a restaurant or a play...The life of the city goes on!' On hearing Mr. Giuliani's plea many British tourists are taking him at his word. They are returning to the Big Apple in droves and spending needed cash in the city's economy. Mr. Giuliani has managed to gain the support of visitors from all over the world, who, thanks to his encouraging words feel that they are in some way supporting their favourite city in its time of need.

5.3   The expanded role of the modern salesperson

Although the primary role of a salesperson is to make sales, to modern marketing orientated salespersons, selling is but one facet of the task. There are many other functions undertaken in the course of customer contact:

5.3.1   Servicing

The salesperson provides services to customers like consultancy, technical advice, after-sales service, arranging finance and expediting delivery from the company to the customer. This kind of activity has increased in lean manufacturing situations.

5.3.2   Prospecting

Companies supply their salespeople with qualified 'leads' that may have been obtained from general customer enquiries, but a certain amount of a salesperson's activity should be devoted to obtaining and developing personal leads. Some will result from the salesperson 'cold calling'. Existing satisfied customers are a good source of leads and new prospects can be obtained by asking satisfied customers if they know anybody who might have a need for the goods or services on offer.

5.3.3   Information gathering

Salespeople are in personal contact with potential and actual customers most days. They are in a good position to collect market information and intelligence that might be useful to marketing management:

❑   Marketing plans – salespeople can contribute to marketing plans by giving details of customer preferences and requirements on matters like price, credit, discounts, promotions, market segmentation and timing of marketing efforts.

❑   Sales forecasting – by asking about likely future purchases, salespeople can gather information of use in forecasting which is central to marketing planning.

❑ New product development – existing customers can provide salespeople with ideas for new products or improvements to existing products.

❑ General marketing research – salespeople can provide information about market conditions, competitive developments and customers. Customers may have a multi-sourcing policy and by probing, the salesperson may be able to gain information about competitors' activities.

5.3.4 Communicating

Salespeople use many forms of interaction with customers as well as verbal communications e.g. reports, charts, models, diagrams, video, internet, PowerPoint presentations. These media are used with customers and at exhibitions, trade fairs, etc.

5.3.5 Allocating

There are occasions when the salesperson may have to perform an allocating role. During times of shortage (perhaps resulting from an industrial dispute, shortages of raw materials, production problems or unexpected demand) salespeople may have to evaluate customer loyalty and future sales potential and allocate stocks accordingly.

5.4 Communication and the salesperson

Communication is a two-way process because, important as it is for the salesperson to talk, it is just as important to listen. *Listening skills* should be developed. It is too easy to switch off when someone is talking a lot. The professional salesperson actively listens to what customers are saying, and this requires a conscious effort.

CASE 5.2

American Express uses personal selling at motorway service stations to increase credit card applications.

Travelling on British motorways can be unpleasant and tiring. Road works are part of the motorist's driving experience. Fortunately British motorways are blessed with a good supply of service stations where the stressed-out motorist can stop for a break, something to eat and a cup of tea. However, if you have stopped at one of the many service stations across the country recently you may have noticed something different. We are used to the AA and the RAC motoring organisations outside trying to persuade us to take out membership. But what we have now are professional sales activities inside the service areas by the food halls and in the direct route of the toilets. The organisation conducting these activities is American Express, and the product on offer is yet another credit card. The sales people are usually two well dressed and attractive individuals who have the skill of gaining a driver's attention no matter how tired they may be. They ask the prospect if they have an American Express card. If the prospect says no, he or she is then asked if they would like to make an application and told all about the benefits of having such a card and the introductory offer available if they sign up. The sales people, usually young and female, are very polite but also persuasive and good at their job. They have a small sales counter with the necessary leaflets and information. American Express have found that this direct selling technique is more effective than mail order in terms of the number of conversions per person contacted.

5.5   The sales sequence

The most important part of a salesperson's position is the sales interview, although other activities now form part of the job. In addition, much time is taken up travelling – sometimes 30% of a working day. Such a diverse range of activities and travelling means that careful planning should take place to ensure that face-to-face contact with customers is optimised. This is achieved by adopting a general plan for all sales interviews and a tactical plan for individual interviews.

The general plan used for all sales interviews is called the *'sales sequence'*. It should be flexible and capable of being adapted to suit individual situations. The general sales sequence is a guide, and this format is adopted by professional salespeople. Listening skills are vital so that the salesperson can interpret verbal and non-verbal clues and adjust the message and approach to fit the requirements of the particular situation. The following format is a general plan for this sequence:

1.   *Preparation* – planning of individual interviews.

2.   *The approach* – the way the salesperson meets and greets the customer.

3.   *The presentation and/or demonstration* – normally the central part of the sales interview and an appropriate time for the salesperson to emphasise product benefits.

4.   *Negotiation* – deciding delivery dates, price, credit terms, etc.

5.   *Closing* – the final bringing together of what has been discussed and agreed, and the time when a possible order can be discussed.

6.   *Follow-up* – An important element of good customer relations (and repeat business) is an efficient after-sales service that is not merely technical support, but part of customer relations management (CRM), also referred to as Key Account Management (KAM) that is company-wide.

5.5.1   Preparation

Preparation for individual interviews means having as much general and personal knowledge about customers as possible (even down to personal idiosyncratic behaviour) so that the interview can be conducted at a more personal level. There follows a checklist of points:

❏   *Company knowledge* includes familiarity with the company's systems, procedures, price, terms and policy on complaints and returned goods. The salesperson needs to be updated on a regular basis (e.g. the company may extend credit terms or alter its quantity discount structure, so it is important that the salesperson knows about this immediately).

❑ *Product knowledge* includes information about existing and new products. Limitations of the product range should also be known. Making exaggerated claims can lead to customer dissatisfaction. Salespeople paid on a commission basis might make exaggerated claims to advance personal remuneration.

❑ *Market knowledge* means an understanding of the general state of the market including new developments in the market and between competitors. Market intelligence is part of the organisation's marketing information system. Salespeople are well placed to act as 'intelligence providers'.

❑ *Customer knowledge* is needed about the size of the company, affiliation to other companies, their bargaining power and markets they serve.

❑ *Buyer knowledge* is needed at a personal level, which may include knowledge of the buyer's family circumstances – perhaps picked up at the last sales interview e.g. at the buyer's wedding anniversary that can provide a caring personal touch. Such preparation can be stored on a laptop computer in the form of a *customer visit record*. Salespersons should keep a file for every live account. Information on such records might include:

A record of previous purchases (particularly the most recent purchase).

Comments made by the prospect that might have a bearing on future visits.

Personal details include basic matters like the customer's name, including first name if the buyer prefers to operate on a personal basis. Names of other people in the purchasing or technical departments visited should be similarly logged.

Customer family details and special interests are useful. This provides good background information that can be used to break the ice.

❑ **Equipment, samples and sales aids**
   ➢ Sales brochures and literature.
   ➢ Handbooks and product specifications.
   ➢ Up-to-date price lists.
   ➢ Samples.
   ➢ Demonstration kits/films/videos/ laptop + spreadsheets.
   ➢ Order book.

❑ **Journey planning**

An organised plan for appointments and other calls on a daily basis is important. Planning should consider both current customers and prospects.

Because sales time is at a premium and because much time is spent travelling it is important that itineraries are well planned. One method is known as *'differential call frequency'*. In many industries it is common for more substantial customers to receive a higher frequency of personal calls other than clients.

5.5.2 Approach

The way the salesperson approaches a prospective customer is a basic sales skill. To evaluate a situation quickly and judge the mood and personality of the prospect are valuable skills. Some pointers are:

- ❑ First impressions are important and the salesperson should be prepared, alert and well groomed in the context of not dressing or behaving in an extreme manner.

- ❑ The opening of the sales interview should be pleasant and businesslike. This is important if it is the first interview. In such a situation, opening remarks are critical as this is where first impressions are gained.

- ❑ Business at hand should be discussed as soon as possible to avoid wasting selling and prospecting time, but clearly the salesperson is regulated by the buyer.

- ❑ If the prospect sets a time limit this should be strictly adhered to.

- ❑ If a further appointment is made, this should be noted straight away along with details of the conversation on the customer visit record.

- ❑ Relevant questions should be asked as well as actively listening to answers.

- ❑ Sometimes debts, of which the buyer may be unaware, must be discussed. This should take place at the start. Once the debt question is discharged new negotiations can be undertaken without the complication of previous dealings.

5.5.3 The presentation and/or demonstration

This stage depends on good foundations. The salesperson should have a clear idea of the buyer's requirements and have established the level of explanation required. Presentations are more effective when the needs of potential customers are known and the sales presentation is targeted towards these needs.

During a sales presentation/demonstration, the role of the salesperson is to communicate specific product or service benefits of interest to the potential customer. Products or services have many features, and *customers buy benefits, not features*. A salesperson should examine the product range listing major selling points of each product. Important selling points are those that are unique to the product and give an advantage over similar products offered by competitors. These significant selling points are the *unique sales proposition (USP)*. Product benefits required by the customer should have been identified during the preparation stage. In business to business (B2B) situations common motives revolve around quality and performance, economy and price, reliable delivery, durability and safety.

A good presentation can help overcome objections. If the sales dialogue is carried out on an interactive basis, the salesperson may even find it advantageous to encourage objections, in the knowledge that they can be dealt with adequately. The salesperson should refer to the needs of the prospect and talk at a level of technicality that the prospect can readily understand. Many sales are lost because the salesperson over-presents technical details. If the prospect gives the salesperson *buying signals*, an attempt should then be made to close the sale.

CASE 5.3

Big Issue uses the personal sales approach to gain circulation.

The Big Issue Magazine is a combination of hard hitting current affairs journalism and critical, incisive writing about the world of arts and entertainment. Its high standard of reporting has won the magazine a number of prestigious awards. It is sold on the street by, usually, homeless people, who use their ingenuity to get people to buy the magazine. The magazine is available for order on-line but the most important selling method is face-to-face personal selling. Although sellers are not professional sales people in the true sense of the word, they nevertheless have to learn the main principles of selling face to face to make any money. Different vendors use different techniques, which include singing (very successful) and telling jokes. The Big Issue enables homeless people to earn an income through self-help. The Big Issue is a limited company. The Big Issue Foundation is a registered charity and is independent of the Big Issue Company Ltd. The Big Issue financially supports The Big Issue Foundation and its various social support programmes. The company is a good illustration of the importance of personal selling and also a good example of a socially responsible business.

5.5.4   Negotiation

Negotiation concerns two parties who wish to bring about an agreement that is acceptable to both sides. The seller typically makes a presentation and an offer in terms of price, credit, delivery, etc. The buyer evaluates these points. Each party knows what they would like to achieve from negotiation and how far they are prepared to go in offering concessions. Hence, sales negotiation is a process of presentation, evaluation, counter-proposal and concession. Each party has an optimal result in mind, but

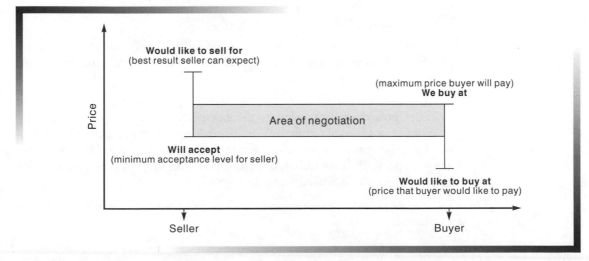

Figure 5.2 'Room for manoeuvre' concept in negotiation

concedes that the achievement of this goal is rarely possible and that they must be prepared to compromise. The gap between the optimal result and the minimum acceptable limit gives each party *room for manoeuvre*. This concept is illustrated in Figure 5.2. The example concerns price, but the concept is valid for any area that is open to negotiation like credit terms, delivery or quality.

5.5.5 Closing

The objective of selling is to obtain an order, so closing techniques should be understood as well as when and under what circumstances each is applicable. Some techniques are:

❑ *Basic close* is when the salesperson sees buying signals from the prospect and starts to fill in the order form. If there is no objection, a sale is achieved.

❑ *Alternative choice* is a *trial close* technique. When the salesperson has received buying signals from the prospect, an attempt is made to close by offering the prospect an alternative choice. (E.g. a prospect shows serious interest in purchasing a new car and asks about delivery: that is taken as a buying signal. The salesperson might then ask: 'What would be your preferred colour?' If the prospect states a preference, a sale is made). The example is a *trial close* (i.e. 'fishing' for a closing signal from the prospect).

❑ *Puppy dog* technique stems from the idea that if you give a family a small puppy to look after for two weeks, they are likely to grow fond of it and be reluctant to part at the end of the period. The same principle is applied to a product that might be loaned for a period. This is often used by firms who offer new equipment free for a 'trial period'. It is then hoped that the prospect will get used to having it and that at the end of the trial there may be resistance to return it as well as the potential for more orders.

❑ *Summary question* is used when the salesperson experiences resistance. The main cause of resistance has been discovered through elimination. For example:

'Is it the price?' 'No!'
'Is it the colour?' 'No!'

Each time the prospect says 'No', a potential cause of resistance has been eliminated. This allows the salesperson to concentrate on the most important area of resistance.

❑ *Similar situation* is best illustrated by an example of a salesperson selling security devices. Upon meeting resistance, the salesperson could point to a similar situation: 'The Howard family in Woodland Meadows said exactly the same as you. They thought it expensive and wanted more time to think. One week later they were burgled!' This technique can be powerful in influencing a prospect's decision, especially if related to an analogy.

These techniques are not exhaustive and the skill is in knowing which one to use in a given situation.

CASE 5.4

Moben Kitchens use personal selling in the showroom and to close the sale.

When selling home improvement products, especially those such as fitted kitchens, which can cost a lot of money, good closing specialists are vital. Many sales people are good at demonstration and general negotiation but it takes individuals with a certain persuasive skill to actually finalise or close the sale. Moben Kitchens are part of the Homefront group Ltd. based in Manchester, UK. The company has over 200 showrooms nationwide, all with a wide range of fully fitted Moben branded kitchens on display. Potential customers can visit the showrooms and see the kitchens. They can talk over their requirements with friendly experts which is usually the first stage of the sales sequence. Moben also use extensive press advertising and prospective customers are invited to Freephone in for a free colour brochure of beautiful kitchens and appliances. Customers are also invited to ask for an appointment and one of Moben's experts will visit the home and discuss requirements. Whether operating in the showroom or in the prospect home there are a special team of selling experts who will usually accompany the negotiator for the final close. A sale is not made until it has been closed. These specialists are in great demand and are only usually brought in at the last minute or in cases where the negotiator dealing with the client is about to lose the sale. Good closers are well paid and are in great demand in a variety of industries such as finance and insurance as well as home improvement sectors. Any situation that requires the prospect having to make a final decision can make effective use of professionals with good closing skills.

5.5.6   Follow-up

It is part of a salesperson's task to provide advice and information after the sale. This might involve persuading the customer to take out a service contract and provide information about service centres, but the idea of *customer care* is a modern technique that encourages repeat business, the techniques of which are expanded later. Excellent after-sales service is vital in securing post-purchase satisfaction and repeat business, especially for major purchases where there might be 'cognitive dissonance'.

5.6   Sales management

5.6.1   Sales force size

Factors to be taken into account in reaching a decision on sales force size:

➢   The company's financial resources.

➢   Numbers of customers to be reached.

➢   Average number of calls required per customer, per week, per month, etc.

➢   Average number of calls that can be made by a salesperson in a given period.

➢   The firm's distribution policy, e.g. if the company operates a policy of selective, exclusive or mass distribution.

5.6.2 Evaluating sales force performance

Looking at sales volumes between members of the sales force is too simplistic. Straight comparisons take no consideration of variations between territories that might be related to differences in market potential and workload. There may be differences in promotional support, competition, time the company has operated in an area and the goodwill that the company has built up. Measures can be qualitative or quantitative:

❑   **Qualitative**

Degree of product knowledge.

Quality of sales presentation and demonstration.

Self-organisation (use of time, journey planning, etc.).

Intelligence.

Patience.

Tenacity.

Enthusiasm, motivation and ambition.

Grooming and general appearance.

❑   **Quantitative**

Sales volume.

Number of orders secured.

Number of new orders.

Number of customers/orders lost.

Number of sales/service calls made.

Expenses incurred.

Amount of market intelligence gathered.

Once potential sales for each area and each salesperson's territory have been forecasted, these are translated into sales targets or sales quotas that each salesperson is budgeted to sell. Area-by-area forecasts represent anticipated contribution to the company's sales and profit. Each salesperson's contribution to reaching targeted sales can be evaluated by comparing actual sales to forecasted sales.

5.6.3 Remuneration of salespeople

Straight salary offers least incentive for salespersons to sell more, but it offers stability and security. This is appropriate when salespersons spend much time on customer care and where customer retention is important. In some circumstances, straight salary is linked to a group bonus whereby all members of a team share a bonus relating to profitability during the previous period.

Salary plus commission (or sales-related bonus) is a popular method of compensation. Some companies use *escalator* commission/bonus schemes where the higher the sales, the higher the commission/bonus pro rata. The ratio between fixed basic salary and commission differs between companies. Generally, the salary element provides a living basic wage, with the commission acting as an incentive. Usually, commission is linked to the sales target or quota system. Once a salesperson sells above an agreed target or quota, then an escalator commission is applied.

Commission only is typically used for self-employed manufacturers' agents. Organisations like life assurance companies and home improvement organisations often employ part-time salespeople on this basis. This method is economic as the cost of each salesperson is directly related to sales. There is an incentive for salespersons to succeed, as level of income is determined by individual effort. The disadvantage is that salespersons feel less a part of the organisation, so after-sales service relationships with customers may suffer, and this is why many such arrangements tend to be one-off purchases.

5.6.4 Recruitment and selection of salespeople

A 'typical' salesperson is difficult to define. The job itself, and the person most suited to it, can vary according to the product or service being sold. The following job description is, therefore, only a guideline.

❑ **Responsibility**

The representative is responsible directly to the sales manager.

❑ **Objective**

To achieve the annual sales target across the product range in the area for which he/she is responsible, as economically as possible and within company policy.

❑ **Planning**

To become familiar with company policy and plan how to achieve the defined objectives within the limits of that policy. Submit this plan to sales management for approval.

❑ **Implementation**
  ➢ Act as an effective link between customers and head office.
  ➢ Organise own travel itinerary.
  ➢ Develop a comprehensive skill in selling.
  ➢ Maintain and submit accurate records.
  ➢ Gather market intelligence and report this to Head Office.
  ➢ Assess the potential of the area in terms of: visits, outlets for company products, activity of competition.
  ➢ Protect and promote the company image.
  ➢ Avoid unnecessary expense.
  ➢ Achieve harmony with fellow staff by setting a good example and maintaining company loyalty.

A checklist for evaluating candidates for a selling position includes:

> Age and marital status.
> Health.
> Interests.
> Education.
> Previous employment and experience.
> Location.
> Clean driving licence.
> References.
> Deportment.
> Intelligence.
> Integrity.
> Motivation.

This is not an exhaustive list, nor are criteria in any ranked order of importance. Most criteria listed apply to jobs other than selling. Such criteria can be incorporated into a rating matrix using an evaluation scale (e.g. excellent, very good, good, fair, poor).

Possible sources of recruitment include:

> Inside staff i.e. current employees.
> Salespeople from outside the company (in many cases from competitors).
> Advertising in the press, the internet and other media.
> Specialist recruitment agencies.

Questions

1. Planning is an essential part of the selling process. What should be included in the weekly calling plan, and what information should be recorded after each visit is made?

2. The primary task of a sales representative is to sell the company's product or service. What additional tasks could a sales representative be expected to undertake and how might they affect their selling role?

3. In order to determine how well or how badly each salesperson is performing, a sales manager needs an appraisal system. Why is this important, and what questions should such an appraisal system be able to answer?

4. How can the sales force contribute to achieving long term relationships with customers through relationship marketing and customer care?

References

Jobber, D and Lancaster, G, (2000), *Selling and Sales Management* (5th edition), (Prentice-Hall, London).

6 Direct marketing

6.1 What is direct marketing?

The term direct marketing refers to a collection of techniques, which, when applied, enables firms to market their goods and services directly to their customers. It is a pro-active approach to marketing that takes the product and/or service to the potential customer rather than waiting for them to come to a store or other point of access. It can be a form of 'non-shop' shopping and is sometimes referred to as 'precision marketing' or 'one-to-one' marketing. Rather than the marketing firm sending out a general communication or sales message to a large group of potential customers, even if these constitute a well-defined market segment, direct marketing tends to target a specific individual or household. In a business-to-business context this would be an individual or a specific organisation or firm. Direct marketing is not just concerned with marketing communications. It is also concerned with distribution. In using direct marketing the firm is making a choice to cut out the use of marketing intermediaries and sell the product or service in question direct to the customer. This has implications for both channels of distribution decisions and logistical decisions.

Direct marketing comes in a variety of forms. It is one of the fastest growing areas of marketing and is being propelled by enormous technical advances, particularly in the field of computer technology.

6.1.1 Direct marketing is not new!

Direct marketing is not new; many companies have sold their products direct to the public for many years, think of some 'brush' and 'perfume' companies that sell products door-to-door for example. Direct mail through the post or even mail order catalogues have been around for a long time and are all a form of direct marketing. Direct marketing originated in the early 1900s, in fact the Direct Marketing Association (DMA) was established in the USA in 1917. Direct marketing became an important force in the UK in the 1950s but at this stage in its development the industry was generally concerned with direct mail, mail order and door to door personal selling. Today the scope of direct marketing has expanded dramatically largely due to the use of the telephone and in particular the use of the internet. Direct marketing includes all of the marketing communications elements that allow the marketing firm to communicate directly with a prospect. This includes direct mail, telephone marketing, direct response advertising, door to door personal selling and, of course, the use of the internet.

Party-plan companies have been selling products directly to customers in people's homes for many years. The telephone has been used for business-to-business sales for a long time, particularly for the regeneration of 'routine' orders and for making sales appointments. It is now being used increasingly in domestic direct-marketing programmes, often to 'follow up' a posted personalised mail-shot. Motoring organisations, such as the RAC and AA in the UK, have used direct personal selling for years to sell membership of their organisations and today use direct mail extensively to keep members informed about product and service benefits. However, today, as already mentioned above, direct marketing has evolved along with the tremendous advances in technology, especially computer technology.

6.1.2   Not all direct marketing is IT driven

However not everything in the modern direct marketing world is IT driven. There is still room for 'old fashioned' tried and tested methods that are well proven and have been used for a long time. Some of the more traditional direct marketing methods are still employed and are still effective; door to door selling for example is still widely used by many companies. Traditional direct mail and telephone marketing techniques are still widely employed by a wide range of direct marketing companies. Hence modern direct marketing is by no means all 'hi tech', but as with many other areas of marketing and business in general it is tending to move in that direction.

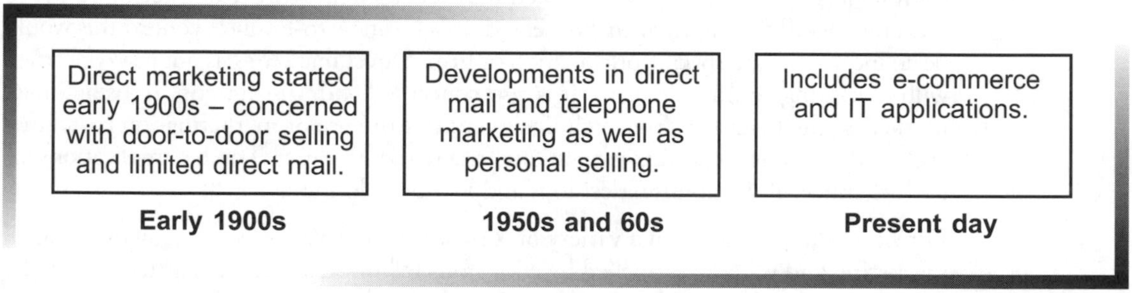

Direct marketing started early 1900s – concerned with door-to-door selling and limited direct mail.	Developments in direct mail and telephone marketing as well as personal selling.	Includes e-commerce and IT applications.
Early 1900s	**1950s and 60s**	**Present day**

Figure 6.1   The development of direct marketing over time, (Lancaster and Reynolds 2001).

6.2   The objective of direct marketing

Much direct marketing activity is intended to result in a sale. In some situations a direct sale result is unlikely or inappropriate. In such cases some other form of measurable response might be used. For example, a direct-mailing campaign and a telephone-marketing programme may be used in the engineering industry to invite and encourage buyers from engineering firms to attend a machine tool exhibition being put on in London. A leaflet drop for double-glazing might contain a free telephone number for the prospect to request a brochure or estimate. The result may not be an actual sale but some specific, measurable action that will hopefully contribute to an ultimate sale taking place at the 'end of the day'.

6.2.1   Strategic role of direct marketing

Direct marketing is likely to form a major part of the communications strategy of many companies and not simply a sort of tactical adjunct. However important direct marketing is to a particular firm, it is unlikely that direct marketing will be used in a vacuum. Other forms of communications are likely to be used in conjunction with direct-marketing programmes even if these are only general corporate advertising programmes. Many firms will use direct marketing predominantly but not necessarily to the exclusion of other communication methods. Direct marketing is often used as part of an integrated customer-relationship management (CRM) programme, which we will discuss at length in the next chapter. CRM programmes, as we shall see, are by their nature long term and strategic in nature.

6.2.2   Formal definition of direct marketing

Direct marketing is broadly defined, in media terms, as any direct communication to a consumer or business recipient that is designed to generate a response in the form of an order (direct order), a request for further information (lead generation), and/or a visit to a store or other place of business for purchase of specific product(s) or service(s) (traffic generation). The emphasis is on marketing communications; in fact direct marketing could equally be called direct-marketing communications, although as we have already seen, direct marketing has other marketing-mix implications, especially for distribution decisions. A leading trade magazine *Direct Marketing* goes a bit further and defines direct marketing as a process that is:

> 'An interactive system of marketing that uses one or more advertising
> media to effect a measurable response and/or transaction at any location,
> with this activity stored on a database.'

Chris Fill, a best selling author on marketing communications, describes direct marketing as:

> 'Direct marketing is a strategy used to create a personal and intermediary
> free dialogue with customers. This should be a measurable activity and it is
> very often media based, with a view to creating and sustaining a mutually
> rewarding relationship.'

The goal is to provide the customer with information relative to their needs and interests. A recent profile on the direct and interactive marketing industry offers a helpful way of looking at it as a cyclical process with six distinct phases:

❑   The creative stage and design phase where the marketing plan is constructed and appropriate media channels are selected.

❑   Data compilation where both internal data, such as customer lists and outside data from a database company or list broker, is assembled in preparation for the next stage in the programme, being;

❑ Database management...where the information is 'mined', 'fused', aggregated or disaggregated, enhanced and standardised for use in the programme.

❑ Database analysis...fine tuning the database which further focuses on an optimal target market.

❑ Execution and fulfilment where customer inquiries and orders are acted upon and the information on response rates is collected for final post programme analysis.

❑ Finally response analysis where the results of the campaign are examined for effectiveness before this cycle begins again.

6.3   The Direct Marketing Association (The DMA)

The Direct Marketing Association (The DMA) is the oldest and largest trade association for users and suppliers in the direct, database and interactive marketing fields. Founded in 1917, the DMA has more than 4,700 member organisations, commercial as well as not-for-profit, from the United States and over 53 nations on six continents. Their mission is to encourage the growth and profitability of their members and their adherence to high ethical standards. To achieve this the DMA:

❑ Provide strong leadership in government and public affairs representation, public relations and communications, adherence to established ethical guidelines, self-regulation, and the identification and promotion of new and best practices to project and grow the business.

❑ Promote an environment in which users of direct/interactive marketing and their suppliers will develop the necessary skills to prosper.

❑ Assist members to understand consumer and business customer needs and concerns regarding direct/interactive marketing and confirm that members respect and act on those needs and concerns.

6.4   The use of direct marketing using different media

We will start with the use of the telephone or 'telemarketing', which is an important direct marketing tool and has been in use as such for some time, particularly in industrial and business to business marketing. We will then examine developments and the use of direct mail, which again has seen enormous growth in its use as a direct marketing tool over the last 30 years and continues to go from strength to strength. Telephone marketing and the use of direct mail were two of the main pillars of the direct marketing industry when the international Direct Marketing Association (DMA) was established in the USA in 1917. Moving on from direct mail we will look at some of the quite staggering developments in the use of the internet in direct marketing. Topics will include database marketing and the techniques of data mining and data fusion, which are central to the direct marketing revolution when using this medium. From there we examine the use of direct personal selling which is well established as a direct marketing tool and quite literally formed the 'bedrock' of the direct marketing industry at the time of the establishment of the DMA in 1917.

To finish this chapter we look at direct-response advertising, concentrating mainly on television direct response advertising but also covering newspapers and radio applications.

6.4.1 Telephone marketing

Telephone marketing has been used as a direct marketing tool for many years, although mainly in business-to-business marketing. Every company has a telephone whereas it has only been comparatively recently that most households have had a telephone installed. Telephone marketing is used extensively in business-to-business marketing. Many routine reordering situations can be handled over the telephone without the need for an expensive personal visit. The telephone can be used to keep in touch with customer in between visits. It can be used to make 'cold call' appointments and re-appointments with established clients. In fact the telephone is extremely versatile and can be used in a number of ways as a marketing tool. In consumer markets the telephone is also used extensively and is growing in importance as a marketing tool. Many services, such as banking, are now offered over the telephone and customers can give instructions to pay bills and get a balance on their account by using special access codes. Many companies use the telephone as part of a direct-marketing programme. They may start first with a direct response press advertisement, which gives a free number to call. This usually starts the direct marketing process.

The telephone derives its power as a marketing medium from its transactional nature (i.e. one human being in a *controlled conversation* with another). What originally began as 'ordering by telephone' soon evolved into *telemarketing*, a concept that can be defined as:

> 'Any measurable activity that creates and exploits a direct relationship
> between supplier and customer by the interactive use of the telephone.'
> (Roncoroni 1986)

The American Telephone and Telegraph Company (AT&T) define it as:

> 'The marketing of telecommunications technology and *direct marketing*
> techniques.' (Nash 1984)

Telephone marketing can be divided into incoming and out-going call marketing. With incoming call telemarketing the prospect makes the call to the marketing firm, usually in response to a direct-mail advertisement or direct response television advertisement giving a 'free-phone' or 'toll free' telephone number. Hence telemarketing, as you can appreciate, is often used with other direct marketing tools as a part of an integrated programme. The caller may wish to sign up to a service such as insurance, apply for a loan over the telephone, order a product seen on the television or in a direct-response advertisement, or ask for further details. The call is logged and often recorded. The caller is then followed up by an outgoing telephone call sometime later or sent information through the post. They may even arrange to have a personal visit, from a kitchen surveyor for example. 'Out-going' telephone marketing may simply be the return of an incoming call. Often existing customers are telephoned to ask if they want to take advantage of a special offer. For example if you have taken out a loan with a finance company and have been a good customer, the firm may ring you to see if you want another loan at a special discount rate. A building society or bank may ring a customer to ask if they would like to make an appointment at the branch to have their mortgage reviewed or to discuss house insurance. Out-going telemarketing is used for a wide range of products and services and not just financial services. For example once you have rung a firm to request a brochure for, say, a kitchen range or other home improvement product such as plastic windows, you might receive a call back inviting you to have a 'free' design service or for someone to call around to discuss finance with you.

CASE 6.1

Jacobsons Direct Marketing Services of Dubai bring professional telemarketing services to the Gulf region.

Realising the potential for direct services in the Gulf, considering the challenges that such a closed and private market offered, George Jacob picked up the gauntlet. And so was born Jacobsons Direct Marketing Services LLC. That was in 1986, on a modest scale. The Company is now more than 40 people strong and handles some of the most prominent Blue Chip companies in this part of the world. And is growing in leaps and bounds, constantly making new inroads into every possible aspect of direct marketing. In short, offering its full range of services as a one-stop shop. Jacobsons Direct Marketing Services LLC is based in Dubai. As the firm completes 15 years in one of the richest and fastest growing economies in the world, it looks back at a record that can be matched by few in this arena. The company's experience has been enriched by their knowledge of the people, their customs and lifestyles, their requirements and more specifically, the dos and don'ts of direct selling in this region of the world. Management of the firm believe in Direct Marketing and strive to make it work for their clients! Jacobsons' call-centre has a 20-call-station capacity to carry out in-bound or out-bound telephone campaigns. With appropriate briefing ahead of any assignment, constant supervisor control and executive project management input, a variety of out-bound projects are regularly carried out. These include:

Pre-qualify leads for sales staff and even the booking of their appointments.

Follow-up mail, fax or e-mail campaigns to boost leads.

Generate bookings for client events.

Prospect and develop database profile.

The firm's comprehensive in-bound service platform provides, besides the trained manpower, a dedication of lines for regular or toll-free connections and a high capacity fax pool to:

Handle inquiries generated by direct marketing response advertising and pre-qualify prospects.

Channel feedback related to sales promotions.

Whether for short or long tactical assignments, Jacobsons' trained tele-agents team is proficient in the many languages spoken in the Gulf region. Their experience spans over a variety of projects in both marketing and databases research, which in turn has enriched them with the necessary skills to deal with different kinds of people, situations and themes. This apart, Jacobsons can custom design a telemarketing campaign to meet specific needs from project conceptualisation through scripting, briefing, teleoperation, progress reporting up to analysis. The company provides a very valuable service to the direct marketing industry in this part of the world.

Companies can exploit the telephone as a marketing tool in a number of ways:

❏ **Cost savings**

Telephone selling provides a customised means of communications. Greater sophistication in telemarketing equipment and services, new marketing approaches and developments in applications have turned the use of the telephone into 'telemarketing'. The telephone may not have the quality of a personal sales call but it is significantly cheaper. Sometimes in the initial stages of a direct-marketing programme a personal visit is not necessary or appropriate anyway.

❏ **Supplement to a personal visit**

Professional sales people use a system of 'differential call frequency' to plan their visits to customers. Sales people may have to prioritise their calls on a 'key account' type of basis (See the section on Key Account Management (KAM) in Chapter 7). Although they might be able to visit the less important customers with the same frequency as the more important customers, they can make a telephone call on a regular basis to keep customers informed of things and to build and maintain the relationship.

❏ **Gaining market intelligence**

Marketing firms can speak to their customers on a regular basis, not only to maintain relationships but also to ask questions about their needs and wants and purchasing intentions. This information can be recorded and fed into the firm's marketing information system (MkIS) for future use. Buyer's intentions can be used to produce qualitative sales forecasts for future planning needs. On establishing customer needs telephone marketers can introduce new products to the client and use the call to sell on further product.

❏ **Supplement to direct mail and other advertising**

Many direct mail and other forms of direct-response advertising, on the television, press or radio for example, will carry a 'freephone' or 'toll free' message. This enables the prospect to make telephone contact at no cost to them. The prospect can make an immediate commitment to purchase whilst the advertising message is still fresh in their minds. If they do not ring to make an actual purchase they may telephone for further information which in turn produces a qualified lead for further marketing actions.

6.4.2 Direct mail

What is direct mail?

Direct mail is considered by some to be an advertising medium, but by others to be a quite separate element of the marketing communications mix. Direct mailing is the use of the postal service to distribute a piece of informative literature or other promotional material to selected prospects.

A 'direct mail shot' may consist of anything from a letter to weighty catalogues of product offerings. The most familiar regular users of direct mail techniques in the UK today are probably Readers Digest and the Automobile Association.

Direct mail is a method of communicating a message directly to a particular person, household or firm. As such it falls under the more general heading of *direct marketing* which includes many other forms of direct communication. To avoid confusion, let us distinguish direct mail from related activities with which it is commonly confused:

Direct mail is not:

Direct advertising. This is one of the oldest methods of reaching the consumer. It consists of printed matter that is sent by the advertiser directly to the prospect. This material is often sent by mail, but it may also be distributed by house-to-house or personal delivery, handed out to passers-by, or even put under the windscreen wipers of parked cars. That portion of direct advertising that is sent through the mail is called *direct mail advertising.* Hence some, but not all, direct advertising is a form of direct mail.

Mail order. If the object of a direct mail shot is to persuade recipients to order the product or service by return post, the correct term is *mail order* or *mail order advertising.* Deliveries are made through mail or parcel services or by carrier direct from a warehouse or factory or sometimes through a local agent. Mail order is a special form of direct mail. Mail order seeks to complete the sale entirely by mail, while direct mail is generally supplementary to other forms of advertising and selling. Direct mail is usually a part of a company's general marketing plan, whereas mail order advertising is a complete plan in itself, and companies exist solely to conduct business in this manner. Hence, mail order is a type of direct mail, but not all direct mail is mail order.

Direct response advertising. Neither direct mail nor mail order should be confused with direct response advertising. This is the strategy of using specially designed advertisements, usually in newspapers and magazines, to invoke a direct response rather than a delayed one. The most familiar type of direct response advertising is the *coupon-response press advertisement*, in which a return coupon is provided which the reader may use to order the advertised product or service or to request further information or a sales call. Other variants involve incentives to visit the retail outlet immediately, such as special preview invitations and money-off coupons. Direct mail can also be used for direct response advertising.

6.4.3   The growth of direct mail in UK marketing

Post Office statistics show a continuing rise in the annual volume of direct mail and in the number of organisations using it for business and consumer communication. There are a number of factors that account for this increased usage and acceptance of direct mail as a major medium. One of the most significant is the fragmentation of media:

❑   There are now five UK terrestrial commercial television channels as well as a wide choice of satellite plus cable television being available to subscribers.

❑   In the print media, there has been the rapid growth of 'freesheets' alongside traditional 'paid for' local press, as well as an increase in 'special interest' magazines.

This fragmentation means that media buyers and advertisers either have to spend more money to make sure they reach as wide an audience as previously, or spread the same amount more thinly over a range of media. Developments in the direct mail industry have removed many difficulties that have previously deterred large advertisers particularly in respect of the poor quality of large mail shots – hence such material was dubbed 'junk mail'. IT advances have made it possible to personalise mail shots, targeted to individuals by name. Quality has been greatly improved by increased money and creative intelligence that has been channelled into direct mail.

CASE 6.2

UKDM.co.uk offers direct marketers the resources they need when they need them.

At UKDM they provide every possible resource to guide the direct marketer in the right direction. The firm concentrates mainly in the area of direct mail but offers other direct-marketing services and advice as well. If you have ever needed a mailing list for a campaign but did not know where to look you will love UKDM. If you need to find out about data mining or data fusion but do not know who to ask – go to UKDM. The firm provides clients with a comprehensive supplier directory, which lists suppliers of direct-marketing products and services. The directory covers list brokers, address management, direct mail and telemarketing services. The company's aim is quite simple; they want to be the first place clients think of and come to when they have a direct marketing problem. UKDM aims to give clients a solution to any direct marketing problem. They have gathered the most-up-to-date information about a wide range of direct marketing services. In the firm's 'DM Showcase' on-line service they will answer customer's queries about direct-marketing problems. Information includes what products and services are the most suitable for a specific campaign and how firms can maximise the effect of their direct-marketing budget. UKDM aims to be a one-stop shop for all the direct-marketing trade's needs. In a sense they are the professional direct marketers direct marketer. The firm is new and the range of products and services available are still being developed. However, UKDM will prove to be a valuable resource and a first point of call for many direct marketers needing rapid advice and information.

6.4.4 Uses of direct mail

The range of products or services that can be sold by direct mail is very wide, as are its uses. To help define it more fully, it is appropriate to deal with direct mail to consumers and businesses separately.

Consumer direct mail

The uses of consumer-targeted direct mail are only limited by the scope of marketing imagination. Some of the more common uses are:

❑ **Selling direct:** If a company has a convincing sales message, any product or service can be sold by direct mail. It is a good medium for selling a product directly to the customer without the need for middlemen. The product can be described fully and orders can be sent straight back to the advertising company.

❑ **Sales lead generation:** If a product requires a meeting between the customer and a specialised salesperson (e.g. fitted kitchens and insurance) direct mail can be a useful method of acquiring good, qualified leads for the company's sales people. Sales calls are expensive, so anything that helps improve the call success rate is welcome. A well-planned mailshot can act as a preliminary sieve, pinpointing the best prospects and ranking others in terms of sales potential. The 'warmer' the leads, the more effective will be the company's sales force with fewer wasted calls.

Direct mail creates a receptive atmosphere for the salespeople through *cordial contact mailings* that build on the reputation of the company and through the 'impact' or impression created. Well-executed mailing identify the company in a favourable light to prospects, setting up 'good will' or creating a latent desire that might be triggered into action by a later mailing.

❑ **Sales promotion:** Direct mail can send promotional messages – 'money off' vouchers, special offers, etc. to selected targets. This can be a useful way of encouraging people to visit a shop or exhibition.

❑ **Clubs:** Book clubs are perhaps the best known example of the use of direct mail as a convenient medium of communication and transaction between a club and its members. Other items can be marketed by the club system; particularly 'collectibles' e.g. record 'collections', porcelain and miniatures.

❑ **Mail order:** Some mail order companies use direct mail to recruit new customers and local agents, as well as for direct selling.

❑ **Fundraising:** One of the advantages of direct mail is the ability to communicate personally with an individual. This makes it a powerful method of raising money (e.g. for charitable organisations). It can carry the 'long copy' often needed to convince a recipient of the worthiness of the charity, and make it more likely that the reader might respond with a donation.

❑ **Dealer mailings:** If a product is sold through dealers or agents, they can use direct mail to reach prospective customers in their catchment area, as a producer might.

❑ **Follow-up mailings:** The company's name can be promoted to the customer by following any kind of sales activity with a mailing, e.g. checking that the customer is satisfied with their purchase or reminding them that their car is coming up for its annual service. Customers can be kept informed of new developments, latest products and improved services. 'Exclusive' offers can be made and invitations issued. Using direct mail in this way helps to maintain contact – quickly, personally and effectively and increase repeat sales.

Business direct mail

Business markets are made up of closely defined, discrete groups of individuals. These groups may not be best reached by mass advertising media. Direct mail can be used to accurately identify different market sectors and provide messages appropriate to each sector. Some of the more common uses in this context are:

❑ **Product launch:** Often the launch of a new industrial product or business service entails getting the message across to a small, but significant, number of people who will influence buying decisions (e.g. catering and car fleet managers).

❑ **Sales lead generation:** As in consumer markets, direct mail can effectively reach qualified sales leads for a company's sales force.

❑ **Dealer support:** Direct mail makes it easy to keep dealers, retail outlets, franchise holders, etc, more fully informed of tactical marketing promotions and plans.

❑ **Conferences and exhibitions:** Business and trade conferences and exhibitions are well-established means of communicating with potential customers and business colleagues. Direct mail can be used to invite delegates, who may be attracted if the event relates to a specific theme of direct interest to them.

❑ **Follow-up mailing using the customer base:** Much business takes the form of repeat sales to the customer base. Since these are existing clients it can be worthwhile mailing them regularly, as long as the content of the mail-out relates to something that is new or of specific interest rather than simply junk mail.

❑ **Marketing research/product testing:** Direct mail can be used for marketing research, especially amongst existing customers. Questionnaires can be used as part of a regular communication programme, with levels of response being increased by some kind of incentive. Small-scale test mailings can be made to sample a target market. The results can give a quick and accurate picture of market reaction, with minimum risk. A marketing approach that is successful in a 'test mailing' can later be mailed to the full list.

6.4.5 Direct mail as part of the promotional mix

In both consumer and business markets, direct mail must fit in with a company's other promotion efforts. For example, a television or press campaign can reach a broader audience, and raise the level of general awareness of the company and its products. If such a campaign is added to a direct-mail campaign aimed specifically at groups of people or companies most likely to buy, or to people particularly wanted as customers, the effectiveness of the overall campaign can be significantly raised.

List of respondents to direct-response techniques in other media (e.g. 'couponed' press advertisements or television or radio commercials which give a 'phone-in' number or a contact address) can be used as mailing lists for direct mail approaches.

6.4.6 The use of the Internet as a direct marketing tool

Society is changing at what seems to be an ever-increasing rate. More choice, less time to choose and to enjoy the results of our choice. Everyone seems to have less time even though the futurologists of only a few years back stated that new technology would give us all more time and lead to the 'leisure society'. Customers have more products and service to choose from and more information available to them to help them make their purchasing decisions. Think about the task of purchasing a new mobile telephone for example. The products are so sophisticated today, there are so many different models and the information available on the capabilities of each model in magazines, on the Internet and in conventional advertising is enormous. Where do you start? Consumers wish to shop at all hours even on a Sunday or bank holiday. Some people want to go to the supermarket in the middle of the night. People do their banking on their mobile telephone, research house purchases on the internet and book their air tickets through the television offers using Teletext.

CASE 6.3

Direct Response Services Inc. of Beverly Hills, California

DRS are a full service marketing and advertising agency, founded in 1994, with special emphasis on direct marketing and Internet-based marketing. The firm takes pride in the services they provide, using proven direct marketing techniques to help clients acquire new customers, retain and increase profits from current customers, increase their web traffic, and support their sales efforts. They provide a complete range of marketing services that satisfy client objectives, complement their image, and communicate their message. The firm stays focused on cost-effective results. The Internet has dramatically changed the way retailers do business. Customers can now shop for a great variety of products from their home or office, anytime day or night. Research indicates there are over 100 million World Wide Web users and that 60% currently shop online. That number is expected to grow exponentially. DRS advise clients how they should be participating in this retailing revolution. No matter if a company's product is books, flowers, clothing, health food, sporting goods or any number of other products, Direct Response Specialists can assist with Internet direct-marketing programmes. Within a matter of weeks, firms can be marketing their products online to current and new customers using the DRS turnkey package of services. While DRS has experience in many product and service categories, they have major knowledge and marketing background in the following areas:

Retail	Business-to-Business	Package goods
Telecommunications	Emerging technology	Software
Consumer electronics	Financial services	Insurance
Fund raising	Lead generation	Traffic building

Seth Godin, author of *Permission Marketing*, said that the average consumer sees 3,000 marketing messages a day. To reach its audience a message has to be relevant and well targeted. Godin is working to persuade some of the most important firms in the world to change the way they relate to their customers. His argument is both simple and radical: conventional marketing communications, particularly conventional media advertising, is not as effective as it used to be. This is partly because there is much more of it for consumers to see and digest, and partly because people have learned to ignore it. The rise of the internet also means that companies can go further than conventional communications would allow them to in the past.

There is a new group of products and services that relies on customers registering their interest in them with the company. Amazon.com, for example, encourages its customers to review books and publishes their comments on the web site so both the firm and other users can read them and make use of them. A US airline invites customers to register their preferences for last minute offers via its web site, and then emails potential customers with details of weekend breaks at their preferred resorts. These are classic examples of the precision that can be achieved with direct marketing.

Potentially the internet is going to be the most powerful direct marketing tool the world has ever seen. In another ten years or so owning a computer workstation which is wired to the Internet will be as common as owning a television is today. The children being taught at school using the new technology today and playing computer games at home will take the use of the Internet as a 'shopping medium' for granted. The Internet is not a fad or short-term trend, it's a major technological development that is here to stay and will continually evolve. This is the beginning of the next business resolution that will affect the way you live, work and possibly play, for the rest of your life. The technology involved in setting up the Internet has demonstrated to management that it will significantly change the way people interact with each other, particularly so in the sphere of direct marketing. The Internet crosses the boundary of geography, politics, race, sex, religion, time zones and culture. Technology, of any kind, helps to make possible and, hopefully, improve the way we work. Without it many of the things we do – and often take for granted – would be at best difficult, and often impossible. For example, much of advertising relies on communications technology; effective distribution and logistics relies on transport technologies; marketing research and analysis increasingly relies upon computing technology.

E-marketing, based on internet technology and the variations that have been developed from the original Internet concepts such as the intranet and the extranet, which connects and links employees, customers, suppliers and partners. The internet has reduced the planet into a 'global village', accelerated the pace of technology, opened up tremendous possibilities for direct marketers, and altered the way they think about doing business. It has started the new revolution in direct marketing, some say the most important revolution since the invention of commercial advertising, the 'e-commerce revolution'. It is the revolution people can no longer ignore anymore.

6.5   Database marketing

The improvements in database software and related computer technology have revolutionised the direct marketing industry throughout the world. Nothing has driven the direct marketing industry forward more than developments in information technology and especially in the development of database software and applications. Database marketing is a marketing and sales system that continually gathers, refines, and utilises information and data that then drives relevant marketing and sales communications programs. It is often used extensively, but not necessarily exclusively, in direct marketing programmes. Examples of this are sales calls, direct-mail pieces, and advertising to selected companies in order to acquire new customers, retain customers, generate more business from existing customers, and create long-term loyalty. The world of sales and marketing is changing all the time. The Internet, e-commerce, the continuing rise of direct marketing and the increasing marketing emphasis on customer retention over customer acquisition are only a few of the salient factors affecting the way firms carry out business in the modern world. Firms have to move very fast, keep up with the latest developments and trends and invest in the most relevant software and systems to stay ahead of the competition. You will notice that 'database marketing' is two words. The first word implies that data is organised and stored in a computer system. The second word implies that firms use this data in their marketing and sales programs.

Database marketing is much more than just a data retrieval system. While direct marketing describes a collection of marketing communication tactics (such as direct mail, response advertising, etc.), database marketing describes a way of organising a company's total marketing and sales process.

6.5.1   What does database marketing allow you to do?

Database marketing is all about focusing and targeting. Databases take the 'guess' out of marketing programmes. They do not necessarily provide perfect accuracy but they do allow for significant improvements in both accuracy and efficiency if used properly. Many companies do a sort of 'hit-or-miss' marketing, for want of a better phrase. That means that management often makes decisions based on intuition or instinct rather than on hard facts based on clear 'scientific' evidence. Hence instead of predicting their target audience based on hard facts they make their best 'guesses' about whom their target audience is and what their audience wants. This process of 'best guessing' can be very expensive in terms of wasted direct mail shots and other forms of communication, and wasted time and effort.

As already referred to, database marketing lets you work more intelligently; it gives you the tools to make more accurate assessments. It lets you take the information you already have in your customer or sales-lead databases, analyse it to find the patterns in it, such as purchasing associations and relationships, and use the information you gained from your analysis to produce and instigate better marketing and sales programs. 'Running better marketing and sales programs' simply means targeting specific groups with specific messages about products that are important to them rather than giving them irrelevant and uninteresting information. If you are able to target the right industries with the right messages about the right products, you will spend less sales and marketing resources marketing to companies and/or individuals, that are never going to buy. Hence you will have more resources to spend on the prospects that are most likely to buy, increasing the return on your marketing and sales investment.

6.5.2 Basic principles of database marketing

Below are some illustrations of the possible applications and basic principles of database marketing. They are not intended to be exhaustive or definitive but they do serve to illustrate the main principles:

❑ First of all find out what characteristics your best customers have in common so you can target your next programs to prospects that have those same character- istics. See exactly which market segments buy from your firm. You might think that you already know your best market segments, but through analysis you could uncover market segments that you have sold a significant amount of product to but did not realise it. This process may enable the firm to improve its segmentation of the market by refocusing and redefining existing segments or may highlight totally unexpected new segments.

❑ Ascertain whether different market segments buy different products from you. This information will allow you to spend your marketing and sales resources more effectively by marketing each of your products to their best potential industries, individual firms or individual people. Learn which market segments bring you the most revenue and which ones bring you the highest average revenue. This is what differentiated marketing is all about; dividing the total market into segments and then having a slightly different marketing strategy for each segment.

❑ Find out what types of industries, firms or individuals respond to what types of marketing communications so you can decide where to spend your advertising and marketing resources the next time. Find out which market segments not only respond to your programs but also actually buy, and which buy from you repeatedly. Again, these might be very different demographic profiles or differ- ent in some other way which may be commercially exploitable, and you might decide to modify your targeting tactics and only market to the segments that buy repeatedly or at least reasonably frequently.

❑ Calculate the average lifetime value of your customers. This can be done using discounted cash flow procedures (see Chapter 7 where this is discussed in greater depth). You can use this information to find out which customers are not living up to their potential and devise marketing and sales programs to encourage them to buy more. Identify new customers and create programs that will encourage them to buy again. Reward your most frequent buyers and the buyers that bring you the highest revenue. The concept of 'lifetime' value is central to the idea of customer retention and long-term relationship marketing. The subject of relationship marketing is covered in more detail in Chapter 7.

6.5.3 Direct personal selling

Marketing communications can be classified as personal or impersonal forms. Much of conventional advertising would be classified as impersonal. Personal selling, as the name suggests, is personal and involves some form of interaction with a prospect, sometimes referred to as a 'dyadic relationship'. This interaction can be at a distance, over the telephone for example. However, the majority of personal selling is carried out on a face-to-face basis. In fact, this face-to-face dimension is one of the key strengths of personal selling. Personal selling can be more expensive for direct marketing firms on a cost-per-contact basis but sometimes there is simply no substitute for the personal approach. Both firms and customers benefit from the direct personal-selling approach. Consumers benefit from direct selling because of the convenience and service it provides to them, including personal communication, demonstration and explanation of products to a higher standard than in conventional stores or through printed media, usually home delivery sometimes by the sales person who took the order, Kleeneze Household Products for example (see Case 6.6), and satisfaction guarantees given in writing and on a face-to-face basis. It is different from conventional shopping and cuts out the need for marketing intermediaries thereby saving the customer money. Many people find it more convenient, cheaper and more interesting than conventional shopping.

The task of selling differs according to the products or services being marketed. In some situations the task of selling is more a position of keeping customers satisfied and the task will then call for more skills of personality and 'caring'. In other situations, contractual negotiations might be the main emphasis of selling where skills of prospecting, negotiating, demonstrating and closing a sale will be a greater element of success. In organisational (including industrial) marketing, great reliance is placed on personal communication. For FMCG products a lot of faith is placed on above- and below-the-line communication. In organisational selling the proportion of selling within the total market budget often outweighs all other marketing expenditure. Direct selling is a specific form of selling. Not only is it personal but also direct and constitutes a rapidly expanding channel of distribution for the marketing of products and services directly to consumers. Moreover, direct selling provides a channel of distribution for companies with innovative or distinctive products not readily available in traditional retail outlets. It may be that the products on offer are produced by a relatively small firm that cannot afford to compete with the enormous advertising and promotion costs associated with gaining space on the retail shelves of major retail outlets. Hence the customer gains by being able to purchase products that would have been unavailable if the marketing company had to operate through more conventional retail outlets. Direct selling enhances the retail distribution infrastructure of the economy and plays an important part in the retail distribution system of the country. It is particularly useful for elderly and infirm people and potential customers who find it difficult to get out of the house. It serves consumers with a convenient source of quality products that may not be available elsewhere.

Direct selling can best be described as the marketing of products and services directly to consumers in a face to face manner, generally in their homes or the homes of others, at their workplace and other places away from permanent retail locations. Direct sales typically occur through explanation or personal demonstration by an independent direct salesperson. These sales people are commonly referred to as direct sellers.

Independent direct sellers are those individuals engaged on their own behalf, or on behalf of a direct selling company, selling products and services through personal sales contacts, and are commonly referred to in law as independent contractors. Essentially, this means that the company whose products they distribute does not employ these independent sales people, but rather they are independent business people operating their own businesses and responsible for their own affairs. This usually means that they have a higher level of motivation and often strive to give a better service and a higher level of customer satisfaction than 'employees' selling for another organisation. These independent direct sellers have an opportunity to earn substantial profits from their business operations, and also have to accept the responsibility for the risks associated with operating an independent business such as keeping records for tax and insurance purposes and paying National Insurance contributions. They also have to comply with the Health and Safety regulations of the country they are operating in and the Codes of Conduct for a particular industry or professional body, e.g. The Direct Marketing Association or The World Federation of Direct Selling Associations (see sections 6.3 and 6.6).

CASE 6.4

Direct Multi-Level Marketing (MLM) delivery system has allowed household products firm to grow exponentially.

Multi-Level Marketing (MLM), sometimes referred to as 'network marketing', like many commercial innovations was pioneered in the USA. However, the method has been exported to the UK and now a number of mainly direct marketing companies use the method with great effect. One of these is the firm Kleeneze that originally started out in business selling brushes direct to the public. Kleeneze, the household products firm, has pioneered the use of multi-level marketing in the distribution of household related products. Kleeneze is a founder member of the Direct Selling Association (DSA) and as such adheres to a strict code of Business Practice and Ethics. The firm is a publicly quoted company on the London Stock Exchange. The firm has a reputation, built up over many years of successful trading, of being committed to innovation and quality. All their products are fully guaranteed. All of the firms products are environmentally friendly, biodegradable and the firm does not test any of its products on animals.

What has changed dramatically from the company's early years is the method of distribution the firm employs. Kleeneze has now changed over to Multi-Level Marketing (MLM), as a distribution system. The system harnesses the entrepreneurial power of individuals by allowing them to become a registered Kleeneze agent by effectively running their own network marketing business under the banner of the Kleeneze corporate brand name. Kleeneze is a direct selling business, engaged in the network marketing of its products and business opportunity. The MLM system employed offers the opportunity of economic independence, personal growth and professional development. The programme offers an opportunity for all those who seek an outlet for their own commercial and entrepreneurial drive. Rewards can be substantial. Part time agents, selling via catalogue door-to-door can earn £200 per week. The big rewards come from developing the network of agents and managing them as a team. People start off as a 'direct agent' and can progress to full 'distributor'. The distributor gets downstream commission from all other agents recruited on the basis of their sales. The distributor also gets further secondary downstream commission on the sales made by further agents recruited by the original agents, and so on. Some 'full-time agents' can realise over £100,000 per year pre-tax.

The products and services sold by direct sellers are as varied as the people involved in the direct selling industry and include: insurance, mortgages, and financial services in general, cosmetics and skin care products; laundry and personal care items; vacuum cleaners and home appliances; household specialities; household cleaning products; food and nutrition products; toys, books and educational products; and clothing, jewellery and fashion accessories; just to mention a few. Sometimes, these products are sold in the context of group presentations (Party Plan). Tupperware Ltd, produce a range of products, which are basically a selection of kitchenware and food and drink storage boxes. The company is a classic example of a party-plan selling strategy used by a successful firm. Often goods and services are sold on a person-to-person basis (one-to-one). In a Party Plan approach, the direct salesperson demonstrates products to a group of guests, invited by a host in whose home or other location the direct selling demonstration takes place. By contrast, other direct sellers will often explain and demonstrate the products they offer to consumers in the comfort of the consumers' homes, at a time, that is convenient for them on a personal 'one-to-one' basis rather than in a group. Avon Cosmetics uses freelance salespeople or agents to visit people in their own homes and to demonstrate and explain the use of a range of beauty products. Direct selling provides important benefits to individuals who desire an opportunity to earn an income and build a business of their own. It offers the prospect of self-determination and financial independence. It also offers an alternative to consumers who want something different from the traditional shopping centres, department stores or other forms of conventional shopping. It offers an alternative to traditional employment for those who desire a flexible income earning opportunity to supplement their household income, or whose responsibilities or circumstances do not allow for regular part-time or full-time employment.

6.6 Multi-Level Marketing

Multi-Level Marketing (MLM), like many innovative business systems, has been developed in the United States and exported to other parts of the world. Some people are very suspicious of MLM and sometimes confuse it with what is known as 'pyramid selling', which is an unethical business practice, banned in the UK. *An important component of the Direct Selling industry* is *Multi-level marketing*. It is also referred to as network marketing, structure marketing or multi-level direct selling, and has proven over many years to be a highly successful and effective method of compensating direct sellers for the marketing and distribution of products and services directly to consumers. Unlike 'pyramid selling' MLM is an ethical business system that uses the principle of 'team building' to sell products and manage the sales force. The direct selling people making up the sales force are usually self-employed people working on a freelance basis for commission on sales.

People usually start by selling goods and services to the public, often in the first instance people they know such as friends and work colleagues. They then move on to not only sell themselves but recruit others to sell as part of their team. They not only receive commission on the goods they sell themselves but also earn substantial 'down stream' commission on the products the people they have recruited have sold. Eventually they may move away from selling directly themselves and concentrate on managing others in their team. As the team grows so does the downstream commission due to the original team organiser. In the end the team leader may have a network of dozens of direct-selling staff at different level in the hierarchy. Some will be content to sell some product directly to customer on a part-time basis. Some will want to recruit a small team and may work on a part time or full time basis. Some want to be senior team leaders and put in the effort to lead a whole networking team of direct personal selling staff and reap the rewards of substantial commissions based on the selling effort of their team combined with their own motivational, leadership and managerial skills.

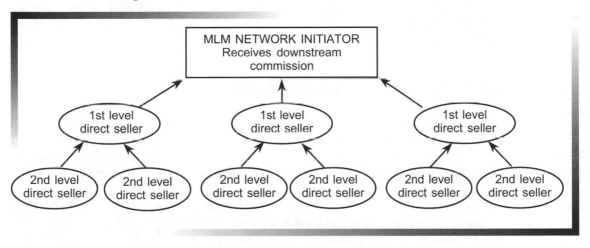

Figure 6.2 The principle of multi level marketing (MLM) showing the team originator receiving downstream commissions from those lower in the network (Lancaster and Reynolds 2001)

6.6.1 The World Federation of Direct Selling Associations

History and mission

Founded in 1978, the WFDSA is a non-governmental, voluntary organisation representing the direct selling industry globally as a federation of national Direct Selling Associations. The United States Direct Selling Association serves as the Secretariat for the Federation and is based in Washington DC. The mission of the WFDSA is to support direct selling associations in the areas of governance, education, communications, consumer protection and ethics in the marketplace and to promote personal interaction among direct-selling executives regarding issues of importance to the industry. There are presently over 50 national DSAs represented in its membership, and in 2001 it is estimated that worldwide retail sales by its members accounted for more than $95 billion US through the activities of more than 25 million independent salespersons. The World Federation and its national DSAs have always understood the necessity for ethical conduct in the marketplace and, as such, the WFDSA has developed a World Codes of Conduct for Direct Selling which all national DSAs have approved and implemented in their national codes. All direct-selling companies agree to be bound by these codes as a condition of membership in a national DSA.

Background and objectives

The WFDSA seeks to exchange information among its members, foster the highest standards of direct selling practices by adoption and promotion of the Codes of Conduct for Direct Selling and encourage personal relationships and co-operation among people in direct selling. The WFDSA also promotes education about direct selling through programs and funding, relying on the US Direct Selling Education Foundation as a 'centre of excellence' to meet this objective. Every three years a World Congress of direct selling worldwide is organised and held by the WFDSA. The WFDSA regularly publishes a newsletter, *World Federation News*, with an international focus on direct selling for distribution to the member direct-selling associations and their member companies. Any duly constituted association of direct selling companies may apply for admission to the WFDSA, although only one association from each country may be admitted.

6.7 Direct response advertising

There has been an enormous growth in the use of direct-response advertising by marketing firms, particularly direct-response television advertising. Direct-response advertising is a major part of the communication activities classified as a whole as direct marketing. 'What is "direct-response advertising"?' you may be asking, and how does it differ from conventional media advertising? Basically, 'direct-response advertising' uses carefully crafted marketing communications to generate a response directly from the advertising itself; a telephone call to you asking for an appointment or further information; an order in the post or a request for a brochure; a credit card order by phone or post as a result of a specific advertisement; a coupon presented for a discount or free sample; all these are responses to a company being generated directly from the advertising itself, hence the term, 'direct-response'. For example, a product may be advertised on commercial television that you simply cannot by anywhere else. The only way to get the product is to pick up the telephone and ring the 'freephone' or 'toll free' number given in the advertisement. You then give your credit card or charge card details and the product is then dispatched to you by courier or through the post. Credit terms are often available for more expensive items and you can set up a direct debit arrangement over the telephone. There is often a further related 'free gift', such as extra product or an additional product, if you place your order within a short period of time. Such advertising formats are being used more and more within the UK and are already used extensively in the USA.

6.7.1 The need for careful planning

Direct-response advertising is not some form of unusual or magical way of generating business however, it takes planning and preparation to do it right. Marketing, after all, is an on-going process that requires careful preparation. Most importantly, since the firm is generating – and monitoring – responses, management can measure the contacts or income produced by each individual advertisement, commercial or mailing. Conventional advertising is notoriously difficult to evaluate in terms of sales response, and it is usually more appropriate to evaluate the 'communications effect' rather than the 'sales effects' when using such advertising. With direct-response advertising there is a direct association between the advertising and the degree of response, which can be objectively measured. Management can actually see how many sales or enquiries you have managed to generate from a given expenditure. Management can test different advertising in consecutive issues of the same publication, and see which advertisement is most effective. Or schedule the same advertisement in different publications and learn which publication is most effective and efficient in producing the desired response.

6.7.2 Direct response and conventional media advertising

The opposite of direct-response advertising is 'institutional' or 'image' advertising. This form of advertising is really trying to generate awareness or communicate particular product attributes rather than initiate a specific response such as making a sale. Look at the advertisements for a range of products such as new cars, perfume, designer clothes, and brand name jewellery, to name a few common examples. These product manufacturers place advertising filling the page or TV airtime with 'artistic' views of their products, with little or no text. The object of the advertisement is to communicate the brand name and the product attributes. As mentioned earlier it is difficult for the firm to evaluate the specific sales response of such an advertisement because of the problem of 'multiple causation'. The advertisement is probably only one of a number of communications being used by the firm simultaneously. It is difficult to separate out the effects, particularly the sales effects. Because they don't have any response generator or tracking mechanism in place for quantifying sales results it is difficult to ascertain which particular medium is working and which is not. The specific communication effects can be measured and related to the final sale but it is still difficult to measure the exact contribution a particular advertisement has made to the final sale. As previously mentioned, it was Lord Lever, the soap magnate who famously said: 'I know that half my advertising is wasted but I do not know which half.' This is probably true today for many firms attempting to evaluate the effects of their convention media advertising.

6.7.3 Direct response advertising needs to be compelling

Direct-response advertising is different from conventional media advertising. It relies on well-designed, compelling and persuasive text to bring about a specified response. Its objective is not merely to inform but to bring about a desired specific response, which can be objectively measured. With direct-response advertising, creative writers usually use art-work copy, page layout, plus carefully chosen text, to explain all the salient reasons why purchasing a product or service is the right thing to do. After all, once the firm has a prospect's attention through using a direct response communication, does it not make sense to tell him or her, in a persuasive, creative, sincere and truthful way, what is exceptional about the firm's product or service and to encourage the prospect to respond rather than merely informing them about product features or some other product or service information? Direct response advertising is appropriate for a wide range of products and services. It is not a 'catch all' panacea and there may well be situations where the use of conventional media advertising used in conjunction with other communications tools would be more appropriate. When used, direct-response advertising allows the user to gain greater precision in their targeting of the message and allows for more accurate evaluation of the advertising against specific measurable response criteria.

Summary

Direct marketing is a branch of marketing that has gone through radical technological change and seen enormous growth in its use over the last 30 years. It is a very important marketing process and some firms base their whole marketing strategies on direct marketing methods. Worldwide, the direct marketing industry is huge with £ billions spent each year. As marketing firms seek ways of obtaining even more value from their marketing budgets, direct marketing is likely to become an even stronger force in the future than it is at present. Direct marketing refers to a collection of methods that, when used by marketing firms, allows them to communicate with and obtain a direct response from a prospect or customer. It allows firms to target prospect and customers more precisely than conventional non-direct marketing techniques and is sometimes referred to as 'precision marketing'.

Direct marketing techniques and methods are constantly being improved and developed and new techniques and innovative media are likely to be developed in the future. At the present time the main methods employed within the direct marketing industry are the use of the telephone, direct mail, the use of the internet, direct 'face-to-face' personal selling and direct-response advertising using television, radio and publications including newspapers, trade journals and magazines. The industry is being driven by firms' desire for greater accuracy and economy in their marketing operations and by the quite stunning technological developments in information technology that can be applied to direct-marketing methods. Database marketing particularly has revolutionised the way firms use direct-marketing procedures and has increased the efficiency of areas such as direct mail and telephone marketing significantly. However, as we have seen, the direct marketing industry is for from being completely driven by information technology and computers. Some of the tried and tested methods that were being used back in 1917 when the Direct Marketing Association was founded in the USA are still being used successfully today, particularly face-to-face direct personal selling. However even these techniques have benefited from the information revolution in terms of the retrieval of customer information and improved targeting. Direct marketing is a major force within the marketing profession in general and is likely to remain so for the foreseeable future.

Questions

1. Using examples explain the role of direct response advertising within the overall marketing communications-mix.

2. Explain how the use of 'in-coming call' telephone direct marketing differs in its role and use from 'out-going' telephone direct marketing. Use examples to illustrate the points made.

3. Trace the development of the direct marketing industry from the beginning of the twentieth century to the present day.

4. Demonstrate how direct mail can be used with other direct-marketing tools to form a cohesive and fully integrated direct-marketing programme.

5. Explain the term 'multi level marketing' and give the main reasons for its outstanding success as a direct marketing business process over the last 20 years.

6. Outline selling situations where direct personal selling is likely to be more effective than other direct marketing techniques. Fully justify your point of view by reference to specific examples.

7. Discuss how the internet is likely to develop as a direct marketing tool over the next ten years.

References

Dibb, S, and Simpkin, L, (2001) *Marketing Briefs: A Revision and Study Guide*, (Butterworth-Heinemann).

Fill, C, *Marketing Communications: Contexts, Strategies and Applications*, Chapter 28, (Financial Times – Prentice Hall: Pearson Educational Limited 2002).

Godin, S, *Permission Marketing*, (Simon and Schuster, 1999).

Nash, EL, *Direct marketing*, (McGraw Hill, 1982).

Pickton, D, and Broderick, A, *Integrated marketing Communications*, Chapter 28, (Financial Times – Prentice Hall; Pearson Educational Ltd. 2001).

Roncoroni, S, Direct Marketing, *Financial Times*, 15 April 1986.

7 Customer relationship management

7.1 The essence of customer relationship management

Customer relationship management (CRM) was born out of the marketing concept. It is an extension of the marketing concept, which integrates a number of recent developments in marketing along with the increased technical capabilities open to marketing practitioners resulting from developments in the application of IT. From the mid 1980s more attention has been placed on long-term buyer–seller relationships. A new long-term marketing model, *relationship marketing* was introduced, first for service-based industries, then spreading to many other marketing situations.

Parallel with the development of relationship marketing came the development of the *internal marketing* concept as management realised it was necessary to have the correct internal marketing culture if they were to successfully pursue any meaningful external relationship marketing strategy. Marketing also witnessed a major advance in the application of computer technology. This is evident in database management and the storage of information, such as in data warehousing and the manipulation and processing of customer information such as in data mining and data fusion. There have also been significant advances in the fields of customer care and customer service provision. The detailed analysis and tracking of customers, which the new technology has allowed has enabled management to prioritise customers more effectively. This has resulted in the growing importance of key account management (KAM). These strands have been brought together to create a completely integrated approach to marketing, referred to as customer relationship management (CRM). CRM has been constructed as a synthesis from many concurrent developments in the areas of marketing theory and practice. It is the culmination of many different, but related, modern marketing developments. CRM will not be the last word in marketing. The field of marketing will continue to develop and evolve and in a few years time CRM will have evolved into an even more sophisticated marketing paradigm.

7.1.1 CRM as an integrated system

CRM is a comprehensive approach that provides 'seamless' integration of every facet of business that relates to the customer whether this be marketing, sales, customer service or field support, through the integration of people, process and technology. It does this by taking advantage of the innovatory influence of internet technology. The object of CRM is to create a long term, mutually beneficial relationship with customers. CRM is a major part of many companies' e-commerce strategy and their long term 'relationship marketing' strategy. CRM is a business and technology discipline that helps firms in the acquisition and retention of their most important and profitable customers. The CRM concept requires a fully integrated system that turns the organisation into a 'learning organisation'. The marketing firm attempts to learn as much as possible about their customers. This helps the firm to develop and cement long-term relationships. The marketing firm requires information from a variety of sources to carry out this task. The use of computer database technology enables the firm to store, update and profile customer details and likely requirements. Products, services and marketing communications can be designed for specific customers and targeted more accurately. Firms can take a proactive approach to the satisfaction of their customers needs and wants in anticipating what they want and informing them of what is available.

7.2 CRM and customer satisfaction

Companies cannot succeed or grow unless they can serve their customers with a better value proposition than the competition. Measuring customer loyalty can accurately appraise the weaknesses in a company's value proposition and help to formulate improvements. In fact, attempting to measure customer satisfaction and factoring research information on satisfaction studies into future marketing strategies is one of the fastest growing areas of marketing research. Many firms now specialise in this area and many have developed special formulae or metrics which they claim measure the satisfaction 'index' of consumers' perceptions.

Implementing a CRM solution is critical to the future success of marketing firms. But CRM is rapidly evolving from being a purely technology-centred undertaking to a business-value endeavour; there is a change in emphasis in the way firms are looking at CRM. Organisations are moving away from seeing their customers as merely exploitable income sources to treating them as assets to be valued and nurtured.

Providing customers with ongoing value, satisfying to their individual needs, and ensuring they get what they want when and where they want it is critical in today's dynamic and competitive market. If one company fails its customers, there is any number of rivals waiting to take over.

CASE 7.1

Cap Gemini, Ernst and Young offer specialist CRM expertise to a wide range of international clients.

Cap Gemini Ernst & Young is one of the largest management and IT consulting firms in the world and is publicly traded on the Paris Bourse. The firm's head offices are in Paris. The new company combines the resources of Gemini Consulting, Cap Gemini IT Services and, following the recent acquisition from Ernst & Young LLP, Ernst & Young Consulting Services. CRM maximises the value of a company's customer portfolio through more effective and efficient marketing, sales and customer service. Importantly, in an 'e' enabled world, CRM is increasingly characterised by the convergence of these three previously separate business functions into a continuous closed loop process. Cap Gemini Ernst & Young assists its clients in optimising their customer connections. They help their clients to be more accessible, and easier to do business with in their efforts to know, target, sell to, and service their customers and prospects. Cap Gemini Ernst & Young offers comprehensive end-to-end strategy and connectivity solutions that enhance their clients' customer relationships and fully integrate front - and back-office business operations. The firm has an experienced team of consultants with the requisite experience across industries to design and execute complex CRM initiatives. These competencies allow the firm to address all issues relative to CRM including strategy, marketing, implementation, delivery, change management and outsourcing. The company has helped more than 300 clients lay solid foundations for connected customer-centric organisations. They use client-specific tools and accelerators ensure speed to value. These include Call Centre Assessment, CRM Strategy Alignment (CRM Index), and Advanced Development Centres. The CRM Centric Group Facility as well as Cap Gemini Ernst & Young's Accelerated Solutions Environments ensure the firm are providing market-tested client solutions.

7.3   The nature of modern marketing and CRM

The focus of modern marketing is towards the building and maintenance of longer-term relationships with customers. This long term view of customer value and the buyer–supplier relationship is referred to as *relationship marketing* (RM). This has developed out of the more transaction-based form of marketing practised by the majority of firms up to the beginning of the 1980s. In fact, RM was the precursor of what today has developed into CRM. It would be fair to say that relationship marketing is the very bedrock of the CRM paradigm.

The concept of relationship marketing was introduced into the literature by early researchers into customer care such as Berry (1983). The basic marketing concept is as valid today as it has always been, but the processes used to accomplish this have changed. If you look at a standard marketing textbook from the 1980s and compare it with one from today, you will see a number of topics in the more recent version, which were not even mentioned in earlier versions. Topics such as 'Internal Marketing', 'Relationship Marketing', 'Precision Marketing', 'One-2-One marketing', 'e-marketing', 'Green Marketing' and 'Customer Relationship Management' in particular, are all fairly recent additions to the marketing literature. There has been a paradigm shift in the way that marketing firms view their customers, look after them, nurture them and establish relationships with them over the long term. The CRM approach to customers is the culmination of this new paradigm. Basically the focus of marketing has shifted from the shorter term view of customers as the next 'transaction' to seeing customers as a long-term income stream over many years. RM has now been taken a stage further to emerge as a fully integrated CRM concept.

7.4 Customer care and its role in CRM

Customer care is fundamental to the concept of CRM. In fact, the recent developments in RM and its evolution into a totally integrated CRM model is an attempt by marketing firms to provide a superior customer-care experience. Firms attempt to achieve this by actively managing and nurturing the long-term commercial relationship with their customers in a pro-active manner. High quality customer care is the key to achieving many of the business objectives confronting all competitive firms trying to apply CRM principles, such as:

❑ Minimising customer turnover.
❑ Attracting new customers.
❑ Retaining customers over the long term.
❑ Improving profitability.
❑ Enhancing company image.
❑ Improving customer and employee satisfaction.

But high-quality customer care is relative. With new operators and competitive forces constantly coming into play, no firm can afford to stand still. Marketing firms need to know what their customers think of them and whether or not they are offering sufficient levels of care and service. Regular customer care 'health checks' will become an essential part of the operating strategy for firms who need to ensure that they climb as high up the customer service ladder as possible. The cost of replacing customers is much greater than the cost of keeping them; some experts say it costs five times as much to recruit new customers than retain existing ones. If those lost include customers firms can least afford to lose – the most profitable ones – then the impact on profitability is significant. In his book *The Loyalty Effect*, Frederick F. Reichheld provides data supporting this view; a 5% increase in retention can lead to profit improvements of up to 85%. But he also warns of what he calls the 'Satisfaction Trap', which is an interesting concept, particularly for marketing researchers involved in carrying out customer service appreciation surveys. His research shows that 60% to 80% of customers who defect from firms had said in a satisfaction survey just prior to defecting that they were 'satisfied' or 'very satisfied' with the service provided by the company.

Customer purchase patterns themselves seem to provide a more accurate basis for measuring satisfaction than customer surveys. Customer service appreciation surveys are a growing area within the marketing research area. However, according to the work of Reichheld, users of such survey results should use them with great care. Such surveys do not seem to be such a good indicator of customer satisfaction, and hence likely customer retention, as the provider of the research services might claim.

CASE 7.2

Million Handshakes Group provides both CRM consulting services and CRM software solutions that support effective communication with customers.

In today's business environment, competition for customers is at an all-time high. Customer acquisition remains important, but customer retention is essential. Acquiring new customers can cost five times more than retaining current customers. Depending on the industry, customer profit rates tend to increase over the life of a retained customer. So how do marketing firms retain their best customers and gain more revenue while ensuring long-term customer satisfaction? According to Million Handshakes, Web presence is part of the answer. The key to long-term loyalty and profitably lies in maintaining a timely, relevant dialogue with customers that spans traditional and electronic channels. Million Handshakes Consulting group has its headquarters in the Netherlands, but has offices in seven countries, including the UK and USA. The firm provides both consulting services and software solutions that support effective communication with customers. Steinar Cook and Øivind Magnussen founded Million Handshakes in 1996. Cook established the predecessor in 1989 to distribute DBMS software on the Norwegian market. Magnussen experienced the need for CRM solutions through his work as a business consultant, where he gained substantial industrial and technical knowledge of CRM challenges. By 2001, Million Handshakes has established a leadership position in the CRM mid-office market, and has been successful in delivering advanced CRM solutions that manage customer processes across disparate delivery and communication channels. While there are many software vendors focusing on the management of customer interaction in isolated channels like call centres, mail, the Internet or sales force automation, Million Handshakes represents a new breed of solutions able to manage the integration required to create a '360 degree' customer view. They have successfully delivered this solution to leading banks, insurance and utilities companies all through Europe. The company believes that its design, enhanced to support popular new application development and integration methodologies such as XML, is very attractive for in-house CRM development initiatives as well as CRM initiatives supported by major systems integrators. Million Handshakes expect a rapid increase in the need for this object-based infrastructure, as corporations experience even more CRM project failures and towering system integration costs.

7. 5   Relationship marketing: its evolution into CRM

In order to fully understand the significance of the CRM concept it is necessary to have an appreciation of where the concept has come from. CRM has developed out of the earlier marketing concept of relationship marketing. We have already mentioned this fact but it is necessary to investigate this link in a little more detail. A brief history of the development of the relationship-marketing concept will help the reader understand its evolution into a fully integrated CRM system. Relationship marketing is a business concept, which has developed from a growing body of literature expressing lack of satisfaction with conventional 'transactional' marketing. This dissatisfaction applies to all areas of marketing but especially business to business and services marketing where the shortcomings of the more conventional marketing approach was first recognised. In 1954 Peter Drucker said 'There is only one valid definition of business: to create customers. It is the customer who determines what the business is.' Hence customers are central to business and the underlying theme behind relationship marketing is the acquisition, satisfaction and retention of customers. In a sense it is the marketing concept in principle but developed into a format in which it can be applied in an operational setting rather than merely being a concept. CRM takes the concept of relationship marketing and integrates it into a total customer management framework, making full use of the latest developments in information technology.

As discussed in 7.3, relationship marketing came from research by US businesses and universities before the idea was imported to Europe. Some adaptation was necessary because of cultural and environmental difference, and this was covered in the marketing literature. However, the principles and practices of modern marketing developed in the crucible of the USA consumer market did not work quite so well in business-to-business environments or for the increasingly important service sector.

As the western economies reconstructed and developed after the war, agriculture and manufacturing became less important and a smaller proportion of these countries GDP. Such countries are often described by economic commentators as being in the 'post industrial' phase of development. In a post-industrial economy a lot of the jobs are of an intellectual or at least 'brain based' type. Services become the predominant economic activity carried out by human beings. Marketers looked to the conventional wisdom in the marketing literature and found that it no longer fitted so well in the new 'service based' economies and some new thinking was required. In the growing business to business sector of the economy too, there developed a deep dissatisfaction with the conventional 'one sale ahead' transactional marketing approach.

It had been recognised in industrial markets for some time that commercial relationships between buyer and seller organisations required a more long-term 'interaction approach' rather than the short termism of the next sale. It was also recognised that many of the relationships formed between members of the marketing 'team' and members of the buying firm's 'team' were largely informal and unmanaged, even though they were important. This new thinking resulted in the development of the 'relationship marketing' model. This has now been accepted by firms 'across the board' so to speak, and not only by firms involved in the marketing of services or involved in industrial markets. As we have said, this concept has now evolved further into a full system of CRM and is still developing.

Writing on relationship marketing, Gronroos (1990) proposed a marketing strategy continuum, ranging from 'transaction marketing', which was regarded as more appropriate to business-to-consumer (B2C) marketing, particularly in the field of fast moving consumer goods (FMCGs), through to relationship marketing. This approach was seen as more suitable for business-to-business marketing and services marketing. However, relationship marketing is now used in all markets including consumer markets. Copulsky and Wolf (1990) used the term 'relationship marketing' to identify a type of database marketing. In their model the database is used by marketing firms to select suitable customer targets for the promotion of products and services. This use of a customer database is very similar to its use in the modern CRM model. The message sent to customers is 'tailor made' to fit in with their particular needs and wants. The response is monitored and used to produce various measures including the projected lifetime value of the customer, another key CRM concept.

McKenna (1991) linked relationship marketing to the organisational structure of a business. The whole business was organised to produce a relationship-marketing approach rather than it being merely a business process. To summarise at this stage, the major concern amongst practitioners with the conventional marketing approach was that it was too short-term and transactional in focus. This may have worked well over the years in a predominantly business-to-consumer environment but less so for service marketing, industrial and other forms of business to business marketing where the creation and maintenance of long term relationships with customers was crucial for long term commercial success. The modern usage of the term 'relationship marketing' describes a situation where the creation, satisfaction and retention of customers are at the very centre of marketing strategy. CRM is in very many ways similar to relationship marketing and embodies all of the principles of relationship marketing. Some commentators would say that relationship marketing and CRM are the same thing. CRM, however, takes the concept of relationship marketing and operationalises it through the use of sophisticated information technology systems.

7.5.1 Internal marketing and its role in CRM

The whole area of customer care and Customer Relationship Management (CRM) has evolved and developed substantially over the last 20 years because so much of modern customer care and customer relationship management systems are internet based. As we have seen, the subject of totally integrated Customer Relationship Management has itself evolved out of the earlier, but related topic of relationship marketing. As with the subject of e-commerce, some commentators feel that CRM is just the latest management search for the perfect business philosophy, in a sense the latest 'management fad'. Others see CRM as a significant change in the philosophy of business, one that incorporates and consolidates many of the earlier areas of new management thinking such as total quality management, internal marketing and relationship marketing.

Internal marketing is in a sense the 'marketing of the marketing concept itself within the firm'. We read in the marketing literature phrases such as 'customer focus', 'customer driven' and 'marketing-orientated organisation'. These are just meaningless phrases unless they can be put into action in a positive and practical way. The art of achieving this through the creation of the right internal culture within the marketing firm is sometimes referred to as *internal marketing*. As we shall discover, achievement of the right internal attitude is a prerequisite to achieving a truly CRM orientated organisation. Good internal marketing can be viewed as a prerequisite for good, effective external marketing polices. It would be difficult to have one without the other. In a very real sense the internal marketing is actually an intrinsic part of the relationship marketing and hence CRM, process. The principles of internal marketing are being widely adopted by all kinds of firms as they strive to create a truly customer orientated culture within their organisations. More than in any time before, today good marketing is seen just as much of an internal process as an external one.

Firms need to market the very concept of marketing to their own staff and others, the so-called 'internal customers'. Firms need to create the right spirit and internal culture before they can hope for success in their long-term external relationship marketing policies. The internal aspect of marketing is a little different from the external aspect. It has been shown that employees behave toward customers in very much the same way as the management behaves toward them. If they are treated badly they are more likely to treat customers badly. If they are treated well they are more likely to treat the firm's customers well. After all both internal marketing and relationship marketing aims to provide a better internal and external business framework to enable the better care of customers. This is what modern CRM is all about. The relationship between effective CRM and good 'internal marketing' polices is shown schematically in Figure 7.1.

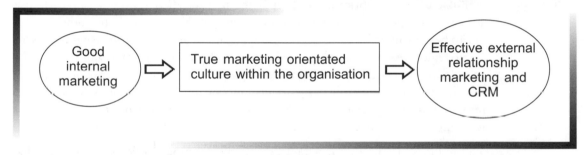

Figure 7.1 Good internal marketing is a prerequisite of effective CRM (Source: Lancaster and Reynolds, 2001)

7.5.2 Internal Marketing and its widespread adoption by firms

Internal marketing takes place at the interface between marketing and human resource management and involves both management disciplines. The application of internal public relations has a salient role to play in the overall process of achieving an internal marketing 'culture' because it too embraces both of these areas of management. Management is discovering that it is all very well to talk about their firm becoming more 'customer focused' or 'marketing oriented' but how do they make it a reality? Whether the firm wishes to employ relationship-marketing policies, engage in social marketing activities, practice 'green marketing' polices, or employ a full CRM programme, those working for the organisation will still need the right sprit, ethos and internal culture. This is where internal marketing comes into the picture.

The trend throughout the world is to pay much more attention to getting the spirit or the culture right before attempting to improve the external-marketing performance of the organisation. Internal marketing has now become an important and intrinsic part of what is considered conventional marketing wisdom. The term internal marketing refers to the process of applying the general principles of marketing inside the firm. Marketing as a business philosophy is concerned with producing the appropriate internal company culture that will result in the firm becoming truly marketing orientated and customer focused. Internal marketing involves much more than simply the application of public relations inside firms. The CRM concept is a synthesis of a number of strands of marketing thought. Internal marketing is a vital component to the successful operation of a truly customer focused CRM programme.

7.6   Supply chain integration and CRM

In 1994 a study was undertaken in the UK by A T Kearney, consultants. It investigated the supply chain from end of line manufacturers right back up the supply chain to sources of raw materials. Its conclusions were that business improvements would be possible not by simply viewing dealings between purchasers and sellers as isolated transactions each time, but by seeking to involve everybody down the supply chain, and hence came the term supply chain integration (SCI). It stated that different supply chain relationships should be possible with some members being content to act as manufacturers and fabricators and supplying to a specification (i.e. seeing their task as being good producers at the right quality and at the right time) but others might like to become more involved in end-use applications and even proffer suggestions for improvement, even though they may be towards the beginning of the supply chain. By considering the entire supply chain new opportunities would present themselves and benefit everybody in the chain. This would improve overall effectiveness in the chain with regard to the elimination of waste and suggesting better ways of doing things, thus reducing overall costs and benefiting the final customer in the process.

The result would be that it would be possible to impel service standards, of vital importance to good CRM, to final customers to superior levels. Marketing firms would achieve this by concentrating the complete supply chain in this direction through mutual co-operation, rather than weakening the attempts of individual elements of the chain through conflicting objectives. The outcome would be the necessity for closer relationships between suppliers and customers. The task would not be easy because of the problems of such integration, and the task of investigating the measures of sophistication that individual members of the supply chain wanted or expected. Following the discussions relating to relationship marketing and SCI it is appropriate to consider the view put forward by Christian Gronroos in 1990, who argued that traditional views of marketing are unsatisfactory in a modern business environment. He emphasised the shortcomings of McCarthy's 'four Ps' and went on to say that more 'Ps' like 'people' and 'planning' and 'processes' should be added as new marketing viewpoints. The basic concept of supplying customer needs and wants in target markets, he states, has always had relevance, but contends that this still views the firm as supplying the solutions and not receiving its ideas from the marketplace. He, therefore, attempted to redefine marketing in a way that applies the principles of mutually beneficial relationship marketing and SCI. Again both relationship marketing and SCI concepts have found their way into the integrated concept of CRM.

7.7 Key account management and CRM

Sometimes marketing firms cannot treat all their customers in the same way even if they would like to. Unfortunately this is rarely practicable, especially in business to business markets where there can be a great disparity in both the size of customer firms and the amount they spend with the marketing firm. Some customers are more valuable than others; this is a commercial fact of life. Often marketing firms are forced, out of necessity, to prioritise their customers and employ differential service level and customer-care programmes concentrating their efforts on what might be regarded as key accounts.

Key Account Management (KAM) is a strategic planning approach that goes beyond traditional marketing to deal with today's complex customer issues. High-involvement relationships with key customers offer major chances to grow business and move forward in the market, and to save costs for both sides. They also require innovation, major investment, and high running costs. A firm's capacity for high-cost, intimate relationships is limited, so the first, crucial decisions focus on the selection and prioritisation of key accounts. This is basically what KAM is all about, the prioritisation of key customers.

Before a firm can decide its KAM strategy, it needs to understand its relationship with each customer, and where the marketing company fits into its business strategy. Key accounts are the heart of a business. How they are identified and cultivated can mean the difference between a thriving enterprise and one that struggles. Most businesses have a few vital customers – those whose business means success or failure. Managing these accounts properly is critically important and can have a significant commercial advantage. For one major industrial cleaning company for example, revenue from its key accounts has grown three times as fast as its non-key accounts. In addition, some of its marginal businesses have grown into £30m+ customers. Yet often a firm's relationship with its most important or key customers is at best ordinary. Key accounts are taken for granted and viewed as dependable cash cows instead of being carefully nurtured and developed. It is hard for senior management to know how well the relationship is being managed for future growth. In recent years, key (or strategic) account management has become a crucial issue for many companies. Driven by some form of 'Pareto' 80/20 rule – 80% of current or potential revenues come from 20% of customers – many firms have come to realise that these customers must be treated somewhat differently from the average customer. Of course, it is one thing to recognise that these accounts should be treated differently, it is quite another to figure out exactly what to do.

Among the sorts of questions companies must answer are the following:

❑ Should we have a key account program at all?

❑ What is the appropriate role for key account teams and what should they be doing?

❑ What is the best way to develop strategy for our individual key accounts?

❏ What systems and process should we put in place to manage our key accounts, particularly in relation to IT?

❏ Should all key accounts have equivalent status or should we prioritise further?

❏ What value should a key account program offer our customers?

❏ What value should a key account program offer our organisation and shareholders?

❏ How many customers should we include in the key account program, and where do we draw the line?

❏ How should we decide which customers to include in the key account program?

❏ How should we organise to manage our key accounts?

❏ How should key account management relate to the rest of the organisation?

❏ How should we recruit, select, train and retain our key account mangers?

❏ How should we reward our key account managers and key account teams?

The above list of points is not exhaustive but serves to illustrate the complex issues management have to address when considering using a key account programme.

CASE 7.3

Wholesale Electro uses simple customer surveys and KAM to boost business.

Wholesale Electro Ltd. (WEL), is a family-owned electrical wholesaler (called a 'factor' in the UK). It is based in West Yorkshire, England and has four branches in the region and an annual turnover of approximately £3 million ($4.5 million) annually. It is a private limited company. Customers include independent (jobbing) electricians, small electrical contractors (usually 2–5 employees) and the maintenance departments of medium and sometimes quite large firms in the area.

The company's project range includes tools and testing equipment, safety wear and general electrical equipment and fittings, e.g. light fittings etc. Such a range constitutes most of that which an electrician or maintenance engineer would need on a regular basis. Particularly expensive equipment or out-of-the-ordinary products can be ordered from the firm's own catalogue or from a range of manufacturers' brochures, which the firm supplies. Orders can be placed in person by calling at the trade counter or by telephone or mail. A technical telephone advisory service is also available.

The company had been trading for six years and in that time had grown from a total turnover of £250,000 in the first year to its present level. Management had thought that it must have been doing the 'right thing', after all the company was successful, but they were not entirely sure. Hence they decided to commission a customer service appreciation survey, which was partly funded under a Department of Trade and Industry Small Firm Marketing Initiative.

The survey involved the use of a postal questionnaire which was administered to all of their existing 1,250 customers. The purpose of the survey was to allow the firm to establish the degree of satisfaction or dissatisfaction with various important elements of the business. In the first two weeks the company received 265 completed questionnaires, the second wave of responses produced another 94, making a total of 359 replies. Questionnaires had been pre-coded to provide the base for the analysis of classification variables e.g. size of firm, type of firm, sales with WEL, etc. By relating their analysis of the questionnaires to specific companies management was able to prepare highly operational action plans for the short, medium or long term and prioritise their customers into key accounts. These plans were customer specific and formed the basis for targeted future marketing improvements and acted as criteria for future evaluation. By concentrating their efforts on key accounts WEL was able to significantly increase business from their existing customer base.

7.8   Integrated customer relationship management

Customer relationship management has developed from a synthesis of relationship marketing, internal marketing and customer care to form a fully integrated system. The ability of firms to use such a system owes a lot to the availability of the appropriate computer-based technologies. However, customer relationship management is much more than just a Web based customer-care programme or an enhanced database-marketing programme. In fact CRM is evolving from a technology-centred scheme to a business value enterprise as firms move from viewing customers as exploitable income sources to important assets that have to be looked after and developed. CRM is a comprehensive approach that provides total integration of every area of business that

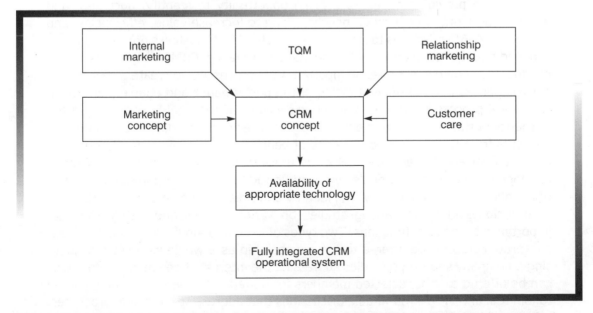

Figure 7.2 Factors contributing to the development of the CRM concept and its practical implementation (Source: Lancaster and Reynolds, 2001).

impacts on the customer – namely marketing, sales, customer service and field support – through the integration of people, process and technology, taking advantage of the communication possibilities of the internet. CRM programmes create a mutually beneficial, on going and long term relationship with a firm's customers, as shown in Figure 7.2

Building high value, loyal, lifetime relationships are the most powerful competitive tool a firm possesses and CRM systems should be designed to achieve this aim. Management should reward staff for doing it right and make sure that they ask customers if they are satisfied with the service, and check their purchasing behaviour to see if they remain loyal. Jeff Bezos (C.E.O. of amazon.com) says:

> 'I encourage everyone who works at Amazon to wake up terrified every morning. They should be afraid of our customers. Those are the folks who send us money. That is why our strategy is to say; heads down, focus on the customer, because the customer needs change at a slower rate.'

Control of the relationship lies in the hands of customers. The marketing firm should help customers train them to meet their needs.

CASE 7.4

CRMBA encourages the use of best practice in CRM amongst its members by offering benchmarking services.

The Customer Relationship Management Benchmarking Association (CRMBA™), is an international organisation based in the USA. CRMBA is part of The Benchmarking Network, Inc. It is an association of professionals in the CRM industry, and is dedicated to providing members with an opportunity to identify, document and establish best practices through benchmarking to increase value, efficiencies, and profits. CRMBA™ mission is to identify 'Best in Class' CRM business processes, which can lead member companies to exceptional performance. CRMBA objectives are to conduct benchmarking studies of important CRM processes; to create a cooperative environment where full understanding of the performance and enablers of best in class CRM processes can be obtained and shared at reasonable cost; to use the efficiency of the association to obtain processes performance data and related best practices from CRM; to support the use of benchmarking to facilitate CRM process improvement and the achievement of accuracy, timeliness and efficiency. CRMBA membership includes individuals who work in CRM in major corporations. Benefits of membership are that CRMBA will identify and present to members opportunities to participate in benchmarking studies on various topics addressing issues of importance to the CRM functions. Two types of benchmarking studies are provided: consortium studies are offered to the membership as a whole with costs divided; single-company sponsored studies addressing the interest of one member company can be offered to other selected members for no fee. Members pay a nominal fee to join real and virtual roundtable discussions that address specific CRM processes.

Ideally, CRM systems help firms provide start-to-finish customer care, from initial acquisition of the customer through to product delivery and after-care services. The value of customers is a long-term concept; lifetime value of customers is now what is important to many firms. This is an important trend that represents the use of knowledge-management practices, such as the use of databases to capture and store comprehensive information about the customer, to build long-term, mutually beneficial, customer relationships. Companies need a CRM strategy because it helps them understand their customer-acquisition and retention goals, which is the whole basis of relationship marketing practices.

7.9 CRM computer software

CRM software brings together data from disparate systems and business units to provide a holistic view of customers and the company's relationship with them. It can help co-ordinate customer contact and relationships across channels (retail, channel, Web) by presenting a unified message regardless of where the contact point is. CRM strategies can be a defence against being the same as every other supplier and can allow the marketing firm to differentiate itself through superior service. For example, if you manufacture a 'commodity-type product' such as welding rods, you can differentiate yourself through better CRM and customer service. CRM is most effective when companies use pro-active strategies to support the sales process through acquisition, retention, and development. Most businesses are moving to web-based CRM, but this does not do away with the need for personal interaction that is so crucial to many companies' sales and marketing. Active CRM technology means that a customer contacting a web site for information can be followed up immediately by a telephone call or some other form of communication. A mixture of communications can be used from the Internet, telephone, direct mail and even personal contact.

Measuring the return on investment is an important first step in determining the criteria against which success of the CMR programme will be appraised. The main quality of any set of measures must be to tell management if each project requirement was achieved. Some common CRM measures include the number of new customers, the cost of acquiring those new customers, customer satisfaction, customer attrition, the cost of promoting products, profit margins, incremental revenue, and inventory turnover. Firms need to consider ways in which Web-based CRM will enhance relationships with their customers and where the service and information provided will be excellent but also where the relationship-management teams really utilise data available to cement and nurture the relationship with their clients. At this point, the e-communication and e-interaction between a firm and its external customers will truly be dyadic.

7.9.1 Data mining

The use of database technologies enables marketers to develop, test, implement, measure, and modify marketing programs and strategies more accurately and more efficiently than non-database methods. The use of databases is a key feature of CRM programmes. Data mining is used as part of these programmes to retrieve and manage customer information for CRM purposes. By applying data mining techniques, marketers can fully harvest data about customers' buying patterns and behaviour, and gain a greater understanding of customer motivations. Data mining and CRM software allows users to analyse large databases to solve business decision problems. Data mining, as the name suggests, involves interrogating a database to discover interesting and hopefully commercially exploitable associations, patterns or relationships in the data. Modern data analysis software such as SPSS allows the user to manipulate, group and correlate data variables and sets. In order to implement successful database-marketing solutions, management needs to know how to carry out certain basic tasks. The list given below is not prescriptive or exhaustive. However, it serves to illustrate some basic principles:

❑   Identify and gather relevant data about customers and prospects to construct the database in the first place.

❑   Use data warehousing techniques, which are systems of data storage and organising, to transform raw data into powerful, accessible marketing information. This adds value to the data collected by putting it in a format so that it can be retrieved and analysed effectively.

❑   Apply statistical techniques to customer and prospect databases to analyse behaviour and attempt to establish patterns, associations or relationships in the data that may be commercially exploitable.

❑   Establish meaningful market segments that are measurable, reachable, viable and commercially valuable.

❑   Score individuals in terms of the probability of their response. This involves prioritising prospects in terms of the probability of purchase and long term commercial value.

Data mining is, in some ways, an extension of statistical analysis. Like statistics, data mining is not a business solution; it is just a technology. CRM, on the other hand, involves turning information in a database into business decisions. For example, consider a catalogue retailer who needs to decide who to send a new catalogue to. The information incorporated into the CRM process is the historical database of previous mailings and the features associated with potential customers, such as age, post code, response in the past, etc. The software would use this data to build a model of customer behaviour that could be used to predict which customers would be likely to respond to the new catalogue. Rather like building a 'virtual customer'. By using this information a marketing manager can target customers who are likely to respond. It provides much greater accuracy and saves time and money.

CASE 7.5

Interface Software Inc., USA supplies computer software and training for firms involved in customer relationship management (CRM).

Interface Software, Inc., is a global leader of Relationship Intelligence solutions for the professional services industries. A critical component to any knowledge management strategy, Relationship Intelligence goes beyond Client Relationship Management software and transforms a professional services firm's internal competitive information about people, companies, relationships, experience and expertise into intelligence. Professionals leverage Relationship Intelligence to uncover new revenue opportunities, differentiate their services from the competition and enhance client service. Innovation is rooted in commitment and Focus Interface Software stands out as a leading innovator catering exclusively to the professional services sector. The firm have been committed to understanding the unique needs of professionals, and tailoring their solutions and services to empower professional services firms to compete more effectively and efficiently. Interface have invested substantial resources partnering with customers to learn how they think, to understand their information requirements and to educate themselves about their concerns. Through this alliance, the company have successfully translated this knowledge into technology that integrates easily into the culture and workflow of professional services firms. Interface Software has also proven itself to be a visionary leader, establishing Relationship Intelligence as a category in its own right. They offer a critical pathway, enabling firms to adopt and implement leading-edge technology that is closely tailored to the way they do business. Interface has offices in Atlanta, Chicago, Dallas, New York, San Francisco, Washington D.C., and the U.K.

7.10 Data fusion

Data fusion is in many ways similar to data mining and again can contribute to the computerised CRM system. As the name implies, data is obtained from a range of different sources and put together, rather like a jigsaw puzzle, to form a complete profile of an individual. For example, you may fill in a loyalty card at a supermarket, which means a lot of your personal information is now on a company database. You may apply for bank account or credit facilities with the same or related company (supermarkets such as J Sainsbury Ltd. offer bank and credit facilities to its customers) and fill in another form and give further personal details. This data may be merged and integrated with data held about you on other personal databases, for example those run by Equifax Ltd. or Experien Ltd, which supplies personal data to firms including financial data such as credit history.

Data from all these sources will be 'fused' together, cleaned using a 'filtering system' and will basically form a complete picture of you as a person and as a consumer.

Sometimes data will be fused together from fragments held on different databases on different people. These people may share similar characteristics and form part of the same market segment. There may be associations between key variables that link a particular consumer to a particular segment. If you have the right value on one or two of these variables you are then treated as if you have the characteristics of the 'virtual consumer' built up from the fused data fragments. Using these techniques firms can attribute a probability to you that you will behave in a certain way as modelled by their virtual consumer profile. Data fusion is a formal framework in which are expressed means and tools for the alliance of data originating from different sources. It aims at obtaining information of greater quality; the exact definition of 'greater quality' will depend upon the application.

7.11   Data warehousing

Data warehousing describes the storage and retrieval system used by organisations for their information. Just as warehouses are used to store goods, virtual warehouses can be used to store data. Just as a conventional warehouse will operate under some form of system so too the data warehouse. In a conventional warehouse you will see storage and retrieval equipment, materials handling equipment, information systems and so forth. So too in a data warehouse, although these are likely to be software applications. Data warehousing is not new. Enterprises have engaged in the transformation and replication of data for decades. It wasn't until the early 1990s that the name 'data warehousing' was introduced into the business lexicon. There are many reasons and benefits for using a data warehouse.   Consider a host of other long-term benefits for an organisation:

❑   Data integrity and quality. Surface and deliver consistent, accurate and reliable information to the business community – so you'll always get consistent answers.

❑   Easy integration and process automation. Maximise existing hardware, software, data and people, and manage, locate and document code across your enterprise.

❑   Cost effectiveness and higher productivity. While users exploit information and improve processes on their own, IT is free to focus on running operational systems. Information is available, accessible and timely to the business community with minimal impact on your transaction systems.

Data warehousing systems and technologies are changing and improving all the time. Information is the lifeblood of successful marketing and never more so when a firm is using a CRM systems approach. Along with other developments such as data mining and data fusion, data warehousing forms yet another strand in the continually developing and fully integrated CRM approach to business.

Summary

Marketing thought has moved away from the conventional transactional approach and into a more long-term relationship approach. The term 'relationship marketing' was used to describe this new 'world view' of modern marketing. This has developed further and made even more extensive use of the information technology available, particularly database technology. The new holistic, integrated approach to the lifetime management of customer relationships is known as CRM. One of the key principles of CRM is to develop not only a long-term relationship with customers, but also a long term 'learning' relationship. The marketing firm attempts to understand what the customer wants and is likely to want in the future. This can only be carried out successfully if the marketing firm makes full use of every available source of customer information. This information is usually kept in some form of computerised data warehouse and retrieval system. The data is mined and 'fused' to add value and build up a picture of the target customer. CRM has been built up from a number of 'strands' of marketing thought and developments. CRM is in a continual process of refinement and development as new marketing ideas are brought to bear and improvements in technology improve further the storage, retrieval, interrogation and manipulation of customer information for CRM purposes.

Questions

1. Explain the historical development of the relationship marketing concept from the end of the Second World War to the present day.

2. Compare and contrast the concept of internal marketing with the traditional marketing concept.

3. What are the main component parts of a fully integrated CR M system?

4. Explain how the development of Internet based technologies has facilitated the adoption and application of the CRM concept.

5. Discuss the contention that the CRM concept is more of a step change in marketing philosophy than simply the application of computer database techniques to consumer profiles.

References

Berry, LL, *Emerging Perspectives on Services Marketing,* 'Relationship marketing' (pp25-28), (American Marketing Association, Chicago, 1983).

Copulsky, JR, and Wolf, MJ, 'Relationship Marketing: Positioning for the Future', *Journal of Business Strategy*, July-August, pp16-20, (1990).

Deming, WE, '*The New Economics for Industry, Government, Education'*, (MIT Center for Advanced Engineering Study, Cambridge MA.,1993).

Godin, S, *Permission Marketing*, (Simon and Schuster, 1999).

Gronroos, C, 'Relationship Approach to Marketing In Service Contexts: The Marketing and Organisational Behaviour Interface', *Journal of Business Research*, 20, Jan, (1990).

McKenna, R, *Relationship Marketing*, (Century Business, London, 1991).

Reichheld, FF, and Teal, T, *The Loyalty Effect: The Hidden Force Behind Growth, Profits and lasting value*, (McGraw-Hill, July, 1996).

Tate, S, 'First Union-Using MicroStrategy to Build more profitable Relationships with 16 Million Customers', *Data Warehousing: What works?*, Volume 8, Oct. 1999.

8 Pricing

8.1 The nature of price

Prices are guided and influenced by market conditions, so the achievement of company profit objectives often necessitates compromise over the amount that can be realised. Price is not necessarily the most important factor in the buying decision. For the seller, price determines the amount of profit (or loss), so pricing decisions should be approached in a disciplined manner, for it provides revenue, while the other marketing mix elements represent costs.

Marketing writers criticise cost-orientated approaches to pricing, as costs do not necessarily reflect market conditions – at least in the longer term. Companies can design marketing strategies that put costs into the perspective of a long-range strategic approach. For example, achieving a high market share may drive down costs through economies of scale. An image building strategy may invoke high initial costs, but it allows the company to charge higher prices in the long term. A purely cost orientated approach to pricing is too narrow. Cost is an obvious starting point, and prices charged must ultimately exceed costs if a company is to remain in business. Tellis explains:

> 'A **strategy** is a broad plan of action by which an organisation intends to reach its goal. A **policy** is more of a routine managerial guide to be implemented when a given situation arises. Giving certain price discounts when a certain amount of product is ordered is an example of a **policy**.'

With this awareness of costs, companies can consider price in terms of marketing objectives that are designed to achieve financial goals. Realistic pricing objectives should be well defined, attainable and measurable. Having laid down objectives, the company can use a variety of pricing tactics to achieve them.

As marketers we are interested in the role of price in the buyer-seller relationship. The buyer views price as a cost that is paid in return for a series of satisfactions. Whatever these are, price is usually perceived as a negative factor. The seller sees price as a means of cost recovery and profit. Both buyer and seller need to understand how price works for pricing structures to be implemented and managed efficiently. Economics provides a starting point from which this understanding can be gained.

From economic theory we learn about the concepts of 'utility', 'value' and 'price'. *Utility* is that aspect of an item which makes it capable of satisfying a want or need. *Value* is the expression used to quantify utility, whilst *price* describes the number of monetary units the value represents.

Economic theory suggests a downward sloping demand curve, or the logical assumption that customers will buy more of a product as price falls, as shown in Figure 8.1.

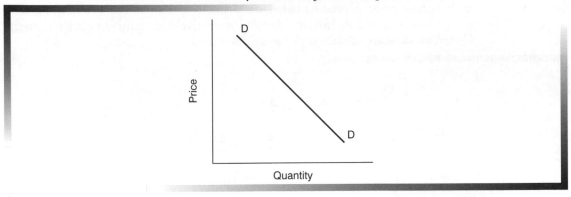

Figure 8.1 Downward sloping demand curve.

Conversely suppliers will be willing to supply greater amounts at a higher price as shown in Figure 8.2.

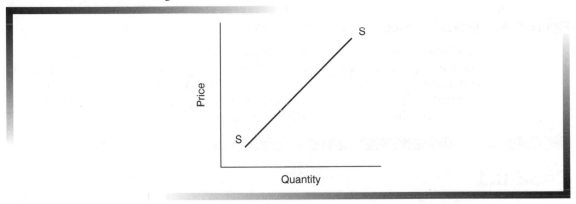

Figure 8.2 Upward sloping supply curve

Where demand and supply intersect is the market price as shown in Figure 8.3. At price 'P', quantity 'Q' will be the amount demanded.

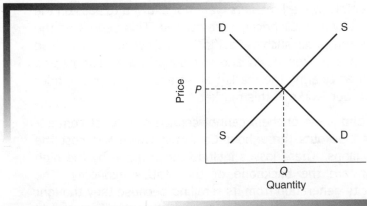

Figure 8.3 Demand and supply curves showing market price

When companies attempt to plot a demand schedule, or demand curve, for a product, they must consider elasticity of demand. This describes the sensitivity of consumers to changes in price. A product has elastic demand when small price changes greatly affect levels of demand. Inelastic demand is relatively insensitive to price changes. These two ideas are explained in Figure 8.4.

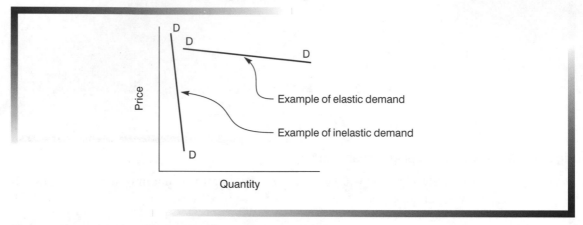

Figure 8.4 Examples of elastic and inelastic demand

Few products have totally elastic or inelastic demand. When demand is elastic, there is usually a point on the demand curve when further price reductions would make little difference to demand. Determining the exact position of this point is important in demand analysis, as it makes little sense to reduce price if this does not result in an increase in sales, sufficient to offset the price reduction.

CASE 8.1

Using price to decrease demand for power – Californians forced to economise on electricity due to punitive price rises.

A deregulation law in California allowed electrical wholesalers, the generators, to increase their prices to retailers. However, retailers were not allowed to pass on the full price rise to end users by law as their prices were capped. This depressed the margins of electricity retailers and some, such as Pacific Gas & Electric Co. have filed for bankruptcy. The market has broken down and the usual law of supply and demand, which is so efficient at clearing the market at an acceptable price under free market conditions, no longer works in this market.

The retail firms are in debt and some of them cannot service their debt commitments. The result has been blackouts throughout California which has cost the golden state's industries $millions. These losses include those made by the high technology industries which are the backbone of the state's economy. The authorities separated electricity generation from its retailing because they thought it would improve competition within the market. They thought that new firms would enter the generation market and bring prices down. In fact, the cost of building generating plant is so high and the political regulation so risky that few investors have ventured into the field. This has left the generators with monopoly power.

The authorities have decided to use price as a weapon to keep demand down. Under the new pricing plan domestic users will be given a baseline for electricity usage. This amount is that necessary to meet the needs of a typical household, and will vary according to location. Very hot areas such as Palm Springs, where households need air conditioning more than in other, colder areas, will have a higher baseline usage rate. Residents that exceed their baseline allocation will see prices rise. Those that use in excess of 130% of their allocation will see prices rise by as much as 47% from the baseline rates. Businesses have been less affected by the punitive price rises as the authorities are worried about exacerbating the prospects of recession in the area. Domestic users are expected to buckle under and consume less electricity.

Companies should establish a cost curve that relates costs to varying levels of output. The economic theory of the firm assumes that companies will attempt to increase output to levels to a point where profits are maximised. This is the point at which marginal costs are equal to marginal revenue, i.e when the cost of one more unit of output is equal to the addition to total revenue that this last unit provides.

A final economic concept is that of *oligopoly*, as many fast moving consumer goods (FMCG) companies operate in near oligopolistic conditions. Here, there are relatively few sellers who make similar commodities and produce below their maximum capacity. Price as an instrument of competition is less effective, so rather than engage in price wars, manufacturers place emphasis on non-price competition. Attempts are made to brand products and engage in above-the-line promotion. Advertising tends to be defensive to retain market share, as the market is saturated with demand being relatively inelastic reflecting regular demand and not new or increased levels of demand.

Examples of such products are detergents, breakfast cereals, soups, soft drinks, car tyres, and petrol. Figure 8.5 illustrates the concept of oligopoly. Demand curve 'D'

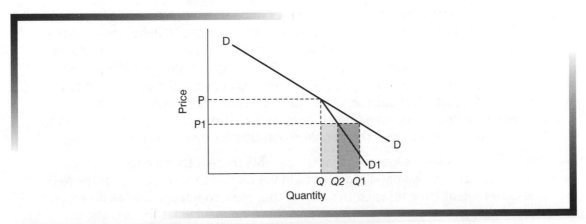

Figure 8.5 The concept of oligopoly

shows that at price 'P', quantity 'Q' is the amount that would be demanded under normal demand considerations. When price is reduced to 'P1', the expectation would be that 'Q-Q1' would be the additional amount demanded. Under oligopoly, the demand curve kinks to 'D1', meaning that 'Q-Q2' is the additional amount demanded, so price competition becomes less effective in producing more sales.

If a company lowers its prices, competitors can be expected to lower their prices. Given inelastic industry demand, this means that the company's own demand curve is more inelastic at lower prices. Oligopolistic situations apply to product groups and industries, as well as local markets. A community might be well served by, for example, many petrol stations or hairdressing establishments competing for business, and in such situations their behaviour equates to oligopoly.

Economics only describes markets to a limited extent as it ignores the effects of sociological and psychological influences on the consumer. When considering price, economics is a logical start and with this as a foundation, marketers have an insight into pricing that can be related to specific pricing situations.

CASE 8.2

India has a competitive price advantage over the West in providing heart bypass operations to private clients.

Because of the underfunding of the UK National Health Service, many patients with life-threatening heart conditions have to wait months for treatment. If they want immediate treatment their only choice is to go private. However, private heart bypass surgery is expensive. Many such patients simply cannot afford it and so have no choice but to suffer in silence. The cost of a triple bypass operation in the private sector in the UK is around £20,000 compared to about £6,000 in India. Flight and accommodation costs will add around another £2,000 to this and it will cost more if the patient stays in India to recuperate. Even so, the operation can still be carried out privately in India for less than half the cost of going privately in the UK.

India offers a price advantage for other types of operations. A double-cataract eye operation would cost £5,000 if it were done privately in the UK whereas in Madras the same costs under £250. A hip replacement in the UK in the private sector will cost a patient £6,500 compared to around £900 in India. Many people from the UK are taking advantage of the huge price differences between the UK and India. It is not only India that offers such services. Other developing counties offer similar price advantages such as Cuba, and Costa Rica as well as former USSR countries including Russia itself which has an international reputation for eye operations.

Some politicians have suggested that UK patients be sent to India for treatment to alleviate the chronic waiting-list problems in the UK and to save money for the NHS. The Government have rejected this saying that they do not see this as an answer to the current NHS problems, though they have not said what the answer is.

8.2 Pricing objectives

The first stage in the pricing process is to establish the objectives the company wishes to achieve. Price is an instrument of the marketing mix that differs from the other elements in that it is a financial, as well as a marketing tool. We should also consider that some pricing objectives might arise from non-marketing sources. For example, in public limited companies pressure may exist to pay a certain level of dividend to shareholders. Price might be seen as a means of recouping recent investment. Finance might decree that price be at a certain level, regardless of marketing. Pricing objectives are established with the market place in mind, as this is a reality of business life.

8.2.1 Return on investment

A basic pricing objective is to achieve a target return-on-investment from net sales. When costs have been established, the company decides the percentage profit it wants to achieve. Whilst this percentage may remain constant, fluctuations in demand will affect the total value of profits made. To achieve this objective the company is likely to be a market leader and less vulnerable to changes in the market place than competitors. Achievement of this objective is easy to measure, but not always practical to achieve for individual products.

8.2.2 Improvement in market share

Improvement or maintenance of market share is a market-based pricing objective. A firm might feel it is earning a reasonable return on investment, but if the market is expanding, existing prices may not encourage a corresponding improvement in market share. A price reduction could increase sales in an expanding market to a level where the return-on-investment increases in monetary terms although percentage return may have fallen. Maintenance of market share is a key to survival, and price carries much of the burden of responsibility. When measuring success, it is relatively easy to establish the size of the total market, and estimate market shares of individual companies operating in the market.

8.2.3 Maintaining price stability

A pricing policy with the objective of maintaining price stability and margins might appear to detract from marketing creativity and free choice. Although some products can be promoted and priced as prestige items, most firms have little or no influence over the general level of prices. They must organise their businesses so costs are at a level that will permit them to fall in line with the prices charged by market leaders. Prices are often 'market led' with little scope for deviation from established price structures. Provided a company's returns are adequate, there is justification for maintaining the status quo by meeting competitive prices established by market leaders. The market or price leaders themselves do not stand to gain much by distancing their prices too much (upwards or downwards) from their smaller competitors. Price adjustments are usually made in response to changing market conditions.

Certain conditions may require an aggressive approach to pricing. During the introduction and growth stages of a new product, price plays a less significant role.

When the product matures, price wars are usually fought. Increases in market share can be achieved by cutting prices, but this should be avoided, as the only winners are end customers.

8.2.4 Growth in sales

The advantages of price stability objectives notwithstanding, under certain conditions a legitimate pricing objective is to achieve a growth in sales. Providing the firm appreciates the competitive conditions under which it operates, a lower price is probably the most effective competitive weapon. If rapid growth in sales is required, price can be used as the major component of the marketing mix. Such a move should be made with caution as sudden price reductions may affect the effectiveness of other marketing mix elements. We should consider that it is easier to implement a growth-in-sales objective by price reductions than to regain previous higher pricing levels.

8.2.5 Profit maximisation

Financial managers are anxious to recoup the costs of development as early as possible in the product's life. Controlling cash flow is, therefore, a common pricing objective. A financial manager might be willing to bear development and marketing costs of launching a new product, but will also highlight a variety of other demands on the company's limited resources.

Most companies have an overall pricing objective of profit maximisation. Market conditions usually make it impossible to maximise profits on all products, in all markets, simultaneously. For this reason, companies employ pricing techniques that promote sales, but reduce profits on certain products in the short term, with the overall objective of maximising profit on total sales. The company's product mix should, therefore, be considered as an entity rather than a series of products whose profits should be maximised individually.

CASE 8.3

London's transport revolution: using price to cut congestion in London.

Motorists who drive into London will have to pay a tax of £5 or risk a heavy fine. The idea behind the scheme, proposed by London's mayor Ken Livingstone, is to price congestion out of the market. If motorists have to pay £5 a day to get into the heart of London they may think twice about it. It is hoped that motorists will leave their cars at locations, at the outskirts of London and use public transport to get into the centre of the City. The London scheme is expected to raise £200 million in revenue which will be ring fenced for expenditure on the city's public transport system. It is hoped the scheme will dramatically reduce congestion, as much as 15% in the first year, and increase the use of buses, trains and especially the Underground.

Many people are against the scheme. London's ring road does not have the capacity to take the added traffic, which is likely to flood out into residential streets just outside the charge zone as people search for a cheap place to park. Some say it is possible that traffic congestion may even increase as a result of the charge. This happened in Nottingham a few years ago when a scheme to reduce congestion in the inner city resulted in total chaos and had to be abandoned. However, others feel that unless we introduce a pricing system we will never be able to control congestion in the UK. The London scheme is seen as a pilot scheme, which if successful will be introduced to other UK towns such as Birmingham and Manchester.

8.3 Steps in price determination

Prices must exceed costs to ensure profitability, so a consideration of cost is a logical first stage in price planning. In line with marketing orientation, pricing strategy should begin with the consumer and work 'backwards'. Pricing should be consumer orientated as the customer is the person who finally decides whether or not the product is purchased. A number of steps should be followed:

8.3.1 Identify the potential consumer or market

The purpose is to focus the planner's mind on the market from the outset. It prevents price from being viewed as separate from other marketing mix elements.

8.3.2 Demand estimation

The likely volume of sales directly affect a manufacturer's costs. Ideally it should provide the company with a schedule of predicted demand levels at differing prices. This establishes the position and slope of the demand curve. The price a company can charge will vary from market to market, within markets and between market segments. This variation calls for market research before the decision is taken to enter a market.

8.3.3 Anticipating competitor reaction

The nature of a competitor's pricing structure is difficult to ascertain. Manufacturers and consumers can easily compare selling prices, but this does not give any insight into competitive pricing structures. Buyers often compound this difficulty by 'inventing' 'special prices' and 'non-existent discounts', not offered by competitors, but stated as being real during negotiation to help in bargaining.

When products are easily imitated and markets are easy to enter, the price of competitive products assumes major importance. Even when products have substantial distinctiveness, it is not usually too long before other companies enter the market.

Competition stems from three major sources:

❑ 'Head-on' competition from directly similar products.

❑ Competition from substitute products.

❑ Competition from products that are not directly related, but which compete for the same disposable income. For instance, watch manufacturers compete with fountain pen manufacturers because their products are often bought as gifts.

8.3.4 Market share and cost analysis

If a company seeks a large market share, prices will have to be competitive. Production capacity should be sufficient to meet demand that anticipated market share might create.

The steps discussed in price determination have concerned the market place rather than the internal workings of the firm. Market considerations should be the major determinant of price, so it would not be appropriate to develop a product whose price did not fall approximately in line with competitive prices.

The company should have established whether or not a potential market is attractive and practical from a basic assessment of costs. If the market is promising, a more detailed cost analysis should be the next step. The likely level of demand should have been estimated for varying levels of output.

There are fixed costs that the company must pay regardless of the level of output (e.g depreciation and maintenance costs of machinery). Variable costs are a function of the level of output (e.g energy and raw material costs and those of additional labour as production levels rise). Total costs are the sum of fixed and variable costs. Break-even point occurs when the number of units sold at a given price generates revenue to exactly equal total costs.

Figure 8.6 shows that demand analysis has predicted that a price level of £1.80 per unit will generate a demand level of 100,000 units per annum. The company needs to know the effect this level of production will have on costs. In this example, the price of £1.80 per unit would be a figure derived from an overall market demand schedule, whilst 100,000 units could represent the share of the total market the company wishes to obtain. In order to ascertain the viability of such a price and level of output, a break-even point is calculated from an analysis of the relationship between costs and output. Fixed costs for production are £100,000. Variable costs rise as production increases and at a production level of 100,000 units, total costs are £150,000. The company now knows that it must charge at least £1.50 per unit to break even at this volume. However, this break-even figure is based on cost. Break-even can be modified by changing the price. Fewer units are required to break even at a higher price.

The company has estimated that £1.80 is a desirable price in market terms. If this price is used with information from Figure 8.6, the following equation can be used to calculate the number of units required to break even at this price:

Fixed costs   =   £100,000
Variable costs =   £0.50 per unit
Selling price   =   £1.80

Number of units required to break even at a given selling price = n

Total costs will equal total revenue when: $100{,}000 + 0.5n = 1.8n$

Therefore, $n = 77{,}000$ (approx) and total costs = £138,500 (approx)

The company had planned to produce and sell 100,000 units. When the price is set at £1.80 per unit, break-even will be approximately 77,000 units. This price provides for profitable production at all points above 77,000 units.

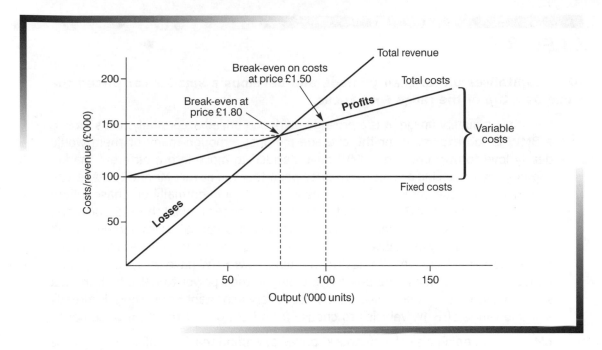

Figure 8.6 Application of break-even analysis

This is a demand-orientated approach to pricing. The manufacturer determines the likely market price and then looks back at the cost structure to establish the feasibility of such a price.

8.4.5 Profit calculation

Pricing objectives differ according to the nature of the market. The cost and demand analysis just described does not reduce flexibility in setting price objectives. It provides management with information it requires to make further decisions. Using the Figure 8.6 example the company could use £1.80 at 100,000 units as its basis for setting a price if the objective was other than to break even. Once equipped with cost and demand data, various price levels that might be appropriate to a chosen marketing strategy can be considered. Several break-even points can be plotted along the line of total cost. As long as output level is to the right of any break-even point, the company will generate profits. The break-even point is thus a function of price that is also a function of the chosen marketing strategy.

We re-emphasise that the determination of price and profit is a practical and not an academic exercise. Marketing practitioners should recognise that profit is the only means of survival for a company and price is the major tool through which profits can be realised.

CASE 8.4

BMW capitalises on its quality image and develops a smaller car priced the same as a top of the range Ford Focus.

BMW has a quality image; it is a prestige mark and priced accordingly. Let's face it, a BMW is too expensive for the average motorist although many of them would dearly love to own one. Now BMW have decided to move into a different market segment by producing a vehicle at a price point that will attract Mr and Mrs Average Motorist. This segment is made up of people who would normally purchase a Ford Focus or a Volkswagen Golf, albeit at the top of the range at about the £15,000 mark. This price point segment has virtually thousands of potential customers in the UK each year and many more if you consider the rest of the world. Business at this end of the market is lucrative with healthy margins. Now BMW have decided they want a piece of the action and are doing everything in their power to get a high market share of this particular price segment. Price is very important here. There is already a whole range of BMW vehicles to choose from but none at the right price point.

BMW is developing a small hatchback, priced at around the £15,000 mark, which is intended to tempt motorists away from their more traditional choice of vehicle. Its size is between BMW's British built Mini and the company's existing 3-series compact model. The new vehicle, the 1-series, will be the same size as a VW Golf – 13ft 7in long, 4ft 8in high and 5ft 8in wide. It is expected to have a 90 brake-horse-power 1.6.litre, a 115bhp 1.8 litre, and a 140bhp petrol engine, along with a 140bhp 2litre turbo-diesel engine version.

The new vehicle will be available in the showrooms in 2004 and is aimed at the younger, aspirational end of the market. A saloon version and other variations are planned if the initial concept is a commercial success. Production is likely to be in Germany.

8.5 Price selection techniques

The chosen price depends on the marketing strategy to be employed. Some pricing techniques pay less attention to demand, concentrating on cost, whilst others put emphasis on the other elements of the marketing mix as well as aspects of consumer behaviour that affect the way price is perceived.

8.5.1 Break-even analysis related to market demand

We begin with the premise that at too high a price there will be no demand, whilst at too low a price the company will make losses. The company must, therefore, choose a price that is acceptable both to itself and to the market place. For simplicity, only one price was considered in Figure 8.6 and there was only one function for total revenue (i.e total revenue = demand x unit price). If demand is estimated at various price levels it is possible to produce a series of total revenue lines. The various total revenue lines can be plotted to form a demand curve for the product in question. Usually a company will choose a price and a corresponding level of demand that will maximise profit. In practice, this may not be possible because of limitations on production capacity, or a need to utilise production capacity as fully as possible.

Whilst demand-orientated pricing is preferable to cost-based pricing, we should be aware of certain practical limitations when it is related to break-even analysis.

Firstly, it assumes that costs are static, whereas costs can vary considerably in a practical setting. Revenue too, is over-simplified, because market conditions can change rapidly. Even if they return to the condition on which the analysis was based, the actual revenue will not be as predicted. If these considerations are taken into account, break-even analysis related to demand is an effective price-selection technique, particularly when costs and demand levels are relatively stable.

8.5.2 Cost-based price selection techniques

These have the advantage of being simpler to administer than demand-based techniques. It is easy for a firm to arrive at an accurate estimation of the cost of producing a unit of production. Cost-plus pricing takes the cost of production and adds an amount that will provide the profit the company requires.

❑   *Mark-up pricing* is a cost-plus technique that is widely used in retailing. The retailer takes the cost price of the product and adds a percentage mark-up to cover overheads and a predetermined percentage profit. Usually mark-up is calculated as a percentage of cost price using the following formula:

（100% + required % mark up) x cost = selling price

Retailers favour mark-up pricing, because it is straightforward. demand. Usually, the faster the turnover, the lower the percentage mark-up. Retailers are in the position of being able to experiment with sales effectiveness at varying price levels and receive quick feedback. Although mark-up pricing prevails in retailing, it is common in manufacturing, because it is easier to estimate cost than demand.

❑   *Target pricing* is another cost-based approach that considers output and costs in determining price. The company decides on a given rate of return or target price and calculates the level of output necessary to achieve this. Break-even analysis is used to determine the level of output where profits will begin. The linear rise in variable costs, as output increases, determines the company's total costs. The company then chooses a price that will produce a revenue line that achieves the target profit.

Target pricing is used by many skill-based and B2B companies. Their price philosophy is 'fair return-on-investment'. The technique has limitations, especially that demand elasticity is ignored.

8.5.3 Psychological pricing

It is the market place and not the company that exerts the greatest influence in price determination. Although an individual company cannot significantly alter the basic market structure, it has some influence if marketing implications are considered. Marketing management is faced with a general level of demand for a product. Inside this demand level are opportunities for strategies to be developed that focus specifically on consumers. The importance that consumers attach to prestige value allows for psychological pricing techniques to be developed. Consumers tend to believe that price is an indication of quality and use this perceived quality to enhance the image of their lifestyles. The purchase of a prestige product becomes an expression of 'self-concept'. 'Designer clothes' are an example of prestige products and their perceived value is greater than cost considerations. Consumers see value in exclusivity and the ability to show that they are able and prepared to pay high prices for fashionable items.

Influences on the consumer that make prestige pricing possible have been discussed in Chapter 3. In order to satisfy the consumer's psychological needs, other elements of the marketing mix, such as promotion and distribution, must support the image reflected by the price. For example, Cartier jewellery and Gucci accessories are only advertised in prestige media, and not in the popular press, nor would we expect to find them in supermarkets.

Demand for prestige goods produces a curve as shown in Figure 8.7. Although demand increases to some extent as prices are reduced, below a lower price further reductions actually decrease the level of demand. This is because the product loses its prestigious image if price becomes too low.

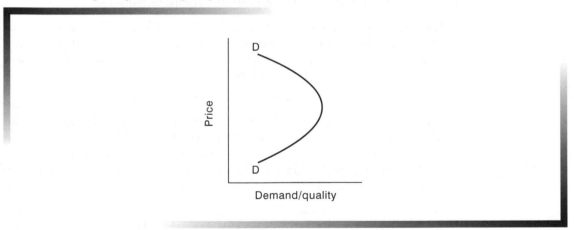

Figure 8.7 Prestige price demand curve

For some products there are price bands within which price reductions have little effect on demand. However, if price is reduced so that it falls into the next psychological price bracket, then demand will increase. This results in a step-like demand curve and is the basis of odd/even pricing (called price lining). Somehow, £4.99 appears a lot less expensive than £5.00. Similarly, for higher-priced products, an even figure reduction appears to encourage demand. The figure of £68 'appears' disproportionately less than its true difference from £70. Odd/even pricing is widely practiced in retailing, although its basis is unclear, and the technique owes as much to tradition as it does to consumer analysis.

8.5.4   Going-rate pricing

Some companies price their products according to the going rate. They must ensure that their cost structures and profit requirements are compatible with this, but having done so, it is a popular method when companies that are 'price leaders' feature in the market. If the main pricing objective is to meet competitive prices, going-rate pricing is appropriate. When companies collectively apply this technique, prices are stabilised and price wars are avoided.

8.6   Pricing strategy

Marketing must devise a pricing strategy that is compatible with strategies attached to other elements of the marketing mix. It is not always possible to set a price and apply this rigidly to all customers in all situations. Demand-orientated pricing sets a base price that the company must endeavour to achieve, but it assumes that price be modified in line with changes in demand. Manufacturers must also consider that customers are not the same. Some will purchase in greater quantities than others or be situated in areas that are more costly to reach.

A company's ability to formulate pricing strategies reflects its willingness to adapt and modify price according to the needs of customers and market conditions.

8.6.1   Discounting

The discount structure a company employs is a major element of pricing strategy. If customers buy products in large quantities, they may reasonably expect to be charged a lower price. The seller may offer discounts voluntarily, to encourage large orders in order to facilitate economies of scale and assist production planning.

Manufacturers also offer discounts to encourage sales of a new product or accelerate demand for products whose stocks are high, perhaps owing to an overall reduction in demand that might be exceptional, or the result of seasonal or cyclical demand variations.

A discounting strategy might be applied to payment terms. It is common in industrial marketing to offer a percentage discount to firms who settle their monthly account promptly. Finance should arrive at a 'sliding scale' for discounts in relation to speed of payment that is a reflection of interest rates. The firm may then not have to wait for 30, 60 or even 90 days for settlement of accounts.

The task of negotiating specific prices usually falls to sales. There are situations where the purchasing power of customers gives a salesperson little alternative but to offer some discount as part of the negotiation.

8.6.2   Zone or geographic pricing strategies

To export, a company should take competition and local conditions into account before deciding a price level. Even within the country of manufacture, customers in some areas may be charged a price that reflects additional delivery costs.

8.6.3 Market skimming and market penetration

In the introductory stage of a new product marketing has two strategic pricing alternatives – marketing skimming and market penetration.

Market skimming implies that a company will charge the highest price the market will bear. A skimming strategy is initially directed at a small proportion of the total potential market. This is likely to be made up of innovators and early adopters, who are receptive to new ideas and whose income and lifestyle makes them less sensitive to price. Diffusion theory is dealt with in Chapter 10 and this suggests that these customer groups influence subsequent buyer categories and the acceptance of an innovative product ultimately filters down to a larger number of consumers. In order to reach this wider group of customers, the company must plan to reduce prices progressively while, at the same time, skimming the most advantageous prices from each successive customer group. The signal for each planned price reduction is a slowing down in sales. The price reductions are successively introduced until the product has ultimately been offered to the bulk of the overall target market. A variation of this skimming approach is to launch a highly sophisticated version of a new product, then reduce the price successively by producing cheaper, simpler, alternative or modified products at each successive stage. For skimming to be successful, the product must be distinctive enough to exclude competitors who may be encouraged to enter the market by the high prices that a company is able to charge in the earlier stages. Other elements of the marketing mix should support the skimming strategy by promoting a high quality, distinctive image. The company must also be prepared and able to forgo high volume production in the initial stages of the product's life, bearing in mind that overall the volume of sales and the price charged must be high enough to achieve profitability. Market skimming is illustrated in Figure 8.8.

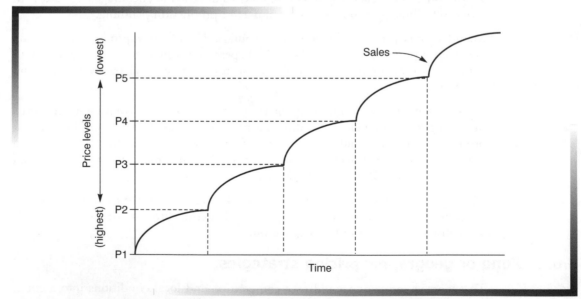

Figure 8.8 Skimming the market

Figure 8.8 illustrates that the first to adopt a new product, as first time adopters and not replacement buyers, might be the upper middle social class 'A' (which might well be the case in high fashion). However, for a new innovative type of computer software, innovator categories (explained in Chapter 10) might be a better indicator of a propensity to adopt. It could be that in this case 'innovators' might well be 'technical' people who may largely belong to the C2 social class. It should also be noted in Figure 8.8 that the first price charged (P1) is the highest and as demand begins to slow at T1, then price is lowered to P2 and so on and price P5 is a final skim.

Market penetration is when a company has a high production capacity that must be utilised quickly, and it is particularly appropriate to the marketing of a new product. A penetration strategy relies on economies of scale to allow high levels of production at a price low enough to attract the greatest number of buyers to the market as early as possible. This, in turn, should preclude potential competitors by erecting price barriers, in the form of large capital set-up costs, to market entry. The longer-term goal is to acquire a high market-share and to hold on to this during the later stages of the product's life through further economies of scale, which may allow further price reductions to fight off competition. Figure 8.9 illustrates penetration pricing and it can be seen that market share is quickly gained through the adoption of a low initial price.

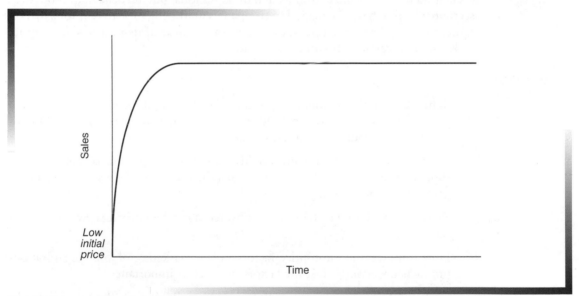

Figure 8.9 Penetration pricing

8.6.4 Discriminatory pricing

Where markets are easily segmented, companies can charge different prices to different segments, even though the product on offer is basically the same. This is called price discrimination. Often, only minor modifications to a product can allow discriminatory prices to be charged. Sometimes discrimination may be based on non-product factors such as the time of year, customer type or location.

'Discrimination' does not mean exploitation, as customers can exercise choice. The manufacturer's reason for discrimination is based on filling capacity and optimising profitability. Volume discounting is a form of discrimination that is not always favoured by smaller customers as their more modest purchasing levels mean that they sometimes do not qualify.

A popular form of discrimination is the many discounts offered to children, students, and older persons for what are similar services offered to the general public. Companies anticipate that these groups may be encouraged to participate in activities that they might not normally afford, thus increasing the company's total market. Such pricing can exploit 'off-peak' usage on a daily, weekly or seasonal basis, thus utilising capacity more effectively. This is popular in the holiday industry, where the objective is to attract customers who might not have considered a particular holiday, had it not been offered at an attractive price. Airlines offer lower rates to 'stand-by' passengers because the journeys are scheduled in any case, so extra sales at however low a price contribute to covering fixed costs. When applying a price discrimination strategy, segments chosen should be easily identifiable and separable so they can be managed and addressed in a manner that distinguishes them from each other.

Although price is important, non-price competition is also effective in achieving sales. It is helpful to understand consumer and organisational buying behaviour motives to ascertain why purchases are made. If a company's marketing mix strategy for a market segment is considered, the role of pricing in the context of its relationship to other marketing mix variables becomes apparent.

Questions

1. Whilst cost considerations form an essential element of the price determination process, a company's costs have little or no relevance to its customers. Discuss in relation to your organisation's customers.

2. Whenever possible, a company should avoid competing on the basis of price, and should compete on the basis of superior value. Discuss the role of price in the price/quality relationship.

3. What factors should be taken into consideration when pricing new products or services?

4. How important are non-price factors in the marketing of your organisations products or services? List the factors in order of importance.

5. Under what circumstances can 'Positively High Pricing' or 'Prestige' pricing be used effectively?

6. Use specific examples to demonstate the price/quality relationship perception of customers in relation to products and services.

References

Tellis G J, (1986) 'Beyond the many Faces of Price: An Integration of Pricing Strategies', *Journal of Marketing*, October, pp. 146-160.

9 Channels and logistics

9.1 The nature of distribution

A *distribution system* refers to that complex of agents, wholesalers and retailers through which manufacturers move products to their markets. Marketing channels are made up of independent firms who are in business to make a profit. These are known as marketing intermediaries or *middlemen*. Distribution outlets can include combinations of owned and independent outlets or franchises. In designing a distribution system, a manufacturer must make a policy choice between selling direct to customers by employing salespeople or using intermediaries, i.e. selling through agents, wholesalers and retailers. The decision is usually based on cost factors that are a function of:

❑ The number of potential customers in the market.

❑ How concentrated or dispersed they are.

❑ How much each will buy in a given period.

❑ Costs associated with the distributive operation (e.g. transport, warehousing and stockholding).

Industrial goods manufacturers tend to use direct selling and deliver direct to the user/customer. Fast moving consumer goods (FMCG) manufacturers tend to use a network of marketing intermediaries because of large numbers of potential customers and their wide dispersion, although there are exceptions like Avon Cosmetics who sell direct to homes through agents.

Distribution arrangements tend to be long term in nature. Because of this, channel decisions are usually classed as strategic, rather than tactical or operational. There are two reasons for treating channel decisions like this:

1. Channel decisions have a direct effect on the rest of a firm's marketing activities.

2. Once established, a company's channel system is hard to change in the short term.

9.2 Strategic elements of channel choice

An important consideration for marketing management when formulating channel policy and the number of marketing intermediaries used is the degree of market exposure sought by the company for its products. Three distribution strategies, resulting in varying degrees of market exposure, can be distinguished.

9.2.1 Intensive distribution

Products are said to be seen by customers as a *bundle of attributes* or *satisfactions*. Producers of convenience goods and certain raw materials aim to stock their products in as many outlets as possible (i.e. an intensive distribution strategy). The dominant factor when marketing such products is their 'place' utility. Producers of convenience goods like confectionery and cigarettes try to enlist every possible retail outlet, ranging from multiples to independent corner shops, to create maximum brand exposure and maximum convenience to customers.

9.2.2 Exclusive distribution

Some producers deliberately limit the number of intermediaries handling their products, as they wish to develop a high quality brand image. Exclusive distribution to recognised official distributors can enhance the prestige of the product. Exclusive (or solus) distribution is a policy of granting dealers exclusive rights to distribute in a certain geographical area. By granting exclusive distribution, the manufacturer gains more control over intermediaries in relation to price, credit and promotional policies, greater loyalty and more resolute selling of the company's products.

9.2.3 Selective distribution

This policy lies between the extremes just described. The manufacturing firm may not have the resources to adequately service or influence the policies of all intermediaries who are willing to carry a particular product. Instead of spreading its marketing effort over the whole range of possible outlets, it concentrates on the most promising of outlets.

Channel members should have facilities to store and market products effectively, e.g. frozen food products require that retailers have adequate deep freeze display facilities. The product may have a carefully cultivated brand image that could be damaged by being stocked in limited-line discount outlets where products are displayed in a functional way to reduce overheads.

CASE 9.1

Family Circle magazine uses selective distribution at supermarket checkouts to get noticed.

Family Circle is a magazine that most people find next to the supermarket check-out. This is rather unusual because most other publications offered by supermarkets are on the other side of the checkout and usually have to be paid for at a separate till. People who are stuck for a long period of time at a supermarket checkout, especially during busy periods, often get very bored. Many people, particularly if they are on their own, as many people are, will pick up Family Circle and start reading an article or some of the advertisements. The magazine has a very broad appeal and has a range of short articles, health advice, shopping suggestions, cooking tips, holiday information and a host of other interesting things including advertisements and promotions.

Many people who pick up the magazine at the checkout for a browse usually find themselves buying it. Either they become so engrossed in a particular piece that they take it home to finish reading it, or they feel too guilty to put the magazine back, having spent so long in the shop reading it. Many simply like what they read and decide to keep the publication, often becoming regular Family Circle readers. Basically, the magazine has made use of an unusual and innovative distribution channel which separates it from the plethora of other magazines on offer in the reading section of the store. However, Family Circle's position at the grocery side of the checkout is not unique any more. More and more publications of a similar nature are finding a place on the checkout sales rack.

9.3 Retail channel systems

Change occurs at all levels in a channel system, but it has been noticeable in UK retailing over the past three to four decades. This period has seen an increased polarity in the distribution turnover of retail firms. At one end of the spectrum there are large-scale operators: multiples, discount chains and the Co-operative movement. At the other end there are many small shops. Some of these are completely independent retailers who purchase from wholesalers and 'cash-and-carry' outlets or who have joint purchasing agreements through 'retail buying associations'. Others are linked to wholesalers through the voluntary chain/group movement, sometimes called symbol shops, e.g. Spar.

Hollander's *wheel-of-retailing* refers to evolutionary change in retailing. The wheel-of-retailing appears to be turning with ever increasing speed with each new retail innovation taking less time to mature, e.g. evidence suggests that it took approximately 50 years for the older-style department stores to reach the maturity (i.e. steady sales) stage; supermarkets took about 25 years and hypermarkets only 10 years.

9.3.1 The search for economies of scale

In a quest for more profits, retail chains devised large-scale methods of operation first through supermarkets culminating in today's hypermarkets (stores with at least 50,000 square feet of selling space) and even larger 'megamarkets'. Each new retailing mode led to greater economies of scale.

9.3.2 The abolition of resale price maintenance (RPM)

Until the mid-1960s, manufacturers' resale prices were protected by resale price maintenance (RPM) under which retailers had to sell at prices stipulated by the manufacturers. If they sold below the stipulated price, supplies could be withheld.

RPM protected small independent retailers from price competition from larger multiples because these larger operators were not legally able to pass on their cost economies to customers. There were some very well-reported case of multiples, notably Tesco, having supplies withheld for selling below a manufacturer's stipulated price (i.e. too cheaply), which was excellent free publicity. Because RPM restricted price competition, retailers relied heavily on non-price competition, and the level of service in many stores was perhaps higher than consumers needed since they would have preferred lower prices.

RPM was abolished by the Resale Prices Act (1964). This resulted in many small shops and wholesalers who supplied them going out of business. The market share that was 'freed up' fell into the hands of more efficient and powerful multiples who used their purchasing economies to compete on price and pass savings on to customers.

9.3.3 Selective employment tax (SET)

This was a tax on 'non-productive workers' (i.e. a tax charged on selective occupations like retailing) that was introduced in 1966. Its effect was to increase shop workers' wage costs by 7%, as it was the employer, not the employee, who paid the tax. SET made labour more expensive and, relatively speaking, capital investment cheaper. This encouraged many retailers (who were the largest employers of non-productive workers) to invest in capital systems (e.g. central checkout systems) that made them less reliant on labour. This gave a further push to the widespread introduction of self-service shopping. Indirectly SET helped multiples to expand at the expense of smaller competitors.

9.3.4 Greater power of multiples

As the power of multiples grew they were able to eliminate traditional wholesalers and purchase centrally, direct from manufacturers. Consumer goods manufacturers could ill afford not to be included in multiples' product lines. Multiples were able to command advantageous discounts from manufacturers. Independents still had to purchase through traditional wholesalers, and even though most formed alliances through voluntary chains (wholesaler sponsored) and voluntary groups (retailer sponsored) they had difficulty in matching multiples' prices. Multiples introduced basic unbranded 'economy lines' during the recessionary period of the 1970s. These 'down market' inferior quality lines were principally cheap, but adequate, food products that large producers would not process (on the basis that they might detract from their branded items) so the task fell to lesser manufacturers.

The early to mid-1980s saw the introduction of 'own label' merchandise, or ranges of brands commissioned and specified by individual multiple chains bearing the multiple's own logotype (logo). The first operator to bring in specified quality 'own label' merchandise was Sainsbury's.

Despite a few manufacturers who do not supply 'own label', in the UK the power within retail channels has certainly switched from manufacturers to retailers (unlike many countries where power still rests with manufacturers of strongly branded products).

9.3.5 Scrambled merchandising

In an affluent society like the UK, consumption of food products is relatively income inelastic. In other words, people do not buy more food when they have more money.

Instead, they tend to 'trade up' and consume better quality foods. In order to expand their businesses, large multiples have diversified, stocking non-food products to further their turnover and profits. Many multiples now sell such items as electrical goods, garden supplies and clothing, and many no longer seem like 'food stores'.

CASE 9.2

BP Petrol Service Stations now sell a range of goods as they move to become a total retail experience for the motorist and non-motorist.

Petrol stations within the UK are not what they used to be. Back in the 1960s a petrol station was a place you went to get fuel for your car and to ask a mechanic for advice if something was wrong with your vehicle. You could buy all sorts of spare parts from the shop including spark plugs, thermostats, fan belts and a range of other similar products. The owner of the petrol station would also make sure you got the right product and may have even helped you fit it on your car. The owner was usually very 'oily' and gave you a certain amount of security and confidence because many people did not know much about fixing motor cars. The 'shop' often offered the motorist a small range of sweets, some soft drinks, and cigarettes. Some even sold bottled gas for camping and that sort of thing, especially if they were situated near the coast or other holiday area. During most of the 1960s garages offered personal service and filled your car up for you. You could just sit in the car. The larger garages, including many owned by BP went over to self-service in the mid to late 1960s.

Today many of the BP Service Stations have an impressive shopping area. There are still some car-related products but these are in the minority in the new shopping environment. You can buy oil, car polish, maps and an emergency fan belt but there is usually no one there to ask for technical advice because the personnel merely work at the checkout. However, you can buy food, micro-waved hot dogs, patio furniture, beer, wine and spirits, newspapers and magazines, frozen meat, greeting cards, flowers and virtually everything else as well as being able to do your National Lottery. BP have a 'scrambled merchandising' policy. They no longer stick to motoring-related products but hope to draw you into the store for a complete shopping experience. And it works. Many people do much of their shopping at a BP Service Station and many people walk to the store from the surrounding area. In many parts of the country the BP Service station is both a petrol station and village store in one.

9.3.6 One stop shopping

Multiples introduced hypermarkets and megastores to capitalise on the concept of 'one stop shopping'. As well as shopping for most of a family's needs, from gardening materials and electrical goods to food in a single location, there is an increasing tendency for customers to shop less frequently (perhaps fortnightly or even monthly instead of weekly). These trends have evolved for several reasons.

Growth in car ownership and two car families. This has brought increased mobility and an ability to travel to out-of-town sites. Such stores have large catchment areas, sufficient to warrant investment in land, building and facilities. Usually, major operators are able to attract ancillary shops such as travel agents, newsagents and florists, to open shops on the same site.

A greater proportion of married women work, so that family time is often at a premium especially if there are children. Time is no longer available for the luxury of browsing.

Universal ownership of freezers coupled with car ownership means that shoppers can transport and store larger volumes of food, thereby benefiting from bulk purchasing. Universal microwave cooker ownership has also boosted sales of 'instant' meals, many of which are cooked from frozen.

A movement of population from urban to suburban centres has occurred (unlike poorer countries where the shift is usually toward the cities). City congestion discourages car drivers who prefer to shop in large out-of-town establishments where parking is adequate and usually free.

The division of labour within marriage is no longer clearly defined. 'Modern' husbands, especially those in the B, C1 and C2 social categories, share roles previously regarded as being the province of women.

9.4   Business format franchising

To franchise means to 'grant freedom to do something' (from the French verb affranchir meaning 'to free'). Franchising constitutes a contractual relationship between a seller (the franchiser) and the seller's distributive outlets (owned by franchisees). The basic features are:

❑   The ownership by an organisation (the franchiser) of a name, idea, secret process or specialised equipment or goodwill.

❑   A licence, granted by the franchiser to the franchisee, that allows the franchisee to profitably exploit that name, idea, or product.

❑   The licence agreement includes regulations concerning the operation of the business in which licensees exploits their rights.

❑   A payment by the licensee (e.g. an initial fee, royalty or share of profits) for the rights obtained.

Franchising has come a long way since its early origins. It was taken from Britain to the USA, where it evolved and developed, and has been re-exported back to the UK in a more sophisticated form.

The modern American concept of the business format franchise has gathered strength in Britain since the early 1960s. The formula is carefully prepared to minimise risk when opening the business. The principle that attracts new franchisees is that other people have followed the same scheme, and since they have been successful, new entrants should also be successful. The franchiser supplies a franchisee with a business package or 'format', a trade name and specific products or services for sale to the general public and is granted exclusive access to a defined geographical area.

9.5 Non-shop shopping

As well as developments of new types of stores in retail channels (e.g. supermarkets, hypermarkets, limited-line discount stores), during the past 40 years, there has been a marked increase in various forms of 'non-shop' selling.

9.5.1 Door-to-door direct selling

This is expensive, but having no wholesaler and retailer margins means that expense is counterbalanced (e.g. Avon Cosmetics and Betterware). It means that manufacturers' agents have to build up clientele among customers in a local community in anticipation that they will purchase from a catalogue on a regular basis.

9.5.2 Party plan

This direct selling method is popular for products like cosmetics, plastic-ware, kitchenware, jewellery and linen products. A 'party' is organised in the home of a host or hostess who invites friends, and receives a 'consideration' in cash or goods based on the amount that these friends purchase. It is sometimes resented, as friends feel there is a moral obligation to purchase.

9.5.3 Automatic vending

This kind of retailing has grown dramatically since the 1960s and is now used for beverages, snacks, confectionery, personal products, cigarettes and newspapers. Vending machines are placed in convenient locations (e.g. garage forecourts, railway and bus stations, colleges, libraries and factories). Automatic vending also supplies entertainment through juke-boxes and arcade games.

9.5.4 Mail order catalogues

Businesses selling through mail order are either catalogue or non-catalogue. The former relies upon comprehensive catalogues to obtain sales, but sometimes use local agents to deal with order collection and administration. Products can be purchased interest-free with extended credit terms for major purchases.

9.5.5 Non-catalogue mail-order

This usually relies on press and magazine advertising, and is used to sell a single product or limited range of products. Craft products are often promoted in this way.

9.5.6 Other direct marketing techniques

The use of direct mail is where a promotional letter and order form is sent through the post. With more effective databases this is now becoming more popular as discussed in Chapter 6. Organisations traditionally using this method include book and music clubs. Television is also used, with orders being placed through a freephone number and a credit card facility.

9.5.7 Future developments

Television shopping via on-line computers is developing and will become a more popular medium along with the internet. As opportunities for leisure activities increase (e.g. sports centres and specialist activity clubs) this kind of shopping will become popular because it will free up more time to pursue leisure activities. This direct method of shopping should make goods cheaper, since orders can be placed directly with the manufacturers without the high costs of intermediaries and associated overheads. Credit facilities are immediately available through electronic debiting.

9.6 Logistics

The organisation must now examine how goods can be physically transferred from the place of manufacture to the place of consumption. Physical distribution management (PDM) is the practical application of logistics and it is concerned with:

'Ensuring the product is in the right place at the right time.'

'Place' has always been thought of as being the least dynamic of the '4Ps'. Marketing practitioners and academics have tended to concentrate on more conspicuous aspects of marketing. Now PDM is a critical area of marketing. Much of its expertise comes from military practice. During the Second World War and the Korean and Vietnam wars, supplies officers performed extraordinary feats of PDM, in terms of food, clothing, ammunition, weapons and a whole range of support equipment having to be transported across the world. The military skill that marketing has adopted and applied to PDM is that of logistics. Marketing management realised that distribution could be organised in a scientific way, so the concept of business logistics developed, focusing attention on and increasing the importance of PDM.

The main reason for the importance of PDM as a marketing function is the demanding nature of the business environment. It was not uncommon for companies to hold large stocks of materials and components. Stocks are now kept to a minimum to save working capital. Responsibility for carrying stock has moved onto suppliers, with each member putting pressure on the next back up the supply chain to provide higher levels of service.

The principal components of logistics and PDM are:

❑   Order processing.

❑   Stock levels or inventory.

❑   Warehousing.

❑   Transportation.

PDM is concerned with ensuring that individual efforts that go to make up the distributive function are integrated so a common objective is realised. This is called the 'systems approach'. As PDM has a well-defined scientific basis, we now present some of the analytical methods that management uses to assist in the development of an efficient logistics system. There are two central themes that should be considered:

1. A successful distribution system relies on integration of effort. An overall service objective can be achieved even though it may appear that some individual components of the system are not performing at maximum efficiency.

2. It is never possible to provide maximum service at minimum cost. The higher the level of service required by a customer, the higher the cost. Having decided on the necessary level of service, a company should then consider ways of minimising costs, which should not be at the expense of, or result in, a reduction of the predetermined service level.

9.7 The distribution process

The distribution process begins when a supplier receives an order from a customer. There is now an expectation that goods will be received at the time requested. *Lead-time* is the period of time that elapses between the placing of an order and receipt of the goods, and this can vary according to the type of product and market.

9.7.1 Order processing

Order processing is the first stage in the *logistical* process. Its efficiency has a direct bearing on lead times. Orders are received from customers, and many establish long-term regular supply routes that are stable, as long as the supplier performs satisfactorily. Taken to its logical conclusion this effectively does away with ordering and leads to what is called *partnership sourcing*. This is an agreement between buyer and seller to supply a product or commodity as and when required without the necessity of negotiating a new contract every time.

Order processing systems should be quick and accurate, as other company departments need to know immediately that an order has been placed so the customer recieves confirmation of the order's receipt and the precise delivery time.

9.7.2 Inventory

Inventory, or stock management, is a critical area of PDM because these have a direct effect on levels of service and customer satisfaction. Optimum stock levels are a function of the type of market in which the company operates. Few companies can say they never run out of stock, but if stock-outs happen regularly, market share will be lost to more efficient competitors. Techniques for determining optimum stock levels are illustrated later and the key lies in ascertaining the re-order point.

Stocks represent *opportunity costs* that occur because of competition for a company's limited resources. If marketing strategy requires that high stock levels be maintained, this should be justified by a profit contribution that will exceed the extra stock costs.

9.7.3 Warehousing

More attention is paid to warehousing in the USA than the UK because of relatively longer distances, and where delivery to customers can take days by the most efficient routes. However, warehousing principles remain the same, particularly when we should consider that the European Union should be viewed as a large 'home market'. Many companies function adequately with their own on-site warehouses from where goods are despatched direct to customers. When a firm markets goods that are ordered regularly, but in small quantities, it becomes logical to consider locating warehouses strategically around the country. Transportation can be carried out in bulk from the place of manufacture to respective warehouses where stocks wait ready for further distribution to the customers. This is a system used by large retailers, although warehouses and transport are owned and operated on their behalf by logistics experts (e.g. BOC Distribution, Excel Logistics, Van Hee and Rowntree Distribution).

To summarise, factors that must be considered in the warehouse equation are:

❑   Location of customers.

❑   Size of orders.

❑   Frequency of deliveries.

❑   Lead times.

CASE 9.3

Yale Materials Handling of North Carolina has been meeting the needs of the materials handling industry with spectacular success for over 125 years.

Yale Materials Handling Corporation offers a comprehensive range of lift trucks that range in capacity from 36,000 pounds upward. The company is one of the most respected names in the global business of manufacturing and supplying materials handling equipment, especially lift trucks for various uses. Specialist lift trucks include 'Sit down rider' trucks (which come powered by electric, gas, LP-gas, diesel or compressed natural gas), very narrow aisle trucks, motorised hand trucks and very big trucks for very heavy lifting jobs. Yale also offer a full complement of services, including fleet management, training, finance, short term and long term rental, repair and service. It also offers a full range of used lift trucks which have been fully reconditioned by the firm's experts. Yale's commitment to offering and delivering the highest quality products and services is shared by the company's extensive dealer network; all of which are fully Yale trained and approved. Yale currently has 223 authorised dealers located within North and South America, 85 dealers in Europe and a similar number in the Asia-Pacific region. Yale has become a global market leader in the lift truck industry by providing a total quality service to its customers. With the firm's durable, reliable and cost-effective range of lifting trucks and other materials-handling products and their comprehensive range of support services the firm is at the very top of the global material-handling suppliers. Yale is a classic example of a fully committed, marketing orientated and customer focused firm. It goes from strength to strength by providing customers around the world with what they want at a price they are prepared to pay.

9.7.4 Transportation

Transportation is usually the greatest distribution cost. It is easy to calculate as it is directly related to weight or numbers of units. Costs should be monitored through the mode selected. During the past 50 years, road transport has become the dominant mode in the UK, as it has the advantage of speed coupled with door-to-door delivery.

When the volume of goods being transported reaches a certain level, some companies purchase their own vehicles, rather than using the services of haulage contractors. However, some large retail chains like Marks & Spencer, Tesco and Sainsbury's now entrust all their warehousing and transport to specialist logistics companies.

For some types of goods, rail transport has advantages. When lead-time is a less critical element of marketing, or when lowering transport costs is a major objective, rail transport becomes viable.

Except where goods are perishable or valuable in relation to their weight, air transport is not normally an alternative form of distribution within the UK where distances are relatively short. For long-distance international routes it is popular, as it has the advantage of quick delivery compared to sea transport as well as lower insurance costs.

Roll-on roll-off (RORO) cargo ferries have assisted UK companies when marketing to mainland Europe. Companies distinguish between European and Near-European markets that can be served by road, once they have crossed the Channel by ferry or Channel tunnel. 'Deep sea markets', such as the Far East, Australasia and America, are still served by ocean-going freighters, and the widespread introduction of containerisation in the 1970s made this medium more efficient.

9.8 The systems approach to PDM

There is a need to integrate marketing activities so they combine into a single marketing effort. As PDM has been neglected in the past, this function has been late in adopting an integrated approach towards its activities. Managers are now more conscious of the potential of PDM and recognise that logistical systems be designed with the total function in mind.

Senior management should communicate overall distribution objectives throughout the company. A systems approach to PDM should encompass production and production planning, purchasing and sales forecasting. Included in the systems approach is the concept of 'total cost', because individual costs are less important than total cost. The cost of holding high stocks may appear unreasonable, but if high stocks provide a service that leads to higher sales and profits, then the total cost of all the PDM activities will have been effective.

PDM as a cost centre is worth thorough analysis, as this function is now a valuable marketing tool in its own right. In homogeneous product markets, where differences in prices may be negligible, service is often the major competitive weapon, and many buyers now pay a premium for products that are consistently delivered on time.

Distribution is not an adjunct to marketing. It has a full place in the mix and is an essential component of marketing strategy. A well-organised business logistics system can supply quantitative data that can be used to optimise the marketing mix as a whole.

9.9 Monitoring and control of PDM

The objective of PDM is:

'Getting the right goods to the right place at the right time for the least cost.'

This seems reasonable, although it does not offer guidance on specific measures of operational effectiveness. Management needs objectives or criteria that allow meaningful evaluation of performance, which is the basis of monitoring and control.

9.9.1 Output of physical distribution systems

The output from any system of physical distribution is the level of customer service. This key competitive benefit is what companies offer to retain or attract business, and should equate to that of major competitors. This level is the time it takes to deliver an order or the percentage of orders met from stock. Other service elements include technical assistance, training and after-sales services. The two most important are:

❑   Reliability and frequency of delivery.
❑   Stock availability and an ability to meet orders quickly.

A company's service policy might be to deliver 40% of orders within seven days from receipt of an order. This is an operationally useful objective that provides a strict criterion for evaluation. A simple delivery delay analysis can inform management whether such objectives are being achieved or whether corrective action is necessary to alter the service level in line with stated objectives. Such an analysis can be updated when the order is despatched. A management report can be generated, from which it can be ascertained whether or not corrective action is necessary.

Days late	Number of orders	Percentage of total orders
0	**186**	**37.2**
1	71	14.2
2	49	9.8
3	35	7.0
4	38	7.6
5	28	5.6
6	14	2.8
7	13	2.6
8	10	2.0
9	8	1.6
10-14	17	3.4
15-21	15	3.0
22-28	10	2.0
<28+	6	1.2
	500	100.0

Figure 9.1 An example of a simple delivery delay analysis

9.9.2 Service elasticity

Costs of customer service can be calculated in terms of time and money. This is particularly applicable in industrial markets where potential customers sometimes consider service to be more important than price when deciding to source supplies. The concept of diminishing returns, for companies wishing to raise their service levels, is illustrated in the following example:

> Suppose it costs a marketing firm £x to provide 75% of all orders from stock, with 60% of all orders being delivered within seven days of receipt. To increase either of these targets by 10% might increase the cost of service provision by 20 to 30%. In order to meet 85% of orders out of stock, stockholding on all inventory items would have to increase. Similarly, to deliver 70% of orders within the specified time may necessitate purchasing extra transport facilities that might be under-utilised for a large part of the time. Alternatively, the company could use outside haulage contractors to cope with extra deliveries, which would add to costs.

Figure 9.2 further illustrates this point. In this example, 80% of total possible service can be provided for approximately 40% of the cost of 100% service provision. To increase general service levels by 10% brings about a cost increase of approximately 15%. 100% service provision means covering every possible eventuality, which is extremely expensive.

Maximum consumer satisfaction and minimum distribution costs are mutually exclusive. There has to be a trade-off and this will depend on the degree of service sensitivity or elasticity in the market. Two industries may use the same product and

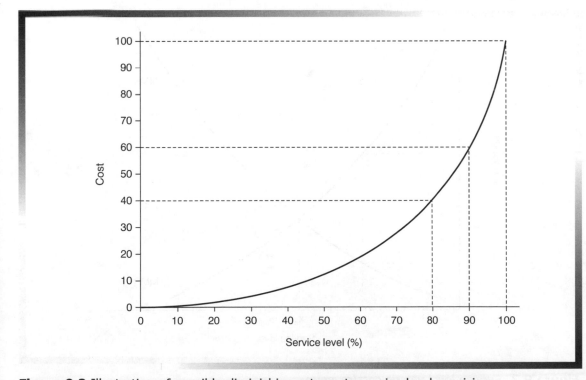

Figure 9.2 Illustration of possible diminishing returns to service level provision

purchase this from the same supplier, but their criteria for choosing this supplier may be different. Both the sugar-processing and oil-exploration industries use large high-pressure 'on-line' valves. A sugar-processing company needs to control the flow of sugar-beet pulp in the sugar making process; an oil exploration company needs to control the flow of drilling fluids and crude oil on an exploration platform. The oil industry is highly service sensitive (or elastic). When dealing with suppliers, price is relatively unimportant, but service levels are critical. Because of the high costs of operations and the potential cost of breakdown, every effort is made to cover every contingency. The sugar-processing industry is more price sensitive and processing is seasonal, with much processing work being carried out over two months. As long as these critical two months are not disrupted, service provision takes a relatively low priority for the remainder of the year.

Service levels should be increased to a point where marginal marketing expense equals marginal marketing response. This follows the economist's profit maximisation criterion of marginal cost being equal to marginal revenue. Figure 9.3 illustrates this point. It can be seen that the marginal expense (MME) of level of service provision x_1 is Y and the marginal revenue (MMR) is Z. It would pay the firm to increase service levels since the extra revenue generated by the increased services (MMR) is greater than the cost (MME). At service level x_2 the marginal expense (Z) is higher than the marginal revenue (X), so service provision is too high. The point of service optimisation is where marginal marketing expense and marginal marketing response are equal at service level x_e.

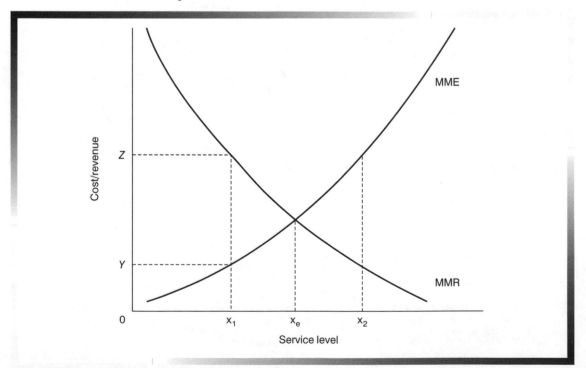

Figure 9.3 Service level versus cost/revenue

9.9.3 Inventory management

Inventory (stockholding) is defined as:

> '*The accumulation of an assortment of items today for the purpose of providing protection against what may occur in the future.*'

Inventory is maintained to increase profitability through manufacturing and marketing support. Manufacturing support is provided through two types of inventory:

1. An inventory of materials for production.

2. An inventory of spare and repair parts for maintaining production equipment.

Similarly, marketing support is provided through:

1. Inventories of the finished product.

2. Spare and repair parts that support the product.

If supply and demand could be perfectly co-ordinated there would be no need for stockholding. However, future demand is uncertain, as is reliability of supply. Hence inventories are accumulated to ensure availability of raw materials, spare parts and finished goods. Generally speaking, inventories are kept by companies because they:

❑   Act as a hedge against contingencies (e.g. unexpected demand, machinery breakdown).

❑   Act as a hedge against inflation, price or exchange rate fluctuations.

❑   Assist economies of purchasing.

❑   Assist economies of transportation.

❑   Assist economies of production.

❑   Improve the level of customer service by providing greater stock availability.

Inventory planning means balancing various types of cost. The cost of holding stock and procurement is weighed against the cost of 'stock-out' in terms of production shut downs, loss of business and customer goodwill that would undoubtedly arise. These various costs conflict with each other.

When conflicting costs just described are added together, they form a total cost that can be plotted as a 'U-shaped' curve. Management's task is to find a procedure of ordering, resulting in an inventory level that minimises total costs. This '*minimum total cost procurement concept*' is illustrated in Figure 9.4.

Economic order quantity (EOQ) assumes that total inventory costs are minimised at some definable purchase quantity, and that they are a function of the number of orders that are processed per unit of time, and the costs of maintaining an inventory over and above the cost of items included in it (e.g. warehousing). It ignores quantity discounts and transportation costs that might significantly increase for smaller shipments. Because of these limitations, EOQ was viewed as a poor manager of inventory. However, better software now allows the use of more sophisticated versions of EOQ. An example of the traditional EOQ method is provided to give an understanding of the principles.

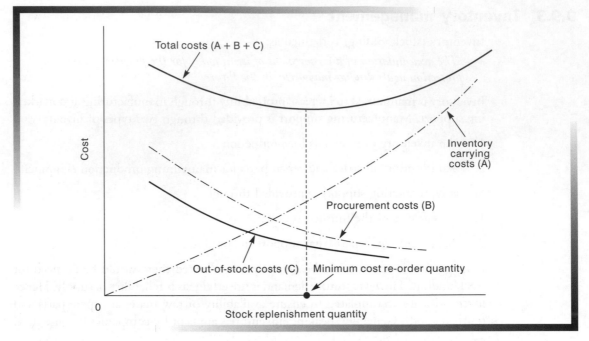

Figure 9.4 Cost trade-off model

The economic order quantity can be calculated using the following formula:

$$EOQ = \sqrt{\frac{2AS}{I}}$$

where: A = annual usage (units)
         S = ordering costs (£)
         I = inventory carrying cost as a percentage of inventory value

e.g. To find the EOQ where the annual usage is 6,000 units, the ordering costs are £13, the inventory carrying cost is 17% (0.17) and the unit cost is £1.30.

$$EOQ = \sqrt{\frac{2 \times 6,000 \times £1.30 \times £13}{0.17}}$$

$$= \sqrt{\frac{202,800}{0.17}}$$

$$= \quad 1,192,941.18$$

$$= \quad £1,092.22, \text{ or } 840 \text{ units at } £1.30 \text{ per unit}$$

The EOQ concept and its variations seek to define the most economical lot size when placing an order. The order point method can be used to determine the ideal timing for placing an order. The calculation uses the following equation:

$$OP = DL_t + SS$$

where: OP   is the order point
         D   is the demand
         L_t is the lead time
         SS   is the safety stock

e.g. To find the order point where the demand is 150 units per week, the lead time is 6 weeks and the safety stock is 300 units.

$$
\begin{aligned}
\text{OP} &= (150 \times 6) + 300 \\
&= 900 + 300 \\
&= 1{,}200 \text{ units}
\end{aligned}
$$

A replenishment order should be placed when inventory level decreases to 1,200 units. The size of the order to be placed when stock reaches this level can be calculated using the EOQ formula.

As with EOQ, the order point method contains assumptions. The order point assumes that lead times are fixed and can be accurately evaluated, which is seldom the case. Despite limitations of EOQ and order point models, the basic principles are valid and form the rationale for more useful computer-based inventory models.

Questions

1. *Retailing* – How do you account for the fact that non-shop selling has, in recent years, been one of the fastest growing areas of distribution?

2. *Channels* – What should an organisation consider when it contemplates changing its channel of distribution?

3. *Distribution* – In what circumstances would a company wish to adopt:
    Intensive distribution?
    Selective distribution?
    Exclusive distribution?

4. *Channel power* – How has 'power' within retail channels switched from brands to retail chains over the past 40 years?

5. *PDM* – Why has the marketing function of physical distribution management (PDM) grown significantly in importance over the past thirty years?

6. *Service provision* – Explain, using quantitative and non-quantitative examples, the idea that diminishing returns can sometimes be faced by marketing firms when raising the level of service provided to certain customers or market segments.

7. *Service elasticity* – Discuss the concept of service 'elasticity' and show how this can be applied by management when setting levels of service and how these are priced in the following sectors:
    (a) Oil exploration.
    (b) A company supplying the automotive industry.

8. *Systems approach* – Outline and discuss the four main components of a 'systems approach' to OPDM.

Reference

Hollander, SC, (1960) The Wheel of Retailing, *Journal of Marketing*, July, pp. 37-42

10 Product

10.1 Defining the product

A diverse range of products/services and markets calls for different marketing mixes. A product is the central focus of the marketing mix as this is what is delivered to the consumer. *Product* and *service* are interchangeable words in the context of this discussion and this is what gives satisfaction to consumers, fulfilling the overall aim of marketing. Product strategy is concerned with how the product is presented to the consumer, how it will be perceived.

Customers pay for something specific and identifiable, but this also includes promotion, availability and perceived value. This is termed a *bundle of satisfactions* that are both tangible and intangible (see Figure 10.1). This broad view of the product/service is important. The marketer must organise the marketing mix to present consumers with an assortment of satisfactions that are appropriate to their needs. The marketing mix creates the product in this wider sense, and it should deliver something that most exactly matches consumer wants or needs.

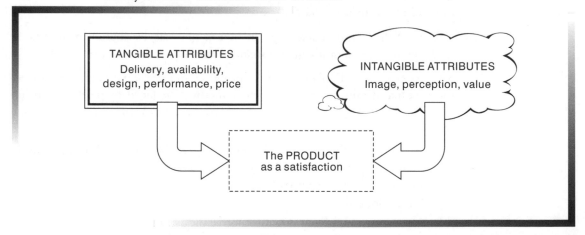

Figure 10.1 Product dimensions – the wider viewpoint

This wider description is known as the *extended product* and represents the sum of marketing effort. Service is included in this description, e.g. a holiday is a leisure market product and an insurance policy is a product in the securities and investment market. To consumers the product is a satisfaction. Although a washing machine is a physical object, the real product features (customer satisfaction) are labour and time saving. A frozen ready-prepared meal consists of ingredients, but customer satisfaction is convenience. To an industrial buyer, the main feature might be speed of delivery or technical support. For marketers, the product is a want-satisfying item; to consumers, it is a satisfaction.

10.2 Product classification: consumer goods

Products have intangible and tangible attributes. With this in mind it is appropriate to consider products in identifiable groups. This is done through a classification that assists market planning. We also assign to each group a customer view of products to ascertain why and how they are purchased.

A distinction is made between consumer goods and industrial goods. Industrial goods are purchased by intermediate manufacturers who use them to manufacture other products. These, in turn, are sold to make other products.

Consumer goods are finished products that are sold to the ultimate user and these are sub-categorised as shown in Figure 10.2:

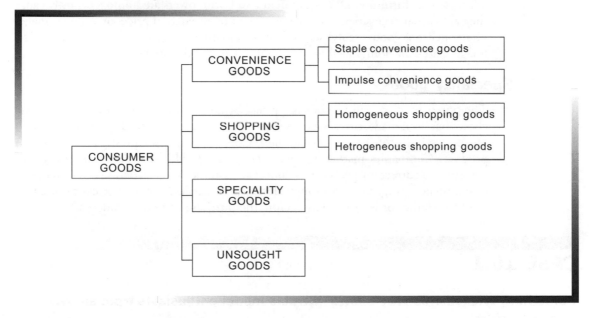

Figure 10.2 Formal classification for consumer goods

10.2.1 Convenience goods

These are relatively inexpensive items, typically part of a weekly shop, whose purchase requires little effort. Consumer decision processes are clouded by the existence of many brands that require comparisons and choices to be made. A task of advertising is to predetermine consumer purchasing decisions so that the consumer buys, or subconsciously notes, a certain brand rather than first considering the generic product and then making a brand-choice decision.

Convenience goods can be divided into staple and impulse purchases. Staple goods are consumed on a daily basis (e.g. milk and meat) where opportunities for differentiation are less. If a sudden need arises that might have been forgotten on a major shopping trip, then even less thought is put into the purchase. Small grocery stores owe much of their trade to the purchase of overlooked items. As the term implies, there is no pre-planning of impulse goods. The decision to buy is often made during a shopping trip and displays, including dump bins, are designed to promote these sales.

10.2.2 Shopping goods

These include major durable or semi-durable items that are more expensive than convenience goods. Purchase is less frequent and is characterised by pre-planning, information search and price comparisons. This infrequency of purchase means the consumer is often unaware of product availability prior to planning a purchase. The quality of sales staff is significant in the marketing of shopping goods. Promotional strategies attempt to simplify the decision process for consumers by ensuring that they have a high level of brand awareness before purchase planning begins.

Shopping goods can be further classified into homogeneous or heterogeneous items. White goods, furniture, DIY equipment and lawnmowers are homogeneous because they are virtual necessities, and are not very differentiated in price, prestige or image. Heterogeneous goods are stylised and non-standard. Here, price is less important than image, and behavioural factors are important in the decision process.

10.2.3 Speciality goods

The purchase of speciality goods is typified by an extensive search. Once a purchase choice has been made, there is a reluctance to accept a substitute. The market is small, but prices and profits are relatively high. Consumers pay for prestige as well as the product. Companies marketing speciality goods should be expert at creating and preserving a correct image. If this is done, the customer's search period can be reduced or eliminated. (E.g. some customers decide on a particular model of car or designer label for clothes or jewellery long before the purchase is even considered.)

CASE 10.1

'Something Wicked This Way Comes' attracts model enthusiasts from all over West Yorkshire.

'Something Wicked This Way Comes' is an unusual name for a shop. The shop is located in Huddersfield in West Yorkshire and offers a wide range of specialist model kits. Customers are usually enthusiasts and collectors. For example, the store offers a range of specialist military models such as soldiers and tanks etc. that the collector can paint themselves and use in battle games and in the reconstruction of war scenes. This is a speciality shop. Very few stores offer the enthusiast the range of products and the people working in the shop are also enthusiasts and can offer advice and take specialist orders from suppliers for goods not stocked. Because it is a speciality store, location is less important than for other products. The store advertises its merchandise on the Web and through specialist magazines. Orders can be taken over the Web and by telephone using a credit card so there is no reason for many customers to visit the store. Those that do come to the store are not put off by its location away from the main shopping precincts of Huddersfield. Because it is a speciality shop, customers are prepared to travel some distance and put up with some inconvenience to indulge their hobby and interact with similar people sharing an interest. Much of the store's business is repeat business, as many customers come back again and again as their collection of model figures or similar products grow. Apart from communicating through magazines and the Web, quite a lot of custom comes through word of mouth as enthusiasts tell others about the store and also introduce friends to the arcane world of specialist model collecting.

10.2.4 Unsought goods

By definition, the customer has not considered the purchase of unsought goods before being made aware of them. Such products often satisfy a genuine need that the consumer had not actively considered (e.g. a life insurance policy, or a funeral).

Consumers can be at a disadvantage when confronted with unsought goods as there may not have been an opportunity for evaluation. They may be faced with a 'special offer' that is often the hallmark of less scrupulous companies. Unsought goods should be marketed sensitively as their promotion often reflects the dubious side of marketing. Methods used are direct mail, telephone canvassing, door-to-door calling and the unscrupulous practice of 'sugging' (selling under the guise of market research).

10.3   Product classification: industrial goods

Only certain goods classed as industrial are directly essential to manufacture. Machinery and raw materials are prime necessities. However, a company could not function without a whole range of other items that, although not integral to the manufacturing process, are essential to the running of the company (e.g. office equipment, stationery and cleaning materials). Goods and services required by industry are shown in Figure 10.3 and classified into appropriate groups:

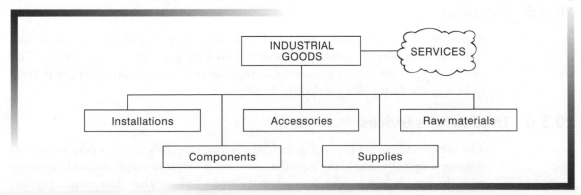

Figure 10.3 Classification of industrial goods

10.3.1   Installations

These are expensive items like plant and machinery required for production. A company might make a mistake when choosing office equipment or building maintenance services which may be costly, but is unlikely to be a serious threat to the company's future. However, if production machinery is purchased that is then found to be unsuitable, this could affect production processes. The purchase of installations should follow an extensive search process. Price is important, but seldom the single deciding factor. Much emphasis is placed, when marketing installations, on the quality of technical support and after-sales service.

10.3.2   Accessories

Accessories are also capital items, but usually less expensive, being depreciated in company accounts over fewer years. Their purchase is important, but not as critical as for installations. Accessories include secondary plant and machinery, warehousing equipment and office equipment and furniture.

10.3.3   Raw materials

Raw materials account for much of the time and work of a purchasing department. A direct relationship exists between raw material quality and the quality of a company's finished product, so quality, reliability of supply, service and price are important. Such produce is purchased continuously, particularly in flow-production situations, so reliable service is critical. Raw material suppliers have opportunities for differentiation on the basis of providing reliable service.

10.3.4   Component parts and materials

Criteria are similar to raw materials, including replacement and maintenance items for production machinery. This category is important in assembly plants where purchases range from computer chips to castings to larger components like car bodies. It includes products that facilitate, or are essential to, the manufacturing process, but which do not form part of the finished product, e.g. oils, chemicals, adhesives and packaging materials.

10.3.5   Supplies

These are the 'convenience goods' of industrial supply, and include items like stationery, cleaning materials and goods required for maintenance and repairs. The purchasing process is more routine. Most supplies are homogeneous and price is likely to be a major factor in a purchasing decision.

10.3.6   Industrial services

The use of external suppliers of industrial services, especially in the public sector, has risen over recent years. Many organisations find it better to employ outside agencies with the expertise they offer, to carry out certain tasks, rather than employing 'in-house' personnel. Cleaning, catering, maintenance and transport are examples. As long as suppliers can meet the standards, it is worthwhile to use outside providers, whilst the company concentrates on its areas of expertise in producing and marketing products.

10.4 New product development

New product development forms part of product strategy as well as being an element of overall marketing strategy. New products are central to a company's continued survival, but their development is a risky undertaking.

In FMCG markets new products appear regularly. Confectionery firms, for example, launch new products, many of which disappear shortly after launch. The development of a new car is a multi-million pound investment, although success or failure is of little consequence to the consumer. For many companies, new products represent 'make or break' decisions.

It is useful to consider definitions of various types of new products:

❑ *Innovative products* are new to the market and completely different alternatives to existing products. Digital cameras are innovative and so was the microwave cooker, and before that the television.

❑ *Replacement products* are new to consumers, but replace current products, usually in a radical way. Photographic equipment has been constantly replaced since cameras were invented. The technology and some component parts of replacement products are innovative in the marketing sense of new product definitions, but the products themselves are replacements.

❑ *Imitative products* are the category into which most new products fall. When a firm has successfully launched an innovative or replacement product, other firms follow. These are described as *me too* products. Not all companies have the resources to develop entirely new products, so it falls to them to be *market followers* rather than *market leaders*. Often, powerful imitators quickly gain market share from innovators.

❑ *Relaunched products* form this final category. The perception of a product is a subjective matter and sometimes a product can be successfully relaunched using a different marketing strategy, perhaps by changing the emphasis of product benefits. It is then classed as a new product, even if its physical characteristics are similar.

The product is central to marketing, for without a product, marketing activity would not be possible. The sale of the product or service provides revenue, and it is the medium through which a company fulfils the marketing concept. Considering the importance of new products and the risks involved in development, it is essential that a development programme be conducted in a scientifically planned manner through a new-product development process. The idea of identifiable phases in new product development was developed by American consultants, Booz-Allen and Hamilton, as explained in Figure 10.4.

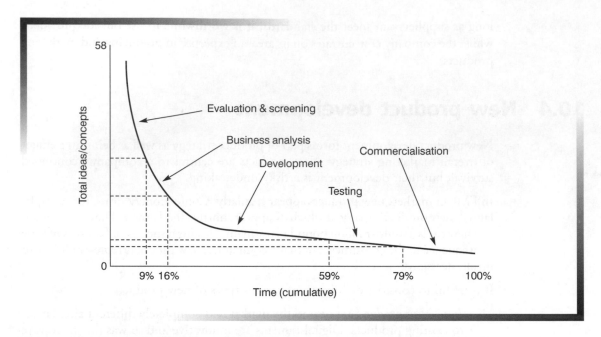

Figure 10.4 Decay curve of new product ideas

This study was done in 1968 and it found that it took 58 new product or service ideas to generate one successful product. The study was repeated in 1981, but it was then found that it only took only seven new ideas to come up with one successful product. However, it is the 1968 study that is the most popularly cited one, as experience suggests that it takes many more than seven new ideas or concepts to produce a successful product.

Refinement has taken place since this experiment in relation to the stages of new product development and the process described in Figure 10.5 represents what is currently viewed as being each of the stages in this process.

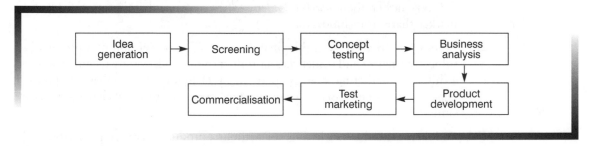

Figure 10.5 Stages in the new product development process

Each of the stages listed in Figure 10.5 is now elaborated:

Idea generation

The attitude of management and the atmosphere in which new ideas are encouraged and created is of prime importance. Ideas come from many sources, e.g. marketing research, research & development and production. Salespersons are well placed for providing customer feedback and reporting on competitive products as part of information collection for market intelligence. Brainstorming sessions can be conducted to focus on new-product development issues. Venture teams and planning committees set up to consider new-product development could include personnel from the shop floor to management.

CASE 10.2

Merck & Co Inc., the USA pharmaceutical company, markets Propecia (Finasteride) as a cure for androgenetic alopecia.

About 40% of the male population lose some or even most of their hair when they get past the age of 40. Although hair loss is not a serious medical condition it can cause embarrassment, loss of self-confidence and, in some people, serious psychological distress. Finasteride is a drug developed by Merck & Co Inc. in the USA, the pharmaceutical company, for the treatment of enlarged prostate gland (benign prostatic hyperplasia). Many men, especially those over 50 years of age suffer from an enlarged prostate which makes it very uncomfortable to pass water when going to the toilet and can develop into prostate cancer. Finasteride helps the prostate sufferer by reducing the amount of the male hormone dihydrotestosterone (DHT) a metabolite of testosterone the male hormone or 'androgen'. DHT also has some causal effect on male pattern baldness (androgenetic alopecia). Merk found that people taking Finasteride for an enlarged prostate also started to grow more hair. They came across this information quite accidentally. The firm was not looking for a hair loss product but on seeing the effects on hair growth the firm decided to market Finasteride are a hair-restoration product. The product is available on private subscription in the USA under the brand name Propecia, but not as yet available in Britain through main stream pharmacies, although a number of UK based companies offer the product by mail order or on the Web. The product comes in 1mg tablet form and the user has to take one tablet every day. Finasteride is sold as the prostate drug Proscar in a 5mg form. Some firms offer Proscar together with a 'pill cutter' which enables the user of Finasteride to have the 1mg dose for about one third of the cost of the branded Propicia.

Screening

Management reduces the collection of ideas to manageable numbers by identifying the most viable to go to the next stage. Typical questions include:

❑   Is there a real consumer need?

❑   Does the company have resources and technical ability to manufacture and market the new product idea?

❑   Is the potential market large enough to generate enough profits?

Concept testing

Here, a small number of key decision makers within the company, and possibly potential customers, are presented with the product idea in a simple format that includes drawings, models and a written description. This is to establish their feelings about the product's potential in the market place. Concept testing uses few resources and allows an organisation to test out initial reactions prior to a commitment to more costly research, design and development.

Business analysis

This stage concerns more detailed financial, rather than practical, concerns. The company estimates demand, costs and profitability that take account of marketing costs as well as costs of raw materials and production.

Product development

The expense, including marketing research and executive time devoted to screening to date, is likely to be small, compared to this stage which involves costs of product development. Through this pre-analysis, the company has minimised risk and isolated and validated a new product idea.

The company now develops a prototype to establish its potential in physical terms, and turns to the market place to obtain feedback. The prototype should correspond as closely as possible to the production model to obtain accurate customer reactions. At this stage it is possible to modify the product.

If it is discovered that its feasibility is deficient at this late stage it should be abandoned, even if it appears to be wasteful, as subsequent failure will be more costly. If this product development stage is successful, the firm will have confidence to go ahead with a product launch.

Test marketing

The purpose of test marketing is to assess the appropriateness of the proposed marketing strategy and tactics, to refine them and to predict the effect of such strategy in terms of market penetration.

For consumer markets, test marketing is made simpler by the existence of Independent Television areas. These divide the UK into well-defined areas that can be used for test marketing. They are appropriate when television advertising forms part of marketing strategy. It is important that a chosen test area should represent the final market as closely as possible.

Test markets are sometimes 'sabotaged' by competitors who increase marketing activity in the test area for a short period with the intention of causing disruption and creating market conditions that are not representative. For this reason, test markets should be unobtrusive and some companies confine test marketing to smaller geographical locations called test towns, like Darlington, Croydon, Bristol and Southampton, as their social constitution typically represents a microcosm of the UK.

In industrial markets, where numbers of customers are less, testing is sometimes conducted through *product placement tests* where a few co-operating customers are provided with the product for a period and give feedback before full-scale launch takes place. This technique is sometimes used for white goods consumer items like washing machines or brown goods items like cookers.

Commercialisation

This is the final stage after various ideas have been filtered. A final proposition has been selected that is acceptable to the marketplace. Test marketing has permitted the company to make any final adjustments to the chosen marketing strategy, and the product can now be 'commercialised'.

10.5   The product life cycle

The *product life cycle (PLC)* is central to marketing strategy. It is based on the suggestion that a new product enters a life cycle once it is launched. The product is conceived prior to *development* and has a 'birth' and a 'death' described as *introduction* and *decline*. The intervening period is characterised by *growth, maturity* and *saturation*. By mapping a product's course through the market, it is possible to design strategies appropriate to relevant stage in the product's life. Figure 10.6 shows the course of the life cycle.

The PLC concept is theoretical and not every product fits into the curve it suggests. The business environment is dynamic, so even basically similar products might react differently during their life span. The PLC is influenced by:

❏   The inherent nature of the product itself.

❏   Changes in the macro environment.

❏   Changes in consumer preferences, which can be affected by the macro- and micro-environment.

❏   Competitive actions.

The market influence on the shape of the curve can influence the time span of the life cycle which can range from weeks to decades.

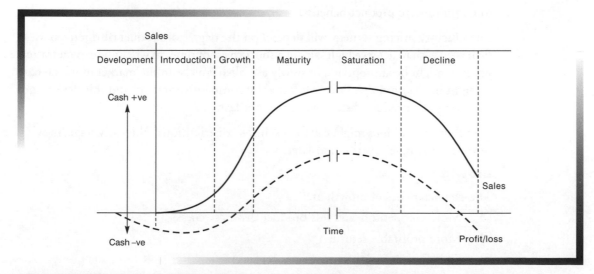

Figure 10.6 Product Life Cycle (PLC)

In strategic terms, marketing management must:

❑ Estimate the likely shape of the curve.

❑ Design an appropriate strategy for each stage.

❑ Identify the product's movement from one stage to another.

The value of the concept is that once a stage has been identified, markets tend to display particular characteristics that suggest certain reactions. We now elaborate the stages that have been highlighted in Figure 10.6.

Development

Naturally, during this phase no sales are made. As time progresses, development costs accrue as can be seen on the lower negative cash-flow curve.

Introduction

This period relates to the launch and its duration depends on the product's rate of market penetration. It ends when awareness of the product is high enough to attract wider user groups and sales begin to increase faster. Typical features of the stage are:

❑ High product failure rate, particularly amongst companies who have not subjected their new products to an effective screening process.

❑ Few or no competitors.

❑ Limited distribution (often exclusive or selective).

❑ Frequent product modifications.

❑ A costly process as development costs have not been recovered, promotional expenditure is high in relation to sales and economies of scale are not yet possible.

The aim is to create awareness that often involves a disproportionate level of marketing expenditure relative to sales revenue. This is seen as an investment in the product's future. Promotion creates this awareness along with the sales function whose task is to communicate product benefits.

Introductory pricing strategy will depend on the degree of product distinctiveness. A firm may wish to achieve high sales in a short space of time, in which case 'penetration pricing' might be appropriate, or slowly establish a niche in the market in which case it might use 'skimming'. Price is affected by competitive activity and this determines how long any product distinctiveness might last.

Distribution decisions might call for 'exclusive' distribution at this early stage, moving towards 'intensive' distribution later.

Growth

The characteristics of growth are:

❑ More competitors and less product distinctiveness.

❑ More profitable returns.

❑ Steeply rising sales.

❑ Company or product acquisition by larger competitors.

Promotional expenditure is still high because it is the best time to gain market share in preparation for market dominance during the maturity stage. Promotional effort moves from creating product awareness to specific brand promotion.

Distribution is important, because during growth FMCG suppliers in particular are in competition with each other to establish dealership and distributive outlet agreements. Once a hierarchy of brand leaders has been established, powerful buyers in retail multiples may attempt to rationalise their list of suppliers.

If a skimming policy is in operation during growth, profits are usually high. The end of growth may feature reduced prices (even though profits may be still high as a result of higher volumes). As the growth period moves towards maturity, market shares may have stabilised and a hierarchy of brand leaders might have emerged.

CASE 10.3

Firms providing video conferencing services and products experience a surge in demand: V-Span of Philadelphia, USA capitalises on the trend.

The problems in the USA have resulted in a dramatic reduction in people's willingness to fly. It is not only the holiday firms and charter airlines that are feeling the effects, but business travel is also reduced, due to an unwillingness to fly, particularly to and around the USA. As the world economy drops down a gear, firms are also looking to save costs as well. This is where video conferencing fits into the picture. The concept of video conferencing has been around for a number of years and some of the more progressive companies, particularly those involved in high technology products, such as telecom firms, have made effective use of this communication tools for some time. For many companies, however, holding important meetings using video conferencing has been something they have only read about in the business pages and journals. However, because of world events ordinary firms are beginning to take video conferencing seriously and are prepared to invest in the equipment or purchase the services of other firms. All companies involved video conferencing equipment or software are seeing an increase in demand for their products and services. The future is likely to hold enormous growth potential for this commercial communication medium for some considerable time to come.

V-Span of Philadelphia, USA is a classic example of a growing band of entrepreneurial companies who are capitalising on the growing demand for video conferences services by clients. The firm has evolved from a video conferencing company into one of the USA's largest privately held broadband communications portals. Put simply, V-Span's technology lets companies outsource their video conferencing needs. V-Span services range from providing a simple connection to managing video conferencing events. Their philosophy is summarised by a statement from the firm's CEO Kenyon Hayward, 'If a company makes semiconductors, we let them focus on making semiconductors, not on video-conferencing work'.

10.5.4 Maturity

Most products are in maturity and a lot of marketing activity is devoted to this stage. The major characteristics of the maturity stage are:

1. Sales continue to grow, but at a much decreased rate.
2. Attempts are made to differentiate and re-differentiate products.
3. Prices fall in battles to retain market share along with falling profits.
4. Brand and inventory rationalisation amongst retailers and distributors.
5. Marginal manufacturers leaving the market when faced with severe competition and reduced margins.

Exponential market growth has ceased, and marketing's task is to retain market share with promotion reinforcing brand loyalty. Further growth is at the expense of competitors so there is a need for sustained promotional activity, even if only to retain existing customers. Deciding levels of promotional expenditure can be a problem as a result of decreased profit margins.

Distribution strategy should aim to retain outlets. A retail distributorship that is lost during maturity is difficult to regain later. To this end, a major thrust of promotional effort may move from consumers to distributors.

10.5.5 Saturation

This is really the second part of the maturity phase, but has its own characteristics. It is when the peak of maturity has been passed, when price wars are common and lower-priced producers have entered the market. They have mastered the manufacturing technology, often in low labour-cost countries. Price wars in this market are the predictable result of over supply. There is an overall reduction in revenue. Although the aim of price-cutting should be to increase sales enough to offset revenue losses, in reality it is often a signal for established players to exit from the market before decline.

10.5.6 Decline

The shape of the PLC curve is not inevitable, but consistently falling sales signify the decline stage. Market intelligence should be able to identify and predict this event, as consumer preferences may have changed or innovative products are in the process of displacing existing products. Characteristics of decline are:

❑ Sales falling continually.

❑ Further intensification of price cutting.

❑ Producers deciding to abandon the market.

A decision to abandon the market poses problems for companies and is often made too late. However, some believe it is worth extending the product's life well into decline because numbers of competitors are falling. A declining market means less competition, but there is residual demand. Price reductions can often be halted or prices even increased, as there are fewer competitors to make a challenge.

Management's attention is likely to move from active marketing to cost control. Cost reduction is always an important element of management activity, but during decline this may be the only method to maintain profitability.

10.6 The PLC as a management tool

There is much criticism of the PLC, and like any theory it should not be taken too literally. (E.g. a product can be prematurely discarded if there is a downturn in sales in the belief that it has commenced its decline, but what might be happening is a temporary downturn at the end of the introduction stage.) The key to the concept's application is an ability to identify the transition from one stage to another through the use of marketing research. Management should then have a framework for using the PLC as a long-term strategic-planning tool.

There might sometimes be an overlap in the lives of two products. The launch of the second product might be funded from the profits of the first product's growth period. Timing of launches should be synchronised within the life cycles of existing products.

In understanding the PLC concept, it is important to distinguish between the specific and the generic product. Following the launch of a truly innovative product (e.g. the video recorder) many imitative products have emerged. Some of these have followed a typical PLC pattern, and others have not. As a generic product, the video recorder has approximately followed a typical life cycle course, with a stretched maturity phase, representing replacement buyers, until an innovative alternative is launched, which may turn out to be the DVD recorder.

Identifying transition from one stage to the next is difficult. In the case of innovative products, there is no information on previous products, so it is unique. Management planners might think themselves into successive stages and ultimately into decline which may not be the case. Critics contend that the PLC is a self-fulfilling prophecy and management might miss opportunities because of too rigid an adherence to the theory. Marketing is a creative process and the PLC concept is merely meant to provide a guide to that strategy.

CASE 10.4

Polaroid's products hit by the new digital technology and its famous cameras go into the decline stage of the product life cycle.

Polaroid, one of the USA's most famous companies is in trouble. The start of its problems can be traced back to the 1990s when the company, famous for instant photography, failed to adequately react to the tehnological superiority and threat posed by the development of digital cameras. Despite spending very little on marketing and developing only a limited range of new products, usually one major development every ten years, the firm was able to create one of the world's best known brands. The secret was superior technology; in fact the whole culture of the firm was based on the development of advanced technology. When a new Chief Executive, Gary DiCamillo, took over Polaroid in 1995 he immediately set about changing this culture from high technology to one based on faster moving consumer products. The range was diversified to take on board products such as the 'Swatch'

watch brand and a range of other novelty products. The company moved away from what it knew best, the development of new technological breakthroughs in photographic processes and equipment. Failing to keep abreast of the new technological developments coming from the digital camera industry meant that Polaroid lost its traditional markets and soon ran out of money to finance further technological developments, although management had some good ideas they were working on. Finally in October 2001 the firm was forced to file for Chapter 11 (USA) bankruptcy protection in order to fend off creditors and be able to find a buyer.

10.7   The product adoption process

The new product adoption process, together with new adopter characteristics, has been introduced in Chapter 3 in the context of buyer behaviour. The PLC concept has considered the product in relation to the market place. The product adoption process, developed by Everett Rogers (1962) is now illustrated in Figure 10.7. From this we discover something about consumers who are market targets. It is a simple relationship, but helpful in allowing us to draw conclusions about the characteristics of the consumers in each adopter category. Consumers do not automatically fall into the same adopter category for all products. An early adopter of new computer software could be a laggard in the music CD market.

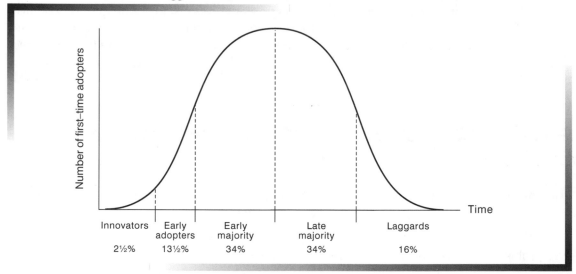

Figure 10.7 The product adoption process

The rate at which an innovative product moves through these adopter categories is called the 'diffusion of innovations' which means:

> '*The extent to which each adopter category successively influences another towards adoption.*'

This is a popular marketing theory, and reference can also be made to the characteristics of each adopter category.

10.8 Product (and market) management

Product management deals with tactical and strategic issues as the product proceeds along the life-cycle curve. The marketing manager delegates responsibility within the marketing function. Some companies employ an advertising manager and a marketing research manager and a sales manager. There is often justification for employing somebody whose role is explicitly concerned with products or brands. How marketing is organised in a company depends on the nature of its products and the markets in which it operates. A simple marketing structure is outlined in Figure 10.8:

Figure 10.8 Functional marketing structure

As the number of product lines increases, responsibility for individual products may become unclear with some being neglected. A product-management structure provides a solution in that a manager is directly responsible for each product's success. It is product managers who decide the level and type of support required from marketing. Figure 10.9 shows their position in relation to other marketing specialists.

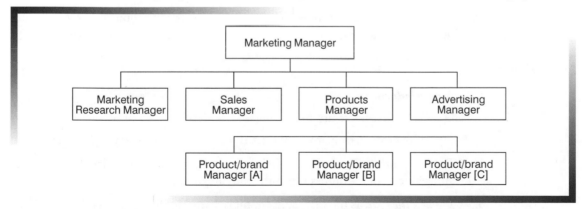

Figure 10.9 Product/Brand management structure

A products manager is responsible for the company's products/brands and is responsible to the marketing manager. Product/brand managers with responsibility for individual brands come under the overall products manager. They are responsible for a brand's welfare, through other functional managers within marketing. The terms product and brand management are interchangeable, but in FMCG markets the term *brand management* is normally used, whereas for industrial products it is usually *product management*.

This system is appropriate when companies have large numbers of products, or where they differ widely. Product managers are not functional experts and must rely on liaison with the other functional managers to execute their ideas, so it is important that individual roles are clearly defined.

The title *market manager* is sometimes used in a similar context to product management. In this case a company markets similar products, but to diverse customer groups. An example is computer applications to banks, educational establishments, public sector and retailing. User needs differ, so a *markets* manager is in charge with individual *market* managers in charge of each market grouping.

10.9   Product line and product mix

The product mix is the assortment of products a company markets. For this assortment to be more easily managed, products are grouped into product lines or groups of products that are similar in terms of their functions or because they are sold to similar customer groups.

A food manufacturer may market a range of beverages along with other products like convenience foods. Beverages can be arranged as a product line. It may even be appropriate to arrange different beverages into their own individual product lines. Thus, the coffee product line might include different varieties of instant coffee, coffee beans, ground coffee and coffee sachets. The length of a product line denotes the number of individual products in the line; the width of the product mix denotes how many lines go to make up the mix.

Marketing management can now view its product mix more objectively and decide whether or not certain lines should be lengthened, shortened or even deleted.

Questions

1. *New products*
    (a)   Why is it necessary for a company to develop new products?
    (b)   How can a company stimulate the generation of new product ideas?

2. *Product classification*: Why is it helpful to have a system that classifies products and services into a number of different categories?

3. *Product life cycle*: Is the PLC concept more useful for looking at sales of products for an individual company or sales of products for an industry as a whole?

4. *Product management*: Do you feel that the product/brand management system only has applicability for fast moving consumer goods, or is there some applicability for industrial products?

References

Rogers, E, (1962) *Diffusion of Innovations*, (The Free Press, New York), p.162.

11 Marketing information systems

11.1 Scope of the MkIS

Marketing research is part of the Marketing Information Systems (MkIS) that collects, processes and co-ordinates information from a wide range of sources. The MkIS is a computer based decision support system and has a number of inputs and one output as shown in Figure 11.1:

Figure 11.1 Marketing Information System (MkIS)

Three inputs can be seen: marketing research, market intelligence and the internal accounting system. MkIS output is used for strategic marketing planning which formulates marketing plans and implements them, but what is planned does not always match what happens. These deviations from what was planned are fed back into the MkIS, represented by a double-headed arrow. Inputs from the internal accounting system relate to factors like sales analyses by time, by product group, by region and by customer type. Market intelligence relates to information that has been obtained principally from the field sales force who, in the course of their work, obtain information about customers, competitors, distributors, etc. and feed this into the

MkIS. Sales forecasting is a marketing responsibility and from the forecast company plans are prepared. The material for sales forecasting is obtained from all three inputs to the system and the forecast also outputs into strategic marketing plans. The MkIS is a component of an organisation-wide Management Information System (MIS).

11.2 Scope and methodology of marketing research

The American Marketing Association (AMA) definition of marketing research is:

> 'The systematic gathering, recording and analysing of data relating to the marketing of goods and services.' (1961)

In FMCG markets in particular, there is little direct contact between producers and consumers. By collecting, analysing and interpreting facts, marketing research can find out what people want and why they want it. Marketing decisions are as good as the information on which they are based. Marketing management is the process of making decisions related to marketing issues. Marketing research is a component of the MkIS and is used by marketing management when planning strategy. Management needs information about its markets, competitors and changes and developments in the external environment to aid marketing decisions.

Marketing information can be expensive to obtain (e.g. a national survey commissioned from a large agency). It is important to generate, process and circulate information correctly. Extraneous data can be expensive and time wasting, so information needs to be managed and controlled like any other area of operation, and marketing research information should be:

- Reliable
- Relevant to users' needs
- Adequate for the type of decisions being made
- Timely
- Cost-effective to obtain.

Marketing research can be broken down into a number of subdivisions that follow. The list is not exhaustive, but it illustrates the areas in which marketing research can aid decision-making.

Product research is concerned with aspects of design, development and testing new products, as well as improvement and modifications to existing products. Activities include:

- Comparative testing against competitive products
- Test marketing
- Concept testing
- Idea generation and screening
- Product elimination/simplification
- Brand positioning.

This last point is important as competitive pressures make it essential that brand-positioning strategies be effectively developed.

FMCG companies spend lots of money on *marketing communications research*. The communications mix (including personal selling, direct mail, exhibitions, sponsorship and advertising) can be more effectively planned as a result of research information. Communications research activities include:

❑ Pre- and post-testing of advertising

❑ Media planning research

❑ Readership surveys

❑ Testing alternative selling techniques

❑ Exhibition and sponsorship evaluation.

Pricing research can be used to:

❑ Help establish a more market-orientated pricing strategy

❑ See what prices consumers associate with different product variations

❑ Establish market segments in relation to price.

Corporate planning research can assist corporate planners in:

❑ Evaluation of companies for acquisition

❑ Assessing an organisation's strengths and weaknesses

❑ Product portfolio analysis

❑ Corporate image studies.

Distribution research includes techniques like *retail audits* that can monitor the effectiveness of different distribution channels and detect regional variations.

Company management needs to communicate the information requirements to market researchers working in the company or in an agency. A research brief should be expressed in writing. Transforming a marketing problem into an all-inclusive research study depends on an ability to communicate the nature of what is required to researchers and there are a number of issues to consider:

❑ Some marketing problems are difficult to define.

❑ The person giving the brief might know little about research or its limitations.

❑ In-company researchers often have a low status, so a full and frank discussion of the problem might not be possible for reasons of confidentiality.

❑ Marketing researchers are often viewed by companies as a 'fire fighters', brought in on an ad hoc basis to solve a problem, with no continuous understanding of the product or market

❑ Marketing personnel sometimes find it difficult to ascertain how accurate data must be as they lack the statistical skills to understand relationships between accuracy, sample sizes and costs.

The task of the brief is to bring the two parties together. A good brief, often achieved only after detailed discussions, should ensure that irrelevant information is not requested and it should:

- ❑ State the population(s) to be surveyed (e.g. consumers not buyers, car owners not car drivers).

- ❑ State the appropriate variables to be measured.

- ❑ Not pre-empt the design of the research, in that many marketing personnel think they know how conduct research, but in practice few can do it properly.

Once the researcher has a brief, it is then possible to prepare a research proposal.

A problem-solving approach to marketing research planning involves six steps:

1. Definition of the marketing problem in specific terms.

2. Refinement of the problem, and its subdivision into individual marketing research problems.

3. Development of a plan for securing facts or information needed.

4. Execution of the plan by collecting facts or information.

5. Analysis and interpretation of these facts.

6. Summary of results in a report.

The objective of this problem-solving process is to identify and isolate any difficult elements, e.g. in a marketing problem like an unexplained sales decline, this can be sub-divided: competitive, market and company elements. Hypotheses are developed and explored in a search for problem elements. Sometimes research is needed, even at this diagnostic stage, to help define the problem.

The starting point should be desk research using secondary data, as it is wasteful engaging in primary research if it has already been done. If this information has been researched on a continuous basis it can indicate trends. Company data is a good starting point for secondary research and the obvious first sources are product, area or territory, customer and time-based analyses of previous sales. External publications are the next resource to investigate, of which there are three principal sources: government/official publications, trade association publications and specialist publications.

When data for a marketing problem cannot be found from secondary sources, the company must then generate primary information usually through a survey that involves four major steps:

1. Setting objectives for the survey.

2. Developing the survey method and sample design.

3. Collection of data.

4. Interpretation of data.

The first is important in cost terms, for without a clear statement of objectives, a lot of interesting, but irrelevant, information might be obtained. There are several methods of obtaining information.

11.2.1 Personal interviews

These may be structured or unstructured and direct or indirect. Direct interviews are used to obtain descriptive information to establish facts. Unstructured direct interviews can be used for exploratory work to make sure that the final questionnaire will be well structured and relevant to the problem. In structured interviews a set of predetermined questions is asked; in unstructured interviews the questions are put as the interviewer sees best.

Advantages of personal interviews are:

❑ Good sample control
❑ More reliable answers.
❑ Allows longer questionnaires.
❑ Greater flexibility.
❑ Observation is possible.

Disadvantages are:

❑   High costs
❑   There might be bias owing to personal contact.
❑   Difficulty in obtaining co-operation from respondents.

11.2.2 Telephone interviews

These are useful when information is needed quickly. As long as not too much information is sought, co-operation can be obtained quite easily, particularly during evenings. Sample bias is a problem as telephone lists only include those respondents whose numbers are in telephone directories and not those who are ex-directory. The sample can be biased as it only includes co-operative respondents. A further problem is that increased use of the telephone to canvass for sales approaches has made respondents wary of such approaches.

CASE 11.1

Business and Market Research Ltd becomes the biggest provincial provider of industrial market research services based on telephone interviewing.

BMR LTD is a very successful provincial market research company based in Disley, Stockport, Greater Manchester. The founding director, Paul N Hague, who gained initial research experience at Dunlop, and Johnson and Nephew started it. Mr. Hague set up the company as an industrial marketing research firm. However, today it provides both industrial and consumer marketing research services to clients. The basis of BMR's initial success was based on the use of the telephone. The firm was established in the early 1970s when the use of marketing research within the industrial sector of the economy was very much in its infancy. The marketing concept was still only just being applied to many consumer marketing firms let alone the industrial sector. Many firms working in the industrial sector of the economy in those days could be classified as either product or sales orientated in their approach to business. Paul Hague saw the potential of applying the principles of what was, basically, social science research methodologies to research into the marketing of industrial products and services. This application of research principles to industrial marketing was already well under way in the USA. The UK usually followed the USA in many of its business trends and applications. Paul Hague realised this and was one of the first people to offer professional marketing research services to industrial clients in a professional manner within the UK. All firms have access to a telephone and most managers have their own telephone and direct number. Most managers in industry would actually prefer to be surveyed by telephone rather than be sent a paper questionnaire through the post. Co-operation and rate of response to industrial telephone surveys is surprisingly good. Many people are only too pleased that you have taken the trouble to contact them and regard them as an 'expert' and are usually prepared to answer questions. Computer aided telephone-interviewing software and equipment also makes telephone interviewing efficient and effective. Questionnaires can be designed to be filled in by the interviewer on a computer screen. The interviewer wears a hand free 'kit' so that they can operate the computer and talk to the respondent. The data is stored and processed as soon as the survey is finished. This quickens the turn-around time, as there are no lengthy postal delays. This makes telephone interviews ideal for situations where the client requires a set of results quickly, such as in the testing of advertising campaigns.

11.2.3 Postal questionnaires

This method offers economy, wide distribution and speed, and interviewer bias is eliminated. If responses are anonymous it will lead to more candid answers. There is, however, usually a high non-response rate. Postal questionnaires cannot be too long, and risks of ambiguity are increased if more than dichotomous (yes/no) questions are to be asked. It might also be difficult to classify respondents, because, unlike personal interviews, probes cannot be used to clarify points of uncertainty.

11.2.4 Panel surveys

For FMCG products, retail store audits are conducted by companies like A C Neilsen and Retail Audits Ltd. Surveys are done on a continuous basis to audit the sales movement of FMCG brands in a selected sample of retailers who are representative of the country as a whole. There are also consumer panels, usually done on a continuous basis, like those provided by the Attwood Consumer Panel (mainly for food products) or Audits of Great Britain (mainly for consumer durables). Consumer panels can be conducted through a diary, questionnaire or home-audit basis.

11.2.5 Marketing experiments

These methods gather primary data in which the researcher establishes a cause and effect relationship among the variables being tested. Experiments can be carried out in artificial 'laboratory' type settings or as field experiments. Test marketing is an example, where researchers choose a representative geographical area, or at least one where they can statistically adjust data to make them representative of a wider market area such as the UK as a whole. The test market then becomes a model of the total market. *Simulated test marketing* is a way of reducing costs, as these are not full test markets and involve surveying a small sample of consumers and showing them samples or pictures of products and ascertaining their preference as if they were shopping.

11.2.6   Sampling

The sample design is a plan that sets out who is to be sampled, how many respondents are to be surveyed and how they are to be selected. Sampling procedures may be on a probability (or random) basis or on a non-probability basis, usually a quota sample. In a probability sample, every member of the population has a known probability of being included and their selection is random. The following sample methods involve probability:

- ☐ Simple random sample.
- ☐ Systematic sample (e.g. every n^{th} name on a list).
- ☐ Cluster sample (blocks selected randomly).
- ☐ Area sample (blocks are geographic).
- ☐ Stratified sample (sampling within strata e.g. different family sizes).
- ☐ Multi-stage sample (random sampling within random clusters).

For a true random sample to be taken from a complete national sampling frame, costs would be prohibitive so the usual method is to take a quota sample.

We should be aware of the difficulties in obtaining information from a sample of respondents. The sample itself may be a source of error if it is not representative. It may start off being representative, but may cease to be so as a result of non-response and possible substitution of other respondents.

CASE 11.2

Political polling firms base results on small representative sample.

Many of the political polling organisations, such as Gallup Poll, Harris Research, and BMRB are commercial market research companies who apply survey techniques to political research. There are many millions of people within the UK who are qualified to vote in the general election, but most research firms base their survey results on relatively small samples of around 1,500 people. The principle of all sampling is that the sample is representative of the population from which it is drawn. A cook in the kitchen samples the soup by taking a small spoonful. He or she does not need to take a whole bowl of soup as long as the sample is representative of the rest. In sampling, it is not the size of the sample that matters, although a larger sample is usually better than a small one, but how representative the sample is. Market research firms can achieve results that are acceptable as estimates in terms of the accuracy of the findings by taking a carefully selected sample. Some firms use random sampling methods that have a mathematical basis. The majority, however, use 'quota sampling' which is really sophisticated guess work. The market researchers do get it wrong from time to time, such as in the 1992 General Election when the Conservative vote was grossly under estimated by the polling firms. However, most of the time, even using quota samples the results achieved by these firms are remarkably accurate considering the relatively small size of the sample used.

11.3   The marketing research process

Whatever the purpose of research (e.g. exploratory or descriptive) it is costly in time and money. The company should explore the problem before investing in a more conclusive research programme. All available facts and ideas should be consulted to build up a picture before conclusive research commences. Exploratory research can give a better idea of the situation and highlight potential areas for investigation. To design an effective survey, you must be informed about the market, the population and the topics of interest, as most surveys are sample surveys rather than census surveys.

Exploratory research is needed, as sample surveys generally include a questionnaire. Before this can be designed (with clear and appropriate questions) it is necessary to have an idea of consumer behaviour and attitudes towards various products including competitors' products. Exploratory research indicates which areas need to be investigated, in what depth and the type of information required (e.g. qualitative or quantitative) as well as the amount of data to be collected. It allows the researcher to arrive at a set of assumptions on which to base the research.

After this first step the research follows a number of stages:

Problem definition

This leads to a preliminary statement of research objectives – usually to provide information i.e. this stage is an identification of information requirements:

- ❑   *What* information is needed?
  Motives – values, beliefs, feelings, opinions.
  Evaluations – attitudes, intentions.
  Knowledge – facts, behaviour, actions.
  Demographic – from specific customer groups.
- ❑   *Why* is information required?
  For prediction, evaluation or planning.
- ❑   *Where* does information come from?
  Secondary data sources, both internal and external to a company.
  Primary data sources (e.g. fieldwork amongst customers, stores, companies).

Review of secondary data sources

- ❏ Company records, reports, previous research.
- ❏ Trade associations, government agencies, research organisations.
- ❏ Advertising/marketing research agencies.
- ❏ Books, periodicals, research theses, statistics, conference proceedings.

Select approach for collection of new/primary information

- ❏ Experimentation.
- ❏ Observation.
- ❏ Surveys – mail, telephone, personal.
- ❏ Motivational research techniques – depth interviews, group interviews, projective techniques.

Research design

- ❏ Methods.
- ❏ Sampling issues.
- ❏ Design.

Data collection

- ❏ Field work.
- ❏ Surveys.
- ❏ Experiments.
- ❏ Observation.
- ❏ Interviews.

Analysis and interpretation

- ❏ Data analysis.
- ❏ Statistical tests.
- ❏ Content analysis of interviews.

Evaluation

Of results of the research and possibly making recommendations to management.

11.4 Methods of collecting marketing research data

11.4.1 Experimentation

Experimentation is used to assess the effect of some element(s) in the marketing mix, e.g. product, package, price change, advertising, type of outlet. There are two types:

1. *Field experiments* are controlled experiments, where a change in an experimental variable(s) is related to a resulting level of sales, advertisement recall/recognition, or attitudes – e.g. coupon trials, split-run advertisements and test-markets.

2. *Laboratory experiments* involve using individual consumers or consumer groups/juries/panels. The researcher has a high degree of control and can introduce and

exclude stimuli to create laboratory-type testing of real-life situations to measure attitudes towards products, prices, packages, advertising or promotion, as well as preferences and intentions to buy.

11.4.2   Observation

Observations can be of people or physical phenomena, observed by people or by mechanical devices and include:

People observing people, e.g. people in shops, children with toys. Only explicit behaviour is measured as there is no interviewer or response bias. Because motivations, preferences, intentions or attitudes cannot be observed, problems might arise when interpreting observations.

Mechanical devices observing people include: the eye camera that observes changes in pupil size when exposed to marketing stimuli; the tachistoscope which is a projection device to present visual stimuli for a short and then increasingly longer periods of time (e.g. to measure brand-name awareness); the psycho-galvanometer that is a device that measures galvanic skin response (e.g. to measure response when exposed to different types of advertisement); tape-recordings (e.g. of sales people with customers); photographic and video cameras.

Physical phenomena observed by people includes analysis of, for example, content of advertisements, store/retail audits, information on brand/stock levels, 'pantry audits' of products/brands in a person's house.

Physical phenomena observed by mechanical devices like traffic counters (e.g. counting the number of people or cars that pass a particular point) and television audience meters for TV audience research that measures when a TV is switched on in a sample of homes and to what channel it is tuned.

CASE 11.3

A.C. Neilsen Ltd. of Oxford, uses retail audits to monitor the consumer's purchasing of brands at the retail store level.

A.C. Neilsen, based in Oxford, are perhaps the best known UK retail audit company. Neilson's have developed their retail audit methods and technology over many years. Basically the retail audit involves the company contacting many thousands of retail outlets on a regular basis, usually every month. Brand managers from fast moving consumer goods (FMCG) marketing firms can contact the company and ask them to monitor the sales of their particular brand in a large representative sample of retail stores across the whole country. For an extra charge Neilsen's will also monitor the sales behaviour of their competitors brands. Extra research can also reveal prices charged, store position, details of sales promotions and merchandising activity and a range of other commercially useful marketing data. All of this data is available on a regular basis, which has the effect of building up a kind of 'moving' picture of brand behaviour over time. In fact, retail audit research is sometimes called 'continuous research' because it is on going over a period of time. The retail audit method also falls under the heading of 'observational' research because people and electronic devices do the observing. Many of the larger supermarket chains have electronic point of sale systems (EPOS), which collect sales data electronically. Neilsen makes use of this in collecting their brand data. For smaller stores a traditional 'stock taking' exercise is undertaken by Neilsen's staff. The results are made available to customers in a short time after the audit takes place and are usually presented and explained by Neilsen's staff at the customer's offices.

11.4.3 Surveys (using questionnaires)

Surveys can be conducted by mail, telephone or personal interview and questionnaires can be self-administered or managed by an interviewer. The choice is determined by: cost, timing, type of information needed, amount of information needed, ease of questioning and accuracy required.

When choosing a survey method, consideration should be given to using pilot surveys, the sample size and methods of analysing the results.

Considerations that should be made under each of the survey methods include:

Postal surveys

❑ Who is the respondent? – industrial buyer? middle class consumer? doctor?

❑ Nature of the survey: Will motivation to respond be high?

❑ Questions: How simple must they be?

❑ Length of the questionnaire: What is the limit?

❑ Response bias (there should be none from interviewers, only from the sample).

❑ To what extent do respondents differ from non-respondents?

❑ Sample selection: Size may be related to expected response rate.

❑ Is a 'list' (of potential respondents sourced externally) being used? How accurate is it?

❑ Should respondents be provided with prepaid reply envelopes?

❑ Response rate: This will affect cost/value of the survey. If relatively slow, it may be appropriate to send reminders to follow up non-respondents.

❑ Importance of cover letter requesting co-operation and/or instructions.

❑ Cost: Should be relatively low per response.

Telephone surveys same considerations as above, plus:

❑ Who is the respondent? Are telephone subscribers who are not ex-directory representative of the required population?

❑ Telephone contact is impersonal. How important is the credibility of an interviewer?

❑ Questions should be short and simple.

❑ The interviewer can only talk to one person at a time (usually). Is it the right one?

❑ The respondent cannot consult other people, company records, etc.

❑ This method is relatively cheap and fast.

Personal interviews similar considerations, plus:

❑ Who is the respondent?

❑ Where is the respondent: in the home or office? in the street? in a cinema queue?

❑ Factors affecting motivation to participate in an interview are shown in Figure 11.2) which gives an outline of the problems of personal interviews.

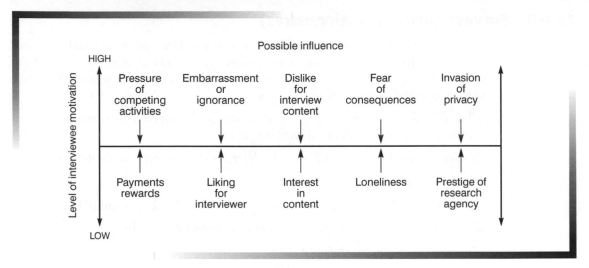

Figure 11.2 Factors affecting interviewee participation

❑ Response bias in reaching the sample – non-contact, interviewer error, refusal to be interviewed.

❑ Bias in response – incorrect and/or untruthful answers, omissions, interviewer's perception of the interviewee.

❑ Who is the interviewer: Salesperson? Housewife? Freelance researcher? – What qualifications and training do they need?

❑ The cost of this method is usually high.

Issues in relation to actual questionnaires include:

❑ *Types of questions* – open ended or structured e.g. yes/no, multiple-choice, rankings, paired comparisons, checklist asking 'which of these....'

❑ *Wording of questions* avoiding ambiguous questions so they have the same meaning for all respondents. Respondents' ability to answer will relate to their level of education and language. Questions must be self-exploratory and fully understood. Respondents' willingness to answer (e.g. they may be reluctant to answer questions on personal matters such as income). Avoid influencing the answer (e.g. 'Do you brush your teeth every day?')

❑ *Sequencing of questions* (and alternatives within questions). Initial questions should provide motivation (and encourage further co-operation) and questions should follow a logical order – from general to the specific. Rotate questions/sub-questions to eliminate bias. Place personal questions at the end, or 'bury' them in the middle.

❑ *Scaling techniques for attitude measurement* usually determine content and direction of attitudes rather than intensity. More commonly used techniques are: paired comparisons, Likert summated ratings (agreement on a five-point scale), Thurstone's equal appearing intervals (paired comparisons), Osgood's semantic differential: a bipolar scale used to measure opinions about ideas, products, brands, stores or companies, Guttman's scalogram, Stephenson's sort technique.

❑ *Other considerations* include: length of questionnaire, use of cue cards (e.g. rotating lists of alternative responses), aids to recall (e.g. pictures of advertisements), presentation of the questionnaire especially if it is to be self-administered, methods of coding and analysis of data will affect design and structure of questions.

11.4.4 Motivational research techniques

These techniques aim to uncover underlying motives, desires and emotions of consumers that influence their behaviour. They attempt to penetrate below the level of the conscious mind and uncover motives that consumers are unaware of or deliberately conceal. Techniques used include:

❑ *Depth interviewing* that uses interviewing and observational methods. The interviewer selects topics for discussion and through unstructured, indirect questioning leads the respondent to express motives, attitudes, opinions and experiences in relation to advertisements, products, brands and services.

❑ *Group interviews or discussions* or *focus groups* where the interviewer moderates and stimulates discussion, to encourage freedom of expression and interaction between individuals.

❑ *Projective techniques* can help reveal what a respondent may cover up in direct questioning. Examples of such techniques include:

➢ Verbal projection – for example, asking 'Why do you think people do....?' i.e. asking about someone else with the expectation that answers will actually apply to respondents themselves.

➢ Word association tests.

➢ Sentence completion exercises (e.g. 'People buy on credit when ...', 'Prices are high because ...').

➢ Response to pictures (Thematic Apperception Tests (TAT) where respondents give a description of a pictured situation based on their own experience and attitudes).

➢ Interpretation of ink blots (Rorschach tests).

11.4.5 Questionnaire design

The objective of a questionnaire is to design questions that have the same meaning to everybody. There are basic rules in questionnaire design that are elaborated.

The general layout of a questionnaire is shown in Figure 11.3.

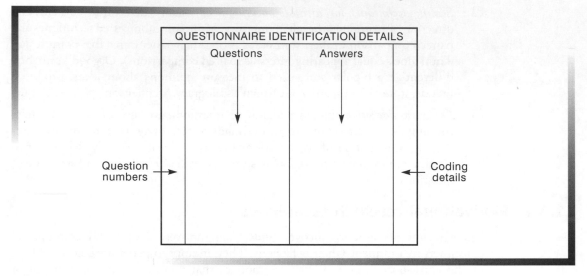

Figure 11.3 A specimen questionnaire layout

- ❑ Each question should be numbered.
- ❑ Use capital letters for the main sections.
- ❑ Instructions to be given to the investigator concerning the conduct of the interview.
- ❑ Alternative routes in the questionnaire should be in bold face, capital letters and underlined.
- ❑ Arrange answer codes (for data processing purposes) answer boxes, etc. as near to the right hand side as possible.
- ❑ Lines drawn at suitable intervals can bring clarity to questionnaire design.
- ❑ Arrows can be used to indicate routes through 'skip' questions.

There is no single rule that can be used to decide which type of question is most suitable to obtain specific types of information. The following types of questions are most commonly used:

- ❑ Open-ended questions that provide a clue as to what type of answer might be expected from the respondent. For example, a question which begins 'What do you think of ...?' will bring forth comments over a full range of opinion. With a large sample, the mass of diverse data collected cannot be statistically analysed, since verbatim answers can only be hand-summarised.

- ❑ Unaided recall questions where the rule is not to mention the nature of answer material and to avoid asking leading questions like: 'How did you travel to the station to catch this train?'

- ❑ Dichotomous questions offers two choices – 'yes' and 'no'. A third answer ('don't know') is implicit. It has been found that as long as the researcher does not mention this alternative, then people who understand the question simply choose one of the two alternatives.

- ❑ Multiple-choice ('cafeteria') questions are where the informant is given a graduated range of possible answers from which to choose a preferred response. The possibilities are listed in rank order from one extreme to the other. It may be necessary to reverse the order on half of the questionnaires in order to prevent listing bias.

- ❑ Thermometer questions have evolved from multi-choice questions that seek to minimise the disadvantage of a distinct classification. Informants are asked to rate their feelings on a numerical scale like 1 – 10.

- ❑ A checklist is best prompting respondents' memories and lessening interviewer bias. Too many items to compare may lead to 'fatigue' on a respondent's part leading to a preference for earlier items. Bias can be lessened by rotating checklist items during a survey.

Additional rules include:

- ❑ Use simple words that are familiar to everyone e.g. shop – not outlet; shopkeeper – not retailer.

- ❑ Questions should be as short as possible.

- ❑ Do not ask double-barrelled questions, e.g. 'Have you a radio and television?'.

- ❑ Do not ask leading questions, e.g. 'Do you buy instant coffee because it is the simplest way to make coffee?'.

- ❑ Do not mention brand names, e.g. 'Do you consider Philips to be the best audio equipment?'.

- ❑ Do not ask questions that might offend, e.g. 'When did you last wash your hair?'.

- ❑ Avoid using catch phrases or colloquialisms.

- ❑ Avoid words that are not precise in their meanings, e.g. 'Does this product last a reasonable length of time?'.

- ❑ Direct questions do not always give the expected response, e.g. 'Are you married or single?' does not cover possibilities of divorce or separation.

- ❑ Questions concerning prestige may not be answered truthfully, e.g. 'Have you a teletext television receiver?' can be better asked by: 'How many hours per day on average do you watch television?' followed by: 'Do you watch teletext transmissions i.e. Ceefax or Oracle?'.

- ❑ Only questions that respondents can answer from knowledge or experience should be asked, e.g. A householder should not be asked if they prefer cooking by gas if they have never experienced cooking by other means.

- ❑ Questions should not depend on memory.

❑   Questions should allow a single thought to be created in a respondent's mind. Where multiple thoughts are created, confusion can result, and inappropriate answers given that do not represent a respondent's opinion where the respondent has to choose between possible answers. This particularly applies to questions commencing: 'Why ...?'.

❑   Avoid words with an emotional bias, e.g. use Conservative/Labour and not Tory/ Socialist.

The first question should be easy to answer to gain the confidence of the informant and require a factual answer. A questionnaire should begin with easier questions and proceed to more difficult ones later, with questions of greatest importance being about one third of the way through. Personal information (age, address, name, occupation, etc) should appear at the end of the questionnaire unless has to be obtained at the beginning of the interview, perhaps for quota sampling purposes where this information must be ascertained beforehand to see if a respondent fits into the required quota profile. Transition from question to question should be smooth and logical. Any 'jumps in thought' should be introduced before the next question is asked.

Recording answers can be done by:

❑   Writing a number.

❑   Putting a cross (✗) or a tick (✓) in a box.

❑   Underlining correct answers.

❑   Crossing out incorrect answers.

❑   Writing in a predetermined symbol.

❑   Circling a number or letter.

❑   When open-ended questions are used, enough space should be allowed for answers to be recorded verbatim.

A questionnaire should be as short as possible related to data to be obtained. For an investigation among householders, an ideal limit is what can be reasonably printed on both sides of an A4 sheet. For on-street interviews, a side or so of an A4 sheet is reasonable. If the interview schedule is lengthy, appointments should be made, and in such cases interviews should not exceed one hour.

The following lists basic questions that should be addressed:

1.   Is each question clearly worded?

2.   Does it break any rules of question design?

3.   Is each question concerned with one single factor?

4.   Are the questions ones that will elicit answers necessary to solve the research problem?

5.   Is each question unambiguous and will both investigator and interviewee have similar understandings of a question?

6.   Are all the possible answers catered for?

7. Are recording arrangements foolproof?

8. Will answers to each question be in a form in which they can be cross tabulated against other data on the same or other questionnaires?

9. Will the answers be in a form that will allow some to be checked against established data?

11.5 Marketing research planning

Investigations can be divided into four phases: planning; execution; analysis and reporting:

11.5.1 Planning

Specification of the purposes of the survey

It is important to be clear about the research problem and then determine which aspects might be solved using survey techniques. A basic question is: 'Is a sample survey the most appropriate method?'

Definition of the population

Categories or types of respondents to be included in a survey and its scope are determined broadly by the purpose of the survey. However, marginal categories require special consideration because:

❑ Excluding them may simplify the survey (and make it cheaper) without affecting the outcome.

❑ Including marginal categories may be valuable where relationships are discovered between sub-groups of the population and variables being measured.

❑ In some situations multi-phase sampling might be the best solution.

Determination of details of information to be collected

This lists information needed to solve the original problem. The list should be comprehensive. A selection should then be made within the limitations of the survey (e.g. expense and time required).

Practicability of obtaining required information

Each item of information selected should be considered in terms of how practical it is to obtain, given the level of accuracy required. It should be asked:

❑ Do respondents have the knowledge required to answer the questions?

❑ Will it involve them in a lot of effort?

❑ If information is to be obtained by observation, can it be measured accurately?

Methods of collecting information

Here consideration is given to different modes of collecting information and sampling issues.

Dealing with non-response

Unless non-response is confined to a small proportion of the whole sample, results cannot claim any general validity. This problem becomes acute in postal surveys where response can be very low. In such cases follow-up letters/calls may increase response rates.

Sampling frame

The structure of a survey is determined by the sampling frame. Until this has been decided detailed planning cannot be undertaken. The frame should be up-to-date, complete and not contain duplications.

Pilot study

The practicability of any survey is best checked by a pilot survey that is designed to check:

(a) **The questionnaire**

- ❑ Use a broad quota sample, especially using those who might find responding to questionnaires difficult.
- ❑ Researchers should be check the meanings of words, respondents' train of thoughts, and record all that is said to help in any subsequent refining of the questionnaire.
- ❑ The final pre-test should use the finally approved questionnaire.

(b) **The sample**

- ❑ Check the ease of obtaining the smallest sub-group required.
- ❑ Check numbers of interviews that are possible in the time allowed.
- ❑ Check that the selection process and call-back/substitution procedures (e.g. if the chosen respondent is not available) are feasible.

(c) **The survey contact**

Check additional fields of enquiry shown up in (a) and also the appearance and 'feel' of the pilot results. Sometimes results obtained at this pilot stage might reorient the basic approach to the survey.

11.5.2 Execution

The execution of a survey involves:

1. Administrative organisation to cover supervision of field operations, the investigations, follow-ups, check calls, etc. and the task of collation, tabulation and computation.
2. Selection, training and supervision of field investigators.
3. Briefing conference.
4. Control and accuracy of field work.
5. Editing of schedules.

6.   Coding of answers to open-ended questions.

7.   Data analysis.

11.5.3 Analysis

Numerical accuracy during analysis can be verified by repetition, cross checks or using different methods of computation to arrive at the same result. If the sampling procedure is defective, results can sometimes be adjusted to compensate for this, e.g. if the sample contains incorrect proportions of certain classes of the population, this can be overcome by weighting the results of the sample.

11.5.4 Report

The following should be included in a survey report:

1   A general description of the survey

- ❑   Statement of its purpose.
- ❑   Description of material covered and nature of information collected.
- ❑   Method of collecting of the data.
- ❑   Statistical accuracy.
- ❑   Period of time of the survey.
- ❑   Cost.
- ❑   Who is responsible for the survey.
- ❑   References.

2   Design of the survey

- ❑   General sampling design issues should be specified.

3   Methods of selecting sampling units

4   Personnel and equipment use

5   Findings of the survey

11.6 Sales forecasting overview

Preparing for the future implies forecasting forthcoming conditions. In everyday life, predictions are made on an informal, subjective basis. If they are wrong we can adjust our personal circumstances. This flexibility cannot be applied in business as decisions are more formal and of greater consequence. The nature of managerial decision-making involves forecasting future conditions for important 'one-off' purposes, e.g. a company may be considering expanding by acquisition, diversifying into a new market or modernising its production processes. These decisions tend to be long-term and strategic, rather than operational.

The sales forecast is the foundation on which company plans are built. The issue facing businesses is not whether to forecast, but how to forecast and how much should be invested in this process.

11.7   Data collection

Once a company has decided how much time, energy and money is to be spent on data collection, it must determine where it will obtain the data. There are two main categories of existing data:

1. *Internal data* generated within the company, e.g. previous company plans, sales statistics and other internal records. For certain situations this may be sufficient.

2. *Secondary data from external sources*, e.g. Government and trade statistics and published marketing research surveys.

A third category is that generated specifically for the forecasting task through some form of marketing research such as a sample survey, a test-marketing experiment or an observational study.

CASE 11.4

FT.Com – Financial Times on-line provides up-to-date and valuable marketing-research secondary data at the touch of a button.

The Financial Times is a British institution, although today it is available in many parts of the world and even produces regional editions, e.g. Financial Times India. The 'FT', as it is affectionately called by readers, has always been a valuable source of information for business students and commercial marketing-research firms. The FT provides periodic 'special reports' on markets, industries and countries which are always of a first-class standard. The FT is now available on line as FT.Com. Not only can the internet users keep abreast of the day's news on the computer screen but also all the latest business news is available from all around the world. The on line version of the FT is regularly updated and so the news stories are virtually in 'real time'. The FT on line provides many of its services free of charge. For special reports and other services you have to pay a small subscription fee. The free services are excellent and are conveniently divided into data and information about firms, industries and regions, e.g. UK, USA, EU, world etc. There is also information available on the stock markets around the world, financial and economic analysis, industry forecasts and a plethora of other useful services. The FT on line is really the modern market researcher's dream. So much valuable information from around the world in virtually real time that can be accessed from the convenience of the researcher's office or even out in the 'field' from a laptop and modem connection. The FT offers the researcher a range of secondary data that is equal to none in terms of its accuracy and reliability. The FT on line is one of the most valuable secondary data sources available to the marketing researcher today.

11.7.1   Internal data sources

Success in obtaining past data from within the firm will depend to a great extent on knowing the firm and its staff. Much information can be obtained by consulting heads of departments and other staff. Obtaining access to information may sometimes be a problem so it is important that such exercises have the authority of top management to obtain maximum co-operation.

The first stage is to take a systems-analysis approach and trace the documentary procedures of the firm. The forecaster should look carefully at what records are kept and how data is obtained, altered, processed and circulated throughout the firm. Every document should be recorded, possibly using some form of flow chart. The type of document as well as the function it serves, should be noted as well as its origin and destination.

11.7.2   Data from the sales department

The sales/marketing department is the main point of interaction between a company and its customers. Consequently, it is the chief source of information including:

Sales volume by product and by product group

This information can be combined to give total sales volume, but it also allows each product or product group in the overall product mix to be evaluated in terms of its contribution to total volume.

Sales volume by area

This may be divided according to sales territories, media areas as used by the Joint Industry Committee for Television Advertising Research (JICTAR) or other geographical areas.

Sales volumes by market segment

The basis for segmentation may be regional or, especially in industrial markets, by type of industry. Such information will give an indication of which segments are likely to remain static, which are declining and which show growth possibilities.

Sales volume by type of channel of distribution

Information gathered by type of retail outlet, agents, wholesalers and distributors can contribute to a more realistic forecast. Such information allows marketing to identify and develop promising channel opportunities, resulting in more effective channel management.

Sales volume over time

In terms of actual sales and units sold, this allows seasonal variations to be identified and inflation and price adjustments to be taken into consideration.

Pricing information

Historical information relating to price adjustments by product types allows forecasters to establish the effects of price increases or decreases on demand.

Communication-mix information

The effects of previous advertising campaigns, sponsorship, direct mail or exhibitions can be assessed. Levels of expenditure in marketing communications can be evaluated.

Sales promotional data

The effectiveness of past promotional campaigns such as reduced-price pack, coupons, offers and competitions can be assessed. Trade incentives aimed at distributive intermediaries can also be assessed in terms of their individual influence on sales.

Sales representatives' records and reports

As described in Chapter 8, sales representatives should keep files on 'live' customers. Often such records are kept in considerable detail, ranging from information on customer interests to detailed personal information, as well as information about the customer's firm, its product range, diversification plans and likely future purchases. Even what the customer last said to the salesperson may be recorded.

Enquiries received and quotations sent

Customers submit enquiries asking for details of price, delivery, etc., and records should be kept of verbal enquiries. Customers make enquiries to a number of companies. Enquiries lead to a detailed quotation being submitted to the customer. This information can be useful to the forecaster, especially if patterns can be established in the percentage of enquiries that mature into orders and the time between a quotation being submitted and an order being received.

11.7.3 Data from other departments

Accounts department

The management accountant will be able to provide accurate cost data. Other useful information can be gained from previous management reports. Management information requirements differ between firms, but such reports may contain very accurate information on such matters as:

- ❑ Number of new customers in a given period.
- ❑ Number of withdrawals.
- ❑ Number of items sold by product in volume and monetary terms.
- ❑ Total sales by salesperson, area, division, etc.

Management accounting reports give information on staff matters such as absenteeism. Such information can be useful when attempting to accurately forecast production capacity. Past budgets with variance analysis will show budgeted figures against actual figures.

Purchasing department

Copies of purchase orders, material lists, requisitions, material status schedule reports, information on suppliers (e.g. reliability of delivery, lead times, prices) can be useful. Purchasing will also be able to provide stock control data relating to reorder levels, buffer and safety stock levels, economic order quantities and stock-turn by inventory item. The forecaster may need to take such information into account.

Despatch department

The despatch department will have its own information system detailing goods dispatched and transportation methods as well as advice notes and other delivery documents. Such information may be useful for forecasting in its own right or act as a check on information gathered elsewhere.

Production department

The production department should be able to supply documentation relating to production control, e.g. copies of works orders, material lists and design information. Information will be available on orders placed with the company's own workshops, requisitions for materials to stores, orders subcontracted to other suppliers, manufacturing times, machine utilisation times and order completion dates.

11.7.4   Departmental plans

Not only should historical and current internal information be available to the forecaster, but this should also include short-, medium- and long-term plans relating to individual departments.

These sources are not an exhaustive list of the sources or types of internal information available to the forecaster. Other departments, e.g. human resource management, research and development, work study, etc., may also hold useful information.

11.8   Forecasting methods

11.8.1   Subjective methods

Subjective forecasting methods are mainly qualitative techniques that rely on judgement rather than numerical calculations. They are sometimes called 'intuitive' or 'naïve' techniques and are applied through a mixture of experience and judgement. Subjective techniques include:

Executive opinion (or jury) method and sales force composite

This involves the sales manager making an informed subjective forecast. This is normally done with the field sales force (in which case is it the 'sales force composite' method) and then consulting other executives in production, finance and elsewhere. The group forms a 'jury' that delivers a 'verdict' on the forecast. The final forecast is based on the collective experience of the sales force and the group. Informed opinions of these people provide a means of prediction and it is often used in the final stages of the development of a forecast. Where subjective forecasts have been obtained from various sources, there is a need to assess and evaluate each one before consolidating them into a final forecast.

Customer-use projections

This method uses survey techniques to ascertain purchase intentions of customers and/or users. Such surveys range from a sales representative talking to existing and potential customers and reporting back to head office, to more formal market research surveys. In consumer markets, where the population is large, a sample survey is usually undertaken. Such a survey can be at two levels: customers' intentions to buy; and a distributive intermediary's intention to stock and promote the product(s). In industrial markets, where numbers of customers may be few, sampling may not be necessary. This method is rarely used alone, but more often in conjunction with other methods. Test marketing can be used to produce forecasts where a small representative area is used, and the results form the basis of a forecast.

11.8.2 Objective methods

Objective methods of forecasting are quantitative in nature. Historical data are analysed to identify a pattern or relationship between variables and this pattern is then extended or extrapolated into the future to make a forecast. Objective methods fall into two groups: 'time series' and 'causal' models.

Time-series models

Time-series analysis uses the historical series of only one variable to develop a model for predicting future values. The forecast does not attempt to discover other factors that might affect its behaviour. Because time-series models treat the variable to be forecast simply as a function of time, they are most useful when other conditions are expected to remain constant, which is more likely true of the short-term than the long-term. Hence such methods are particularly suited to short-term, operational, routine forecasting – usually up to six months or one year ahead of current time.

Causal models

Causal models exploit the relationship between the time series of the variable being examined and one or more other time series. If other variables are found to correlate with the variable of interest, a causal model can be constructed incorporating coefficients that give relative strengths to various causal factors. For example, the sales of a product may be related to its price, advertising expenditure and the price of competitors' products. If the forecaster can estimate the relationship between sales and the independent variables, then the forecast values of the independent variables can be used to predict future values of the dependent variable (in this case, sales).

Such techniques include 'moving averages' and 'exponential smoothing' as well as more sophisticated decomposition models and auto-regressive moving averages (Box-Jenkins) techniques that are the subject of more advanced study.

Questions

1. Use examples to illustrate how marketing research can aid marketing decision making.

2. Exploratory research has a specific role to play in the research process. Examine this role and outline the research techniques that might be used.

3. Under what circumstances would qualitative research techniques be more appropriate than quantitative research techniques? Give examples.

4. It is often said that poor forecasting leads to large inventories, costly price markdowns, or lost sales due to being out of stock. Evaluate this view using examples to illustrate your points.

References

'Report of the Definitions Committee of the American Marketing Association' (1961) – (The AMA, Chicago, USA).

Ledbetter, WN, and Cox, JF, (1977) Operations research in production management: an investigation of past and present utilization, *Production & Inventory Management*, 18, 84, pp 84-92.

12 Broader issues in marketing

12.1 Introduction

Marketing attracts condemnation owing to a misunderstanding of its meaning. Marketing orientation puts customers at the centre of business. It grew out of sales orientation whose philosophy is to sell by any means and is associated with 'sharp practice'. Social observers question the ethics of marketing, because in a world of finite resources, it is contended that we might be devoting too much to the fulfilment of material needs by creating unnecessary wants. They argue that resources spent on competitive advertising, branding and packaging are wasteful.

Marketing is not only a business practice. It is a social influence that is used to improve the quality of life in its widest sense. This influence should not seek to patronise, but be employed in co-operation with individuals and groups who are customers of marketing's offerings. The pursuit of customer satisfaction is valid irrespective of profit motives. Marketing is appropriate to the not-for-profit sector, because its practice obliges managers to act with end user needs in mind. Marketing has social consequences and implicit in marketing orientation is a recognition that business responsibility extends beyond a company's immediate customers. People should develop their own opinions and consider marketing from these perspectives. The issue of 'consumerism' is meant to assist this process. The first part of this chapter extends the marketing concept into issues of social marketing and marketing for non-profit making organisations.

The second part examines trading between nations that can be traced back many centuries. Since industrialisation 'trading' has become more complicated. National expectations have risen such that people are no longer content with the basic essentials of life. Manufacturers have responded by producing goods designed to fulfil these higher expectations. For economies to grow and develop, they must earn money from outside their own countries. Governments have an interest in promoting international trade and attempt to ensure that their balance of trade is not adverse.

The marketing concept has developed and been accepted as a way of business that is valid internationally. The pursuit of customer satisfaction, which is demanding in home markets, requires additional skills when operating internationally. A modified marketing-mix is often developed to suit foreign markets and caters for differences in language and culture. International marketing involves precise documentation, and it is often frustrating when dealing with problems not normally encountered in home-based marketing.

12.2 Criticisms of marketing

12.2.1 Customer dissatisfaction

Marketing rarely operates as theory predicts. This does not negate theory, but at best theory can only predict what might happen. The marketing concept is criticised when customer satisfaction is not achieved, but it provides a clear objective against which performance can be measured and remedial action taken. The fact that companies acknowledge the marketing concept and pursue customer orientation does not excuse efficiency shortfalls but, for many, 'marketing' has become a generic term for 'business activity'. Some firms pursue a sales orientated approach whose short-term goal is profit with customer satisfaction being sublimated. Criticisms levelled against such companies include:

❑   Poor product quality.

❑   Misleading advertising packaging and labelling.

❑   Unreliable delivery.

❑   Poor after-sales service.

Consumers have a right to be protected, especially when the product or service is complex (e.g. insurance and credit). Government and consumer bodies have taken steps to enforce protective measures. Consumer sovereignty is a safeguard against malpractice and companies who fail to provide satisfaction will ultimately exhaust their supply of customers.

12.2.2 Limitation of customer choice

The idea that marketing creates monopoly and limits consumer choice is a common criticism. The belief that some companies will become powerful enough to dictate what, how and where consumers buy is an issue. In truth this is rare, as the existence of Anti-trust laws in the USA and the Monopolies and Mergers Commission in the UK is evidence of official concern over the power of monopolies.

Laws and commissions have been established to curtail monopoly by acquisition. A state of monopoly that is reached by continued increase in market share is largely a reflection of consumer choice. In a capitalist system, marketing allows companies who are successful to tend towards monopoly. Critics suggest that pure competition affords consumers more varied choice. This argument has a sound theoretical base, but a condition for pure competition is that buyers and sellers have perfect knowledge and buyers are rational consumers, which is rarely the case. Companies that tend towards monopoly are subject to competition from firms who seek to differentiate and improve their products to gain market share through customer satisfaction. This is a powerful safeguard against risks of exploitation.

This tempering of power was fittingly illustrated during the 1970s and 1980s.

At one point it seemed that a few large bakeries (in a powerful oligopoly) had begun to restrict UK consumer choice to processed sliced bread. This product was initially adopted because it reflected consumer preference. The few companies involved in manufacture felt powerful enough to ignore market segments that preferred other varieties of bread, and made their manufacturing task easier by limiting consumer choice. After some time, these large bakeries encountered powerful consumer resistance. Today supermarkets have in-store bakeries and specialist independent bakers have experienced a revival.

Major breweries reduced their number of product lines and produced what was convenient and profitable, namely keg beer. Breweries now provide beer whose selling points are traditional recipes and regional specialisation. These examples illustrate the power of consumer choice and sanctions against companies who neglected the marketing concept.

In the UK in the late 1970s major banks dominated the consumer marketplace. They were obliged to revise their product offerings because of legislation and new initiatives taken by smaller banks, building societies and the Post Office.

12.2.3   Inefficient utilisation of resources

A popular criticism of marketing is that it is wasteful. Money spent on advertising might better be used in product development or reducing prices. There is a good case where advertising is purely competitive, and in some countries, advertising that relies solely on direct comparison with competitive products is not permitted.

In the UK, the Advertising Standards Authority (ASA) watchdog body requires advertisements to be 'legal, decent, honest and truthful'. The existence of this body is evidence that some companies abuse the power which media expenditure allows them.

Creative and informative advertising plays a valid role in assisting consumer choice. Although it seems wasteful to devote large sums to the promotion of basically similar products, several products would not exist if it were not for the fact that consumers demand product differentiation. Any interference in this process would limit consumer choice rather than promote consumer welfare. Moreover, the situation is self-regulating, as companies cannot devote infinite amounts to advertising. Such expenditure is an extra cost that is governed by the price consumers are willing to pay.

Goods must be transported from manufacturers to users, but critics believe that marketing extends this transportation needlessly because many goods are generically similar. In truth, such goods are usually highly differentiated with respect to style, price and design.

During the past 30 years the retail structure in the UK has altered significantly and we are now served by a small number of national chains. This phenomenon is noticeable in 'do-it-yourself' supplies. Companies set up on the periphery of towns in so-called 'sheds' that are factory-type constructions. The result is that small hardware stores are rare today. Such distribution arrangements are certainly efficient and the success of 'superstores' indicates that consumers are satisfied. In the long term consumers must decide whether convenience outweighs the potential disadvantage of choice restriction. Whilst a complicated distributive structure may appear wasteful, the right of the consumer to 'vote through the purse' is also important.

Distributive intermediaries are criticised, and many retailers boast lower prices because they have 'cut out the middleman'. In many cases such claims are justified, but marketing intermediaries do perform valuable specialist functions that serve both consumers and manufacturers.

Marketing's critics should refer their opinions back to consumer choice. There is no evidence to suggest that in centrally planned economies, the distributive systems used to supply goods and services brings about greater consumer satisfaction. As has been witnessed through the dismantling of Communism, the converse might be the case. The concept of 'marketing' enables consumers to personally apply sanctions against inefficiency and waste.

12.2.4 Effects of marketing on lifestyles and values

The thought that marketing promotes materialism and creates artificial needs and values is perhaps one of the most difficult concepts to argue against. Marketing has been accused of generating a dependence effect by creating and satisfying wants that are not 'original' to consumers. Doubtlessly many marketing activities cater to materialism. It is considerably less certain though that this is wrong in itself and if so, where blame should lie. A defender of marketing might claim that the marketing system reflects society's values. But who should determine these values and ambitions? As consumers we are surrounded with possessions we do not need. Psychologists argue that many material goods satisfy hidden inner needs and anthropologists point out that even amongst primitive societies, value is placed on functionally useless possessions.

Another factor in the 'materialism' discussion concerns quality of life or standard of living. Many consumer goods are materialistic, yet provide a more comfortable way of life, reduce labour and release time to pursue other interests. At a macro level marketing has done much to improve the quality of life, even though the perceived value will differ between different sectors of society.

12.3 Consumerism

The modern day consumer movement had its roots in the 1970s when it was principally involved in specific issues. However, consumerism has been responsible for much of the social awareness displayed by businesses today. Such companies do not view consumerism as a threat, but as a movement that can be responded to positively.

The consumerist phenomenon began to be noticed in the USA in the late 1950s. Social commentators such as Vance Packard and Rachael Carson began to alert the American public to the idea that the business community was more concerned with its own welfare than that of its customers. Vance Packard's book *The Hidden Persuaders* challenged the advertising industry and Rachael Carson's *Silent Spring* attacked the business community for its disregard for the environment. The idea that individuals might combat the power of large corporations had been unthinkable until Ralph Nader published an indictment of the automobile industry, *Unsafe at any Speed* that was particularly aimed at General Motors. This, and other campaigns, signified the foundation of organised consumerism.

CASE 12.1

Which acts as an accelerator or inhibitor in the adoption of new products.

In the UK, the consumer movement was slower to gain momentum than in the USA, and its roots can be traced to the magazine _Which_, published by the Consumers' Association, which was established in the 1960s. The magazine selects, tests and classifies products and services according to their relative performance. Such information was initially received with great interest, as the idea was totally new to British consumers. Perhaps more important than the information that _Which_ provided, was the notion that consumers need not accept the offerings of manufacturers without question and had a right to express opinions about what was being offered for sale. It was no coincidence that companies began to adopt the marketing concept as a business-orientated philosophy at the same time as consumers began to realise the potential of their influence.

Which magazine acts as a 'accelerator' or 'inhibitor' to the general diffusion and specific adoption of new products. Many people experience a degree of perceived risk when considering buying new products, particularly if they are radical techno-logical innovations they really know little about or if they are expensive. To reduce the perceived risk inherent in the purchasing situation they seek expert advice from a source they can trust. These sources are often television consumer affairs programmes such as the BBC's 'Watchdog' programme, or trusted consumer magazines such as 'Which'. The publication gives detailed reports on new products, product modifications and on existing products. Where there are numerous product brands available 'Which' produces a critical appraisal of each brand and gives a detailed comparison. If a new product has a 'good' 'Which' write-up then this will reduce the perceived risk in the minds of potential consumers and increase the probability of the consumer actually buying the product in question. If on the other hand, the new product gets a 'bad' report it is likely to have the opposite effect.

Consumerism can be defined as 'a social movement seeking to augment the rights and power of buyers in relation to sellers'. It accepts that both parties have rights:

Buyers have the right:

❑ Not to buy products offered to them.

❑ To expect the product to be safe.

❑ To expect that the product is essentially the same as the seller has stated.

Sellers have the right:

❑ To introduce any product, provided it is not injurious to health and safety, and provided potentially hazardous products are supplied with warnings.

❑ To price products at any level.

❑   To say what they like in promoting their products, provided that messages are not dishonest or misleading.

❑   To spend any amount of money in promoting their products as well as incentive schemes.

The idea of 'consumer sovereignty' is central to arguments defending marketing; it should not be underestimated and is the consumer's chief weapon against business malpractice. A problem is that some companies deliberately set out to deceive customers. Consumerists, therefore, emphasise that the obligation is on businesses to provide satisfactory goods in the first place, and it should not be the responsibility of customers only to be able to embargo goods or services after having been initially disappointed. The consumer movement supplements the basic buyers' rights just described, by specifically stating what should be expected of the seller.

In 1962, President John F Kennedy, in keeping with the climate in the USA that had been laid down by the likes of Carson, Packard, and Nader, made a declaration on consumer rights that still underpins modern consumerism:

❑   **The right to safety**

Consumers should be able to expect that there are no 'hidden dangers' incorporated into a product. Companies must seek safe alternatives to components that are known to be harmful. The drugs Thalidomide and Opren have provided test cases in this respect. Polyurethane foam in upholstery was found be a fire hazard. Some manufacturers argue that consumers are unwilling to pay higher prices that product improvements would require, and in many cases, legislation is necessary before steps are taken to reduce risks. Consumerists can at least alert buyers to potential risks before they choose between economy and safety.

❑   **The right to be informed**

Whilst consumerists can increase consumer knowledge for many products, consumers do not have the time, skills or knowledge to make choices or understand product information if it is of a technical nature. Consumers have the right to expect sellers to provide easily understood information about their products so they can then make reasoned decisions.

❑   **The right to choose**

To make a reasoned objective choice, consumers should be able to distinguish 'real' competition in manufacturers' promotions. Products should be presented in such a way that is simple for consumers to relate quality and quantity to cost before making purchases.

❑   **The right to be heard**

Consumers have the right to express dissatisfaction to suppliers and others so attention can be focused on poor service and product performance. This implies the existence of mechanisms for redress should a product prove unsatisfactory.

In addition to Kennedy's rights, two more rights are now added to reflect modern circumstances:

❑ **The right to privacy**

With the information revolution has come an increase in direct marketing through database management. Much promotional material that is distributed in this way is beneficial to consumers and it is possible to make directly targeted approaches that are more likely to fit class and consumption profiles. However, some people take the view that using their details in databases is an invasion of privacy and view it as 'junk mail'. They now have the right to remove their details from such mailing lists through the Data Protection Act.

❑ **The right to a clean and healthy environment**

Ecological awareness is a significant issue. Organisations like Greenpeace and Friends of the Earth have shed their nonconformist image and achieved respectability they did not possess 20 years ago. It is through many issues that have been their concern that environmental legislation has followed. The Government has introduced a voluntary Environmental Initiative in which companies can apply for certification that their manufacturing processes are environmentally friendly, and then advertise this fact.

Whether consumers are better served today because companies have made voluntary changes, or because of coercion, is not important; the fact is that consumers do receive better treatment. Companies should develop their own customer orientation and concern for consumer welfare, but to protect consumers from companies who have not accepted this challenge, it has been necessary for Government to take action. In the UK the legal system has always taken an interest in fair trading, and the 1970s especially witnessed increased concern spurred on by the consumer movement. The following consumer protection statutes provide an insight into this development:

Aerosol dispensers (EEC requirements) regulations (1977)

Babies dummies (safety) regulations (1978)

Business advertisements (disclosure) order (1977)

Consumer credit (credit reference agency) regulations (1977)

Consumer Protection Act (1987)

Consumer Safety Act (1978)

Cooking utensils (safety) regulations (1972)

Cosmetic products regulations (1978)

Electric blankets (safety) regulations (1971)

Fair Trading Act (1973)

Hire Purchase Act (1973)

Night-dresses (safety) regulations (1967)

Price marking (bargain offers) order (1979)

Pyramid selling schemes regulations (1973)

Resale Prices Acts (1964 and 1976)

Supply of Goods (Implied Terms) Acts (1973, 1982)

Toys (safety) regulations (1974)

Unsolicited Goods and Services Acts (1971 and 1975)

In the UK there is no single consumer protection law. The two most pertinent statutes are the Sale of Goods Act that has been continuously updated since 1893, and the Trade Descriptions Act (1972). The Government established the Office of Fair Trading in 1973 and appointed a Minister for Consumer Affairs together with the Consumer Protection Advisory Committee, designed to monitor the activities of the business world and publish information in consumers' interests. All local authorities have Trading Standards Departments that oversee proper execution of Weights and Measures and Food and Drugs Acts and act in an advisory capacity in cases of dispute. This task was initiated by Consumer Advice Centres from 1972 until their abolition in 1980 on the basis that consumerism was beginning to protect consumers too much, to the detriment of manufacturers.

When the impact of the consumer movement was first felt, many companies felt threatened. In reality it helped business to identify its shortcomings as well as real needs of consumers. Many companies adopted a positive stance, and instead of concealing product defects, made safety, honesty and service product 'features', including initiatives in areas of labelling, pricing and credit agreements.

Consumerism is now involved with broader socio-economic issues as well as consumer protection. There is a positive feeling about environmentalism. Consumer bodies discuss such issues with Government. Consumerism has progressed from specific issues, affecting small sections of society, to an involvement in issues that affect society as a whole. Marketing has undergone a similar evolution. A new perspective on the marketing concept is being adopted that still relates to customer satisfaction, but this is taking place through a social as well as customer orientation.

12.4 Social marketing

Marketing is a management system with customer satisfaction being the object of marketing effort. Extending this definition adds to marketing's remit, but the objective of customer orientation is unchanged. The concept of social marketing argues that business activity should be acceptable to society as well as targeted customer groups. It is a study of marketing within the total social system. A need for marketing to be socially acceptable has existed as long as trade has been practiced. The recognition of the role of social marketing has gained momentum during the past 25 years owing to two factors:

During the twentieth century, a major thrust of business activity was providing basic commodities. Disposable income was limited. In the 1950s and 1960s the aftermath of World War Two restricted the availability and means of obtaining luxury goods and services. During the past 25 years, living standards have improved to such an extent that the basic needs and wants of most people have been fulfilled. We are now able to choose how to spend disposable income. The affluence of the current post-industrial society has brought with it social costs that are linked to changes in society's value systems. It is not the task of marketing to dictate what is good or bad for society. The remit of 'social marketing' is to question whether certain products and services have a detrimental effect on society. Social awareness should be used to establish whether consumers really receive satisfaction and if products provide benefits to the quality of life, or whether they are simply for short-term gratification. Critics of marketing contend that marketing is partially responsible for 'cultural pollution'. Social marketing does not imply 'guilt', but its existence suggests that such views should be respected.

Another spur to the growth of social marketing concerns scarcity of basic resources relative to the abundance of manufactured goods, as well as the way goods are produced. Marketing's success in providing for material needs and wants has also contributed to their existence. Environmentalists are concerned with issues like pollution, waste, congestion and ecology. Social marketing recognises that it is not enough to provide customer satisfaction if, in so doing, society is adversely affected. The social marketer's task is to find new products and production methods that do not pollute or deplete scarce resources.

Two issues face twenty first century marketing practitioners:

Causes of industrial pollution are easy to identify and often an alternative process can be devised that eliminates the problem. Such remedies can be costly, and the issue is whether consumers are prepared to pay for a safer environment and who should bear this cost. The issue of lead in petrol was an example of social marketing in action. The help of government (in keeping the price of unleaded petrol lower than that of leaded petrol) enabled a compromise to be reached that provided a needed product at a reduced social cost. Oil companies were prepared to invest in research into unleaded petrol, in return for which consumers were asked to accept modifications in product usage.

The second question is a philosophical issue that relates to issues like whether government or religion should influence our lives. Consumers are responsible for their own social and moral welfare, but what steps do they take to minimise pollution or reduce wasteful consumption of energy? Often an external body co-ordinates such actions. Consumerists call for social responsibility in business, but say little about a need for consumers to accept shared responsibility.

Marketing is a social force that transmits a standard of living and reflects cultural values and norms. Marketing can use its influence to work for social good in areas where it is accepted that there is scope for improvement. For example:

- ❑ Automobiles (pollution, congestion and safety).
- ❑ Foodstuffs (additives, preservatives and pesticides).
- ❑ Packaging (non-biodegradable materials).
- ❑ Manufacturing (pollution, noise and safety).

Social marketing addresses these issues by providing customer satisfaction at a reduced social cost. Consumerism and government legislation have partially coerced companies into a more socially responsible approach to their activities. Many companies have made voluntary moves towards social orientation. Manufacturers pay attention to packaging design by providing goods in less wasteful, easily disposed of, packages. Aerosol manufacturers have discontinued using a propellant that damaged the earth's ozone layer. While acknowledging that product costs and performance are keys to success, producers have been urged to take on responsibility and liability for the products they sell.

Marketing's critics argue that examples of social orientation are attempts to gain popular approval. Whether these initiatives are from within the company or from external pressure is irrelevant to consumer satisfaction. Progress in social orientation is likely to be more enduring if business is the initiator of social change rather than change being imposed by external agents like government legislation. Although social orientation benefits consumers, marketing practitioners face considerable problems when implementing socially orientated strategies. In particular, many socially desirable modifications involve extra costs for which consumers are not prepared to pay. Car production is an example of an industry that is able to provide added safety and comfort features like traction control, air conditioning and airbags on luxury models, but which cannot easily be incorporated into price-sensitive models. Marketing must find ways of improving products at minimum cost, but consumers should be prepared to make a financial contribution towards their own welfare.

Marketing's social responsibilities imply a transition from a 'management' orientation. This does not suggest that profit is unimportant as it is the essential element of a company's survival.

12.5 Marketing in not-for-profit organisations

Non-profit organisations perform roles that cater for social rather than commercial needs. Their social orientation already exists and what is needed is the adoption of managerial marketing techniques to accomplish their tasks more effectively.

Parallels can be drawn between the functions of profit and non-profit sectors. Non-profit organisations have 'products' (usually services) and 'consumers' (users) and they function through organised structures of purchasing, production and personnel. A parallel for 'selling' is not readily seen. For example, in a public hospital, 'customers' have little opportunity to exercise choice because of scarce resources and one hospital not really acting in competition with another. Marketing implies customer satisfaction and, in this respect, those who are involved with consumers in non-profit sectors have roles similar to those of sales personnel in that they are the last link between the organisation and the user. In this sense they represent the organisation and influence consumer attitudes towards its service. Non-profit organisations have marketing problems, although this fact is not generally acknowledged. Government has attempted to address this in health care with the introduction of General Practitioner fundholder status and hospital trusts with the object of making them more accountable in financial and marketing terms.

In business, customers have the sanction of placing their custom elsewhere. The public sector receives criticism that is aggravated by the fact that in most cases the sanction of choice does not exist. Non-profit organisations are still able to function, but criticism can develop into resentment. If we recognise that not-for-profit organisations have marketing problems, we can then use marketing as a tool for action. The most important element of marketing for non-profit organisations is 'communication'. Businesses find customers and communicate with them to make sales. In the non-commercial sector it is easy to lose touch with customers and the idea that non-profit organisations can take their users for granted can be likened to sales-orientation.

Marketing orientation involves defining what the organisation is attempting to achieve, which is similar to defining the market in the commercial sector. A public library does more than provide books. It also serves as a meeting place, a support to local schools and a source of information for a wide range of commercial activities. When seen through a marketing orientation, libraries are involved in providing leisure and information.

Non-profit organisations should fulfil their functions through the marketing mix. Apart from 'price', mix elements are no different to those for commercial products or service marketing. The emphasis in the marketing mix varies according to the task. A police force may place emphasis on public relations to foster a favourable image of the police within a community to facilitate the task of policing. The police visit schools so children get to know them better and understand their place in the community. Police forces hold 'open days' and run PR campaigns and see their task as far broader than catching criminals.

12.6   Quality and marketing

Marketing must be integrated throughout the company. Designers should understand customer requirements and translate these into products that customers need. The exclusivity of 'marketing' should be removed from the marketing department, because it is what everybody should do in the interests of maximising customer satisfaction. This gives rise to the idea of the 'part-time marketer' (PTM) where everybody in the organisation is responsible for satisfying customer needs. Similarly, the concept of total quality management (TQM) is that everybody in the organisation is responsible for the image and service that the company puts forward. These two aspects are inseparable in providing lasting customer satisfaction.

In order to break down departmental barriers, so staff from different departments work together to tackle problem solving (known as 'continuous improvement processes'), many companies have set up quality improvement teams so that synergy exists and interfaces between marketing, production, quality, purchasing and human resource management. The role of marketing in quality improvement teams is to be assured that the organisation is doing the right things in building customer valued quality products.

Best practice benchmarking (BPB) as defined by the DTI (1993) involves the formation of a project team comprising people from multifunctional areas like marketing, production, quality and purchasing. The team's task is to obtain information on products or companies that have a higher level of performance or activity and to identify areas in their own organisation that need improving. The team is given a facility for research on product development and quality. Because of the benefits of shared knowledge in this multifunctional team, companies that implement BPB find that this drives members of the team to meet and exceed new standards.

It is now recognised that there must be a change from a production/cost-dominated strategy towards one of servicing the diverse needs of customers through marketing. This process of interdependence has led to the development of 'relationship marketing', which involves building long-term relationships with customers through a deliberate philosophy of customer retention. As the strategic geographical focus of companies has changed from domestic to international, the marketing concept has transformed from a transactional to a relationship focus. Customer-focused quality is important as it involves moves towards customer targeted activity. As we move towards a global economy, customers demand even better quality and put increasing importance on reliability, durability, ease of use and service.

Schill and McArthur (1992) contend that a new philosophy emanated in the 1980s, known as the 'competitive strategy' era. An integrated/functional role with the task of formulating and implementing corporate competitive strategy led marketing theorists to take on a new dimension known as 'strategic marketing'. This attempted to integrate manufacturing, finance, human resource and other functions with marketing to support a cohesive competitive strategy, focusing on matters like cost leadership and product differentiation. The idea was established that company-wide solutions were necessary in providing solutions to customers' problems.

The alignment of manufacturing and marketing strategies contributes to the overall success of the organisation. Market led strategies are based on growth. The relationship between marketing objectives and manufacturing strategies is critical, affecting the success of the organisation, but the nature of this relationship is not well defined. Piercy (1991) refers to the 'strategic internal market' that should have the goal of developing a marketing programme aimed at the internal marketplace in a company that parallels and matches the marketing programme aimed at the external marketplace of customers and competitors. This model comes from an observation that the implementation of external marketing strategies implies changes of various kinds within organisations, in the allocation of resources, in the culture of 'how to do things' and even in the organisational structures needed to deliver marketing strategies effectively in customer segments.

The role of marketing should be one of co-ordination across the company's functional units. This is critical because each department is likely to have different views of customers. Sheth (1992) says:

> 'It will become increasingly important for the left hand to know what the right hand is doing, especially in the market boundary of front line personnel in procurement, manufacturing, selling and service market offerings.'

The social, ethical and economic issues of marketing look at managerial systems from a 'bird's eye' viewpoint. If we broaden our marketing scope further we must turn to other disciplines to gain an objective view of marketing's place in society. The role of profit in marketing assumes a capitalist economic system. A study of politics and economics allows us to consider other systems. The ethical and moral questions raised by marketing can be considered through reference to sociology that helps us understand how and why people react to marketing activity.

Quality as well as marketing must permeate manufacturing operations and this has given rise to the notion of TQM and the PTM. As marketing becomes central to commercial and non-commercial activity so its role changes from being a function of management to that of a far broader philosophy that has total quality as its driving force.

12.7 International marketing

12.7.1 Multinational, international and export marketing

Confusion exists between 'multinational marketing', 'international marketing' and 'exporting'. Multinational marketing refers to companies whose business interests, manufacturing plants and offices are spread throughout the world. Although their strategic headquarters may be in an original 'parent' country, multinational companies operate independently at national levels. Multinationals are not really exporters as they produce and market goods within countries they have chosen to develop.

The difference between exporting and international marketing is less obvious. A company that engages in simple exporting might consider it to be a peripheral activity. Most firms have some export involvement, and the term 'exporting' is commonly applied to firms whose export activity represents less than 20% of turnover. This implies their international activities are sporadic and lack commitment to the degree of modification they should be prepared to make to their products and marketing mix strategy to sell successfully overseas. When overseas sales account for more than 20% of turnover, it is assumed that a company has made a strategic commitment to overseas involvement and is then regarded as engaging in international marketing, implying:

- ❏ A strategic decision has been taken to enter foreign markets.

- ❏ Necessary organisational changes have been carried out.

- ❏ Marketing mix adaptations for overseas markets have been made.

- ❏ The company has made 'attitudinal' adjustments appropriate to an international marketing strategy.

In essence, international marketing is concerned with any conscious marketing activity that crosses national frontiers. Multinational corporations and exporters represent extremes on the international marketing spectrum. International marketing uses the same marketing concepts as national marketing. Management must set objectives that international strategy should achieve and this should be implemented through the marketing mix and be organised so it is appropriate to the market being considered. It is likely that an individual marketing mix strategy will need to be developed for each market. Marketing research, advertising and promotion, product design issues, packaging and sales management all possess the same rationale in both domestic and international marketing; what differs is the way these functions are performed. An advertising campaign or marketing research survey can be more complex in international markets. Language and culture account for the principal differences. Physical communication can sometimes pose problems. Whatever market is considered, the underlying marketing concept does not change.

Some firms actively seek overseas involvement. Products or services they offer may be so specialised that the domestic market will not provide sufficient sales. This is commonplace in industrial markets where specialist manufacturers make few domestic sales as unit value might be high and repeat purchase rates low. Some companies even establish on the basis of having identified a buoyant foreign market. Most companies, however, begin overseas involvement on the basis of a well-established home market. The decision to 'go international' might be due to a variety of reasons:

Saturation of the home market: Many companies in mature markets find that scope for growth is limited. Competitive action may threaten market share. International opportunities are sought to maintain the viability of existing production. Such action might also extend the product life cycle.

To facilitate growth: Growth markets may present a situation in which a company that does not grow with market trends becomes smaller relative to competition and less able to compete in terms of lower costs and innovation. Access to overseas markets facilitates growth by providing new outlets.

To achieve lower unit costs: The core business may remain in the domestic sector whilst new international markets afford an opportunity to increase production and lower overall unit costs. This might allow a company to keep pace with market expansion and even permit expansion of domestic market share, providing overseas returns are sufficient to make a contribution to fixed costs and cover the variable costs of increased production.

Depressed demand in the home market: Some companies regard overseas markets as marginal cost areas. At times of depressed demand in the home market, exporting can maintain production capacity and make a contribution to fixed costs. This 'hit and run' strategy depends on the market in which the company is involved. For price-sensitive commodities this can be viable. However, true international marketing depends on long-term involvement, and such a tactic implies short-termism.

Implicit in the definition of international marketing is the idea that exporting is a pursuit that accounts for a small part of a company's overall affairs. The implication is that exporting does not involve the company in any major modifications to its home-based marketing. The term 'international marketing' is used to describe activities of firms that have made a positive decision to enter overseas markets and are prepared to implement whatever is required to achieve success in such markets.

Initial sporadic exporting sometimes provides a basis for further involvement, and a decision has to be taken on whether to develop this activity or not. As exports grow, a company is more likely to adopt an 'international marketing' philosophy. The company can initiate this commitment by making gradual changes, but at some stage a decision has to be made to devote more marketing effort to exports. A gradual evolution towards export commitment may be punctuated by these actions:

❑   Allocation of employees with responsibility for aspects of exporting like documentation, shipping and customer liaison.

❑   Minor modifications to payment terms and conditions.

❑   Involvement in export marketing research.

❑   Engagement of overseas agent(s) and/or distributor(s).

❑   Product modifications to suit individual overseas markets.

❑   Participation in international promotion, trade fairs and exhibitions.

Companies such as Ford, IBM, McDonalds, Shell and Mitsubishi can be described as multinationals. Although they have their 'roots' in a single country, whose headquarters may still hold strategic power, they are multinational in nature because their activities are worldwide and because they have established themselves in countries on an equal footing with indigenous companies. They operate as national companies in everything but name. If such companies decide to divert their resources from one country to another, the consequences for local communities in which their operations decrease or cease can be severe.

If the trend towards worldwide standardisation of products (e.g. cars, hamburgers or clothes) continues, and cultural groups grow increasingly alike in their tastes as societies become more 'cosmopolitan', the importance of multinationals is likely to increase. The rise of multinationals means that in product terms certain goods have 'global' appeal. These goods are successfully marketed in all countries with little or no attention to product or image modification. This is the phenomenon of global marketing.

In most countries one can see local people wearing Levi jeans, driving Ford or Toyota cars, drinking Coca-Cola and listening to Sony personal stereos. Companies that achieve global standardisation simplify their marketing task and effectively create competitive barriers. This is a trend that seems likely to increase with the growth of multinational activity.

12.7.2   Strategic international marketing

An 'international mentality' is an intangible attribute and just as an understanding and acceptance of the marketing concept should permeate a firm, those involved in export activity should extend the concept overseas with a committed approach to their markets. Once the 'international decision' has been taken, overseas customers should expect the best service a firm can offer. It is by providing service at least as good as local suppliers that the international marketer can succeed. The mentality required means a genuine interest in overseas customers and their countries and a willingness to adapt, as well as a high degree of patience and tolerance.

International strategy formulation typically takes the following course:

1. *Investment analysis* – can resources be better employed by adopting a strategic alternative, say in the home market?

2. *Market selection* – which markets appear most likely to fulfil the company's overall strategic objectives?

3. *Broad-based functional decisions* – how will the marketing mix be employed in order to implement the strategy?

The chosen strategy should possess specific objectives to permit subsequent measurement of results. These objectives must be realistic and within the capabilities of the firm and take account of the environmental factors of the market. They should also be consistent and not conflict with each other. Typical objectives include a specific return on investment (ROI), a specific market share percentage and a specific time scale.

Only through a strategic approach can a company objectively assess its situation and plan an international marketing strategy. The amount or 'level' of investment is a key strategic issue that is governed by the method of entry into the market and the way in which the international marketing mix is employed.

12.7.3 Organisation for international marketing

Export documentation is complex and requires specialist expertise. Staff must be trained or recruited to carry out this work. Some firms manage their own freight forwarding which demands specific skills. As exporting increases, it might be necessary to establish a complete export administration department.

Communication between the company, its customers and intermediaries might seem obvious, but the speed of response to e-mail, fax, post and telephone messages is a measure of a firm's efficiency. When communication is efficient, it denotes a businesslike attitude. Rapid response to requests for samples or technical information demonstrates that the company is interested in its customers. The fact that a customer is far away can have the effect of decreasing the urgency of any request. The company should implement systems and procedures to ensure that communication, in the sense of customer liaison, is efficient.

How the company organises its salesforce (i.e. the people directly concerned with customers and intermediaries) and how agents and distributors are selected and managed, is important. Some firms approach overseas markets directly whilst others employ commercial agents and distributors to act on their behalf.

Overseas agents are usually nationals of the country concerned. They can be individuals or companies. Their role, supported by the supplier, is to identify customers and provide on-location representation for the supplier. Agents are paid on a commission basis. Distributors operate by purchasing from the manufacturer and then reselling after they have added a mark-up for their services. The market for industrial goods lends itself more to agency agreements than consumer goods where distributorships are more common.

The agent/principal relationship is vital to success in any overseas operation. While agents are not direct employees they should be afforded the attention and co-operation that employees can expect. The agent should be able to demonstrate to customers a positive relationship with the principal in the form of a true partnership.

Apart from financial reward, agents can be motivated by regular contact and sales support, prompt replies to queries, invitations to the principal's premises and regular updates on company developments. The agent should respond by providing feedback and information about the marketplace. Agents should develop long-term objectives that benefit themselves and their principals in the form of a partnership that normally implies territorial exclusivity in relation to the product or service being represented.

The criteria for agent selection are similar to those applied to the appointment of any employee. Most agents have more than one principal and their existing activity should complement, but not compete with, what is proposed. The agent search process is often carried out through commercial contacts, but can also include advertising or the employment of consultants to prepare a short-list of potential agents. Government agencies such as the British Overseas Trade Board (BOTB), Chambers of Commerce and British Consulates in relevant countries can be useful contacts.

The appointment of distributors follows a similar process. The firm requires an overseas distributor who has relevant experience and contacts and whose existing activities are in harmony with the proposed product range. The chief differences are related to the fact that, unlike agents, distributors purchase goods from the supplier. They usually contract to maintain agreed minimum stock levels. Although the distributor reduces risk and financial outlay for the supplier, losing 'title' reduces the control the supplier has over marketing.

'Direct investment' implies a semi-permanent diversion of funds and expertise so the company is no longer transporting finished goods from the home base to export markets, but is manufacturing outside the home country or engaging in co-operation with foreign manufacturers. This is normally considered when the firm's level of international involvement has reached a point where it is no longer practical to continue the physical transfer of goods from one country to another. Sometimes direct investment provides a method of entry into overseas markets that bypasses the export evolution process. By purchasing a foreign company, or by entering into a licensing or industrial co-operation agreement, a company gains immediate market access and revenue from abroad without necessarily having had prior international involvement.

Licensing is much favoured by Japanese companies, and this involves one company allowing another to use a trademark or patent, or a manufacturing process, design or recipe, for which the user company makes a payment. It is a relatively easy method of entry into foreign markets and it provides immediate revenue.

International co-operative ventures involve sharing technology or manufacture between two companies from different countries. As well as sharing knowledge and expertise to mutual advantage, both companies benefit from sharing costs. Joint venture operations involve two companies joining together to manufacture and market their products as one. They differ from co-operative ventures in that the companies are effectively merging, rather than sharing, their expertise. Often a new company is formed in which neither party has an overriding shareholding. The maintenance of a 50:50 holding interest helps to ensure that conflict between the two parties is minimised, although in some countries, particularly in the Middle East, there is an insistence that the 'local' partner has a controlling interest (i.e. 51% or more).

12.7.4 International marketing mix, information and strategy

The company must develop a 'mix strategy' to achieve strategic objectives. The elements are the same for international or domestic marketing and any home-based mix is likely to require modification for international marketing.

Product

Physical changes are not normally a major source of problems to a company that has international intentions. More difficult are intangible factors like image and product positioning. Packaging is a major element of the product that can be affected by legal and cultural aspects of the international market. For example, package sizes produced for the home market may not correspond to those in another country. In some countries, colours have religious significance, and it would be offensive to associate some colours with material goods. Climate can be a factor when considering package type. For instance, in warmer more humid climates, chocolate bar manufacturers put an extra layer of wrapping around the silver foil to prevent the product from melting. In industrial markets, some countries may be unable to handle goods packed in their existing form because of a lack of appropriate materials handling equipment.

CASE 12.2

MacDonald's differentiates its product mix on an international basis.

Many people regard the fast food chain MacDonald's as a good example of a firm using undifferentiated marketing strategies. In fact, closer inspection will reveal that this is far from the case and that there are quite significant differences in the firm's product mix within different countries or at least overseas regions. The firm is perhaps best known for its 'hamburgers' which are actually made from beef. Many people are aware, however, that the firm now offers 'veggie' burgers and chicken-based products. In the UK other ranges were introduced partly because of the BSE scare and people's reluctance to consume beef. Many people in the UK will still not touch beef. Even looking at the basic 'burger' product we can see many product adaptations in different parts of the world. In Canada the burgers are far bigger than they are in the UK. In India the firm offers a range of vegetable-based burgers to the Hindu community and a range of Halal-based meat products to the Moslem community, the same in Pakistan. In Israel the burgers are 'Kosher'. In France customers can obtain alcohol with their meal and a range of salads are available for starters. Whereas the basic concept of burger based fast food is the same wherever MacDonald's operate in the world, the firm has gone to a lot of care to ensure that the original USA based fast food concept is acceptable to the tastes and religious sensitivities of the local population.

Labelling is a product-related issue where local convention might dictate modifications. In some countries levels of literacy may require that important information be relayed graphically. Language presents an obvious need for label modification. Firms with wide international involvement tend to repeat information in a variety of languages relevant to their major markets, in a move to accommodate those markets as well as reducing the number of label modifications. A brand name that sounds innocuous in the home market may have a different significance in another language. Even logos might possess negative connotations.

Dealing in many markets allows a company to pursue a variety of product policies. At any single point of time it is likely that a single product's life cycle position may vary in different markets and countries. This implies that marketing mix and product decisions should be adapted accordingly.

Promotion

As well as the issue of language, most advertising must be modified to suit its target market. Cultural attitudes to family life, behaviour, good manners and sexual equality vary widely. Legal restrictions may forbid comparative advertising or restrict broadcasting time. This compounds the issue of copy translation and message. Unless it is carefully conceived and checked out by nationals of a country, the message and advertising copy might be totally misdirected. Whilst media available can vary between countries, the major criterion for media selection is universal. The appropriate medium is that which reaches the highest number of prospects within the target market at the most cost-effective rate, taking into consideration the specific task that advertising is designed to achieve.

Sales promotion needs to be tailored to the market. Although standard techniques can be employed, where the product is distinguishable as 'imported', the promotional emphasis is normally centred around some form of joint effort organised by an agency of the exporting country (e.g. a Trade Association or a Chamber of Commerce). Large retailers in the target country might be persuaded to host in-store promotions that feature a variety of products from a particular country.

In industrial markets, trade fairs or exhibitions are valuable promotional tools. Companies can participate individually or through some co-operative venture. Participation in such events is often made more attractive by government aid or sponsorship. Exhibitions provide the company with an international meeting point for seeing a large number of customers in a short time.

Distribution

As well as physical distribution and logistics, the company must consider whether to use agents or distributors or to sell direct. In general, transport decisions are clear and can be refined as the company gains experience. Perishable products should be despatched by the fastest means. Expensive airfreight would not, on the other hand, be appropriate for bulky, low value products.

The idea of 'total distribution' or a systems approach as discussed in Chapter 9, is especially applicable to international marketing. In commodity markets, or where there is local competition, service is frequently the major competitive tool. A company that consistently delivers on time will build up a level of loyalty that may never be achieved by promotion. The organisation of the distribution mix is a function of the product and market type, and, where international markets are concerned, distribution is a high profile element of the overall marketing mix.

Price

While opportunities for product and price differentiation in overseas markets are apparent, it is a feature of the twenty first century that, in general (and especially in consumer markets), product standardisation is increasing. This means that a company often has little option other than to charge a price established by competitors. In such situations it is essential that cost structures have been examined and the expected return on investment is considered to be acceptable before market entry. When a company is obliged to operate within a predetermined price framework, it should attempt to differentiate its products by means other than price.

Procter & Gamble is a successful international company that gains high market share through an emphasis on promotion rather than price. International markets can offer special opportunities for obtaining high prices due to prestige or novelty associated with the country of origin. Burberry clothes have a 'Britishness' sought after throughout the world. The French have a reputation for high quality cosmetics. International sales of some whisky brands are as much due to Scottish origins as to taste.

The main issues of international pricing are the price quotation where the main terms used in export/import transactions are:

❑ *Ex-works* where the importer is solely responsible for transport and insurance from the supplier's premises.

❑ *FOB (free on board)* where the supplier is responsible for the costs of transport and insurance until goods are loaded prior to export. Once loaded onto a ship or aircraft, the customer assumes responsibility for further costs.

❑ *CIF (cost, insurance and freight)* where the supplier's quotation includes all costs of delivery to a port convenient to the customer. A typical quotation may read 'CIF local port', but often the port of destination is specified.

❑ *C & F (cost and freight)* is where insurance is not included in the price. This might be because the government of the importer insists on using the country's own insurance facilities. Sometimes the government of the importing country might specify the shipping line that the exporter must use.

❑ *Delivered client's warehouse* (sometimes termed *rendu* or *free delivered*) is typical when trading within Europe where lorries deliver 'door-to-door'. The supplier is responsible for all costs, including customs clearance, but excluding any local duties or taxes.

❑ More specialist quotations include *FAS (Free alongside ship)* and *FOW (Free on wagon)*

Payment terms and conditions vary between countries. Thirty-, sixty- and ninety-day credit terms are common within Europe. Discounts for prompt payment vary.

Letters of credit are a normal trading condition in distant markets. They provide protection for both parties because funds are not transferred until conditions are met. Once they are fulfilled the supplier is guaranteed payment by the bank. In some countries, especially those with balance-of-payments problems, payment can be deferred by as much as two years. Financial institutions exist that are able to factor payments to suppliers for a percentage of the cost involved. Means of payment must, therefore, be carefully considered before sales are negotiated.

Currency is an important consideration and hard currencies like the US dollar and pound sterling are 'universal' currencies, but they are not always the most convenient means of exchange. From a marketing perspective, it can be preferable to make quotations in the local currency as long as it is readily convertible and stable. This shows a commitment to the overseas customer. Where local competition is strong, quotations made in local currency can remove one of the distinctions that competition might use to argue against international sourcing. Financially, trading in foreign currencies carries an element of risk that can be offset by buying a currency 'forward'.

International sales management

It is important that the overseas salesperson has sufficient authority to make important business decisions 'on the spot'. This increases the salesperson's credibility and raises the tone of the meeting from what might otherwise appear to be a courtesy visit. The need to make such decisions whilst abroad requires a level of managerial ability not always needed for domestic sales staff. International sales personnel should, therefore, be capable of working with minimal supervision.

Expatriate sales personnel (nationals of the exporting country) can also be domiciled in the target country. Although the business rationale for such an arrangement is sound, management problems can occur. Maintaining an expatriate sales force is expensive and complex. Control is reduced and salespersons may feel personally isolated from the home country. Morale amongst staff living abroad for long periods can be difficult to maintain.

When high levels of sales are achieved in a particular country it might be appropriate to engage national sales personnel. They will be familiar with the language, customs and culture, which expatriate sales staff might never achieve. On the other hand, customers may consider a sales force of local personnel as 'once-removed' from the exporting company, and less directly involved in the marketing process.

Cultural variables can pose problems when devising sales strategies. There should be an awareness of differences in aspects like humour, morality and the role and status of women. Sales personnel must observe rules of local etiquette. Culture is an 'ethnic' rather than 'geographic' factor. A country may contain groups of people with radically different cultures; the Germans and French recognise distinct cultural differences between the north and the south of their respective countries that are not immediately apparent.

CASE 12.3

EBay.com, the Internet based auction house continues to flourish despite the faltering world economy, and spreads its wings internationally.

EBay.com, the internet based online auction house, is continuing to flourish despite the faltering world economy. Not only is the company prospering within its traditional continental American market, but also the company is becoming more international. As of October 2001 around 16% of the firm's revenue is generated from outside the United States. Although still predominantly an American business its way of conducting business seems to be acceptable all over the world. The company has produced a business model that seems appropriate in all of the world's economies whatever the economic conditions and cultural differences. The firm is expecting international sales to grow in the future along with international advertising revenue. In fact this is where the majority of future growth is likely to come from. Unlike most other internet companies that have been shedding workers, eBay now employs 600 more people than it did at the start of 2001, 2,600 in all. Also in a falling advertising market where the outlook for advertising revenue looks weak for many media companies, eBay has increased its advertising revenue by 129% in the last year. Again significant growth is seen in international advertising. The company has over 32 million customers and all of them use the company with one purpose in mind, completing commercial transactions. As the world economy falters, people and firms have more things they want to sell, some may be 'distress sales'. Ebay in this respect is likely to become busier in times of economic slowdown. The company illustrates well the international dimension of Internet firms and that with the right business model firms can operate across international boundaries successfully.

International intelligence and information

The MkIS (marketing information system) should function as it would for domestic purposes, but the breadth of information required is greater and information can be more difficult to obtain. Field research can be frustrated by language problems, in which case it may be necessary to engage local research agencies. In developing nations, organised data collection might not exist, levels of literacy might be low and media available for promotion limited.

At the secondary stage the research process should relate to:

International trade directories and magazines.

Government statistics and reports.

Embassies and consulates.

Published surveys.

'On-line' data services accessed directly or through specialist agencies.

International banks and other financial institutions.

The intelligence system has a vital role to play in monitoring the international environment once business has begun. In the 'home' country, much information available through the media is taken for granted. The international intelligence system should ensure a regular flow of information from countries being monitored. It is part of the role of agents, distributors, sales personnel and other locally based employees to contribute information.

International marketing strategy

Warren Keegan (1969) put forward a theory that is now central to strategic thinking when considering international marketing. He considered the mix elements of product and communication and identified five possible strategies as described in Figure 12.1.

		Products		
		No change	Adapted	New product
Marketing communications	No change	Straight extension	Product adaptation	
	Adapt	Communications adaptation	Dual adaptation	Product invention

Figure 12.1 Keegan's five strategies for international marketing

Straight extension

The product or service and the type of communication message is the same for overseas and home markets (e.g. Coca Cola).

Communications adaptation

The promotional theme is modified and the product or service remains unchanged (e.g. bicycles are promoted as basic means of transportation in developing countries whereas in developed countries they are promoted as a means of recreation).

Product adaptation

The product or service is different for home and overseas markets, whereas the promotion is the same for both (e.g. petrol has a different 'formula' for colder climates than for warmer climates).

Dual adaptation

The communication message and the product are altered for each market (e.g. clothing products where designs are different for each market and promotion can emphasise functionality or fashion).

Product invention

The above strategies are appropriate where product needs and market conditions are similar to the home market, but in developing countries this may not be true. New product development might be required to meet customer needs at an affordable price (e.g. a 'hand cranked' washing machine is an example of 'backwards invention' to suit the needs of countries where there is an uncertain power supply and washing is done by hand).

The decision to enter overseas markets is an important strategic consideration that cannot be effected without preparation and willingness to adapt. An international strategy should be preceded by close examination of alternatives in the home market. Increasing sales volume through overseas markets may only be possible by means of extensive product and marketing mix modifications, the cost of which may negate the expected advantages.

Questions

1. *Use of marketing by non-profit organisations*: Marketing is increasingly being used by non-profit organisations like colleges, libraries and political parties. What is the relevance of the marketing concept to such organisations.

2. *Ethics*: Marketing has been criticised on economic and ethical grounds. Discuss these criticisms, indicating how far you think they are justified.

3. *International marketing*: How can firms increase their involvement in international markets? Discuss the relative merits of the methods you describe.

4. *Information sources*: What limitations or problems are apparent when using International Marketing Research information sources?

5. *Financial implications*: Why does the acceptance of a foreign order usually impose a proportionately heavier financial burden on the supplier than a similar home market order? What steps can be taken to reduce this effect?

References

DTI, (1993), *Best Practice Benchmarking*, (Department of Trade and Industry, London).

Keegan, WJ, (1969) 'Multinational product planning: strategic alternatives', *Journal of Marketing*, 33, pp. 58-62

Piercy, N, (1991), *Market-led Strategic Change*, p367, (Thorsons, London).

Schill, RL, and McArthur, DN, (1992), 'Redefining the Strategic Competitive Unit: Towards a new Global Marketing Paradigm', *International Marketing Review*, Vol 9, No 3, pp 5-23.

Sheth, JN, (1992), Emerging Marketing Strategies in a Changing Macroeconomic Environment: A Commentary, *International Marketing Review*, Vol. 9, No 1, pp 57-63.

13 Marketing strategy, planning and control

13.1 Introduction

Some businesses are led by managers who have a 'feel' for the market, and their intuitive decisions lead to success. Intuition is important, but few of us could say that our intuition is so frequently correct that we could use it as the basis for managing a company. Markets change rapidly and the intuitive leader runs risks that are unacceptable to shareholders as well as employees. Furthermore, if the intuitive leader is suddenly indisposed, what might happen? Some companies simply respond to current demand and, as long as order books are full, they see no need for planning. When sales slow down, they put pressure on the sales force to sell more.

13.2 Strategic planning

Planning systems that have not evolved from the marketplace are often based on the company's budgeting process. Resources are allocated to functional managers on a historical basis and there is no facility to evaluate expenditure in terms of results. So long as the department has not overrun its allocation, everybody is satisfied.

Many managers maintain they are marketing orientated, but overlook the fundamental aspect of a formalised planning procedure that takes into account the firm's environment, its internal resources and its longer-term objectives. Planning is difficult in practice, but its concept is quite straightforward. The planning process is continuous. Throughout the year, information should be constantly collected and analysed and performance should be under constant review. Figure 13.1 outlines the contents of planning, strategy formulation and control. Each of these is important. Strategy formulation is exciting for marketers because of its creative content, but we should not overlook the fact that control provides a means to discover whether the strategy has been appropriate and the information that allows corrective action to be taken. A simple view of planning can be remembered through the acronym MOST:

- ❑ Mission – the business we are in
- ❑ Objectives – what we need to accomplish
- ❑ Strategies – in general terms how are we going to do it?
- ❑ Tactics – in specific terms how are we going to do it?

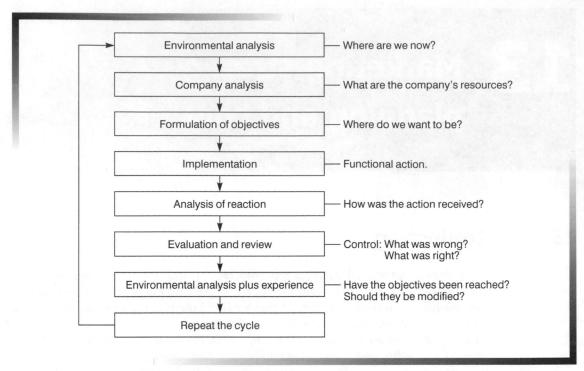

Figure 13.1 A simple planning system

Planning can be confusing because of the many words and titles used in its description. In particular, confusion arises over the meaning of 'strategy' and its use in the terms 'corporate strategy' and 'functional strategy'. It is useful to clarify these terms:

❏ *Planning* is the process of decision-making that relates to the future. The term can be used at all levels in company decision-making.

❏ *Corporate planning* refers to decision-making at the highest levels of management. It is sometimes referred to as 'strategic planning' or 'long-range planning'. It is not concerned with forecasting sales or marketing mix strategies. Corporate planning asks: 'What business are we really in?'; 'What are our basic objectives?'; 'Are our markets growing or declining?'; 'Do new technologies threaten our products?' After analysis, strategic plans can be drawn up from the answers to such questions.

❏ *Operational* or *functional planning* is the process that develops the corporate or strategic plan. A strategic corporate objective may be to enter a new market and achieve x per cent market share with y per cent return on investment within two years. Operational planning will indicate how this should be best achieved (e.g. by adopting a particular marketing mix strategy and financial allocation).

❏ The word *strategy* can be used at an operational level (product, price or advertising strategy) because it describes medium- to long-term actions.

❏ *Tactics* are actions that bring about modifications to operational plans (e.g. a price change or an increase in advertising necessitated by unexpected competitive action). They are essentially short-term in nature.

❑ *Objectives* should be SMART – Specific, Measurable, Achievable, Realistic and Time related

To realise corporate objectives, management must break down areas of responsibility into identifiable and manageable units. This facilitates analysis, planning and control. The business is broken down into 'strategic business units' (SBUs). These represent separate entities to which corporate strategy is delegated. A major criterion is that SBUs should be easily identifiable and represent the key business areas of the company. Although it is not always possible to precisely delineate business areas, ideally SBUs should be single businesses that can be planned independently of the company's other businesses. This suggests that they have an identifiable management, with responsibility for managing and controlling resource allocation, and direct competitors can be identified. For multi-market or multi-industry organisations, SBUs may be entire companies. Single industry or 'product-line dominant' companies might identify SBUs based on specific market areas.

There is a hierarchy of planning as shown in Figure 13.2:

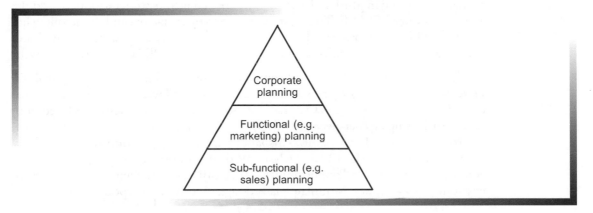

Figure 13.2 Planning hierarchy

This can be expanded as follows:

Strategic corporate planning: define organisational mission; establish strategic business units (SBUs); anticipate change

⇩

Marketing planning for SBUs: set marketing objectives; develop marketing strategy; make formal marketing plans

⇩

Operational marketing plans: The term 'corporate planning' has evolved in line with the increasing size of companies and numbers of multi-product, multi-market companies. Take-overs, mergers and multi-national activity have created a complex business environment, so larger companies are indirectly responsible for the direction of several firms who are often involved in unrelated markets. The task is to define a corporate mission and develop plans that enable this to be accomplished. The mission should be stated in marketing terms to encourage a wide a view of opportunities.

Objectives are defined and communicated to individual parts of the company whose managers develop their own plans for achieving these objectives. Such a process facilitates a marketing mission rather than a product orientation. Whatever the mission, it should serve to generate a common theme throughout the company and motivate staff towards a common goal.

13.3   Audit and SWOT

Having defined corporate objectives and identified SBUs, the company proceeds to the stages of planning outlined in Figure 13.1. The first stage is environmental analysis (sometimes called the external audit) and it is known through the acronym PEST analysis (short for Political, Economic, Socio-cultural and Technological analysis). Some authors cite the acronym as STEP as there is no chronological sequence in how each factor should be considered. Each of these categories should be investigated in turn. These separate PEST factors have later been broadened to include Legal aspects to make the acronym SLEPT. Later, Environmental factors were introduced and the acronym became PESTLE. The most recent is Ecological factors and the acronym has become STEEPLE. However, the introduction of so many extra factors complicates what is a sound tool of analysis, and for most situations, PEST analysis works well.

In addition to the external audit, the company performs an internal company analysis. Here the company analyses its own internal strengths and weaknesses and its external opportunities and threats (SWOT analysis). Strengths and Weaknesses are listed from an internal company perspective and Opportunities and Threats from an external macro-environmental viewpoint. This latter part uses information that has already been identified from the PEST analysis. With this information, planners can then consider the strengths and opportunities of their SBUs, situate them in their respective environments, and then formulate plans designed to realise corporate objectives.

CASE 13.1

J. Sainsbury PLC capitalises on its strengths and decides to offer gas and electricity services to its customers along with the weekly groceries.

J. Sainsbury, a leading grocery multiple, is set to offer gas and electricity services to its customers. The development will make the firm the first UK supermarket chain to offer such services under its own brand name. The firm has secured a strategic alliance with Scottish Power, the energy and water utility company to facilitate the arrangement. The company believes it has the retailing strength and enough customers of sufficient loyalty, to be able to offer utility services of this kind. Other retailing groups are also thinking along the same lines and Argos, the catalogue retailer owned by Great Universal Stores, has similar plans. J. Sainsbury is both a corporate and grocery product brand name that is well respected for representing safety and quality. It is a name people trust. When purchasing electricity and gas people also want a name that they can trust, as has been shown by independent research carried out for the company. Scottish Power's links with Sainsbury's goes back to September 2000 when Sainsbury's gave its reward card holders an extra 5,000 points when they moved their account to Scottish Power.

13.4 Portfolio analysis

13.4.1 Boston Consulting Group (BCG) Matrix

Portfolio analysis was pioneered in the USA by the Boston Consulting Group, and it is sometimes referred to as the *Boston Box*. This method identifies the company's SBUs and places these on a matrix that considers market growth and relative market share.

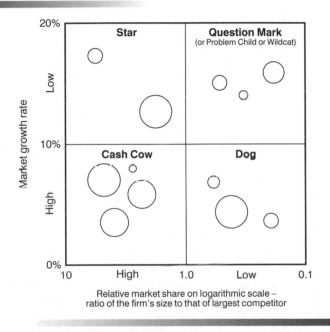

Figure 13.3 The BCG portfolio analysis matrix

Four business types can be distinguished:

❑ *Stars* are SBUs that have a promising future. Significant investments of cash are necessary to develop their full potential. If managed correctly, they will develop into a valuable source of revenue as the market evolves.

❑ *Cash cows* have achieved a high market share in a mature market. They deserve the company's fullest attention because the cash they generate can be invested in newer market areas with high growth potential.

❑ *Question marks* (or *problem children* or *wildcats*) pose a problem for management. Whilst market growth prospects are good, question mark SBUs have a low relative market share. If they are to be moved to the left (i.e. increase relative market share) substantial investment may be required. Based on marketing information, management must decide whether such investment could be better employed supporting other SBUs.

❑   *Dogs* show no growth potential and their relative market share is low. Although they may not necessarily be a 'drain' on the company's resources, they are unable to make a positive contribution to profits.

The BCG model was designed for multi-industry companies and SBUs depicted in Figure 13.3 related to competing companies. BCG analysis is now used within companies where SBUs relate to product lines. The size of each circle represents the value of sales. A major objective of business is to optimise performance so corporate objectives can be realised. An individual company can do little to change market growth, which defines its position on the vertical axis. The options are, therefore, to eliminate unprofitable SBUs from the 'portfolio', or to move them from the right to the left along the horizontal axis (i.e. increase their market share) and increased sales will also increase the size of SBUs.

Suppose the SBUs in Figure 13.3 are twelve individual companies that make up a large organisation. These are the 'corporate portfolio' (called the 'product portfolio' for a smaller company). The upper-left quadrant reveals one small star and one large star, although three large cash cows with a high relative market share are below this complemented by a small cash cow. The company should protect its cash cows and attempt to improve the star situation so that a new generation of cash cows can be developed. The company might have problems when attempting to move the most promising question marks from the right-to the left-hand quadrant. As far as the dogs are concerned, they should be examined individually, to decide whether they should be kept and improved (perhaps in the interests of ensuring a more comprehensive portfolio) or be sold off or liquidated.

The accuracy of any model is only as good as the information on which it is based. A BCG matrix requires accurate market and company information before it can be used as a meaningful management tool. As well as presenting strategic alternatives, a BCG matrix is valuable because it requires objective consideration of the elements of the portfolio in relation to each other. However, it is criticised as being too simplistic as variables used do not take into account the circumstances of growth or market share.

CASE 13.2

The Boston Consulting Group Inc. (BCG) becomes one of the most respected management consultancy firms in the world by providing innovative strategic marketing services to commerce and industry.

The Boston Consulting Group is based in Boston Massachusetts, USA, with offices all over the world, and is perhaps most well known for its BCG product portfolio matrix. The company made its name during the Second World War when the US government asked it to investigate how the country's aircraft production efficiency could be improved. BCG consultants realised that firms in the industry got better at making aeroplanes the more they made and hence experienced learning curve efficiencies. The consultants also identified other efficiencies related to increases in production, including administrative efficiencies. After the war the company attempted to apply the principles it had established to commercial firms and adapted its concepts for use as strategic management tools, especially in the field of marketing, such as product portfolios. Today the firm offers a range of consulting services and not just those based on its famous BCG matrix. The firm is the epitome of a marketing orientated firm. Its range of strategic management services are rated by the world's top organisations as being innovative, meaningful and amongst the best in the world. Today the BCG is a global player in management consulting.

13.4.2 The General Electric (GE) Matrix

General Electric of America's matrix overcomes some criticisms of the BCG matrix by using industry attractiveness and competitive position as its parameters. It was developed by management consultants McKinsey and is also referred to as the GE/McKinsey business screen. This matrix contains nine boxes and offers a wider strategic choice than the BCG matrix by using broader market and company factors. It uses business strength on the horizontal axis and industry attractiveness on the vertical axis.

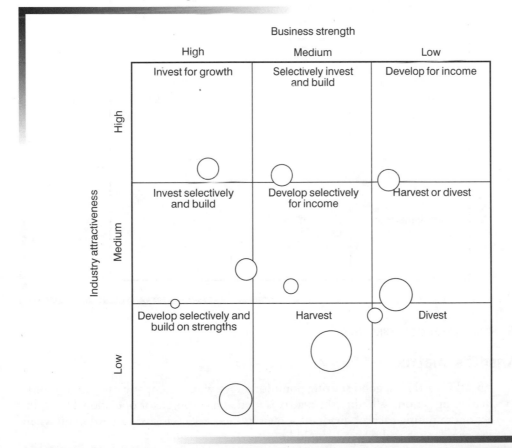

Figure 13.4 The GE matrix. Each box suggests a strategy appropriate for the SBU it holds.

13.4.3   The Shell Directional Policy Matrix

This matrix was developed by Shell Chemicals and was designed to cope with a dynamic market place. The requirement was that each strategy should be evaluated against potential contingencies. Figure 13.5 shows that the vertical axis looks at measures of the company's competitive capability (e.g. market growth, industry situation, environmental issues) and the horizontal axis examines prospects for sector profitability from an industry point of view.

Each SBU is given between one to five stars along each axis. This is then quantified, and the result places each SBU at an appropriate point in the matrix.

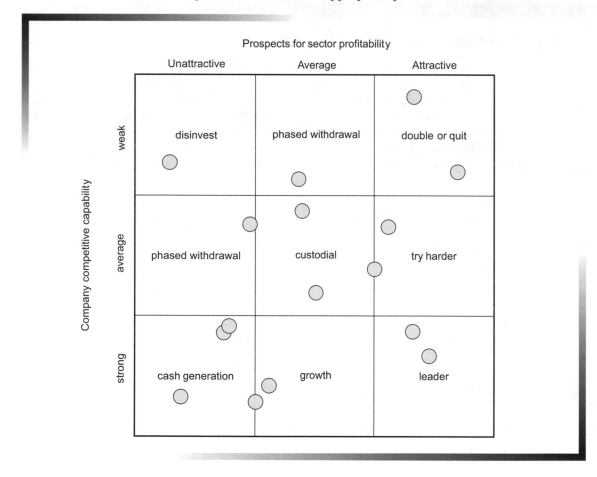

Figure 13.5 Shell directional policy matrix

13.4.4   Ansoff's matrix

Ansoff's matrix is a good starting point for a review of a company's position prior to marketing action. Whether the matrix is used at a corporate or operational level, the act of examining each of quadrant shown in Figure 13.6 focuses attention on where the company is and where is could be.

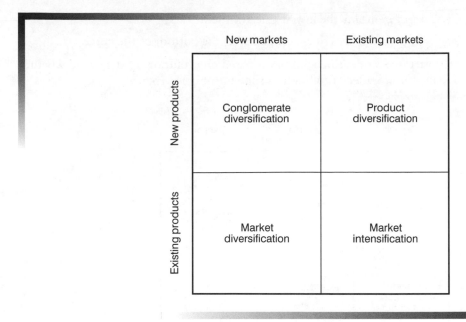

Figure 13.6 Strategic alternatives

13.4.5   Industry/market evolution

Porter proposed that success strategies are not necessarily 'financial' and 'high market share' as shown in Figure 13.7.

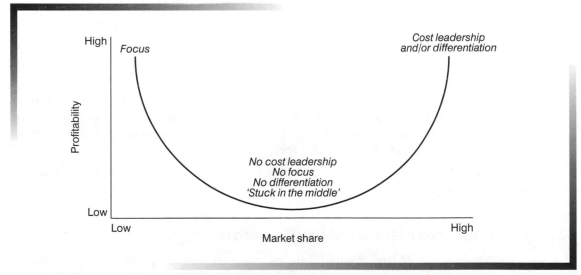

Figure 13.7 Porter's generic strategies

❑   *Focus* means the company consolidates its efforts on a small range of products in a market niche.

❑   *Differentiation* means to establish a unique sales proposition (USP) or feature that competition cannot match.

❏   *Cost leadership* means the lowest price in the market.

❏   *Stuck in the middle* describes companies at the bottom of the curve.

In 1985 Porter further developed his ideas based on evolutionary stages and whether the company was a leader or follower as shown in Figure 13.8.

	Growth (emerging industry)	Maturity (and transition to maturity)	Decline
Leader	Keep ahead of the field	Cost leadership; raise barriers to entry; deter competitors	Redefine scope; divest peripheral activities; encourage departures
Follower	Imitation at lower cost; joint ventures	Differentiation; focus	Differentiation; look for new opportunities

(Strategic position — vertical axis label)

Figure 13.8 Strategic position in industry life cycle

Depending upon whether the company is a 'leader' or a 'follower' depends upon which strategy should be adopted. Individual evolutionary stages are explained:

❏   *Growth* or emerging industry is characterised by conservatism amongst buyers over the attributes of new products and the fact that they might become dated in function or style.

❏   *Maturity* and transition to maturity can mean reduced profit margins as competitors enter and sales slow. Buyers are confident as they are familiar with the product. Manufacturing emphasis is on features and intangibles like image. Attempts are made to serve specialist market segments.

❏   *Decline* indicates that the market is saturated. Alternatives might appear that supplant traditional products and this is when companies should look for other products.

13.4.6   Product (or market) life cycle matrix

Barksdale and Harris combined the BCG matrix with the product life cycle concept to overcome the problem in the BCG matrix that ignores the position of the industry in relation to its stage of development. The matrix is described in Figure 13.9.

❏   *Infants* are in a position where R & D costs are being recovered with high promotional expenditure in terms of educating the market.

❏   *Stars* have high promotional costs, but good future potential once the product/

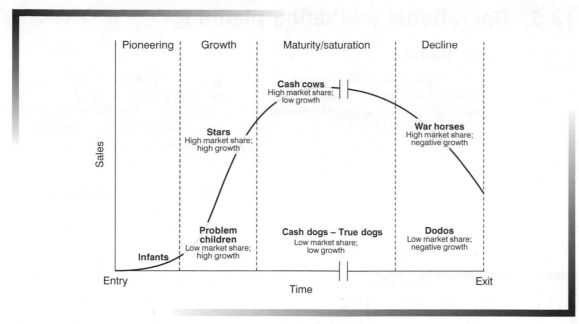

Figure 13.9 Barksdale & Harris BCG/PLC combined portfolio

service has been accepted by the market.

❑ *Problem children* (or wildcats or question marks) are in a high growth situation, but low market share. They are costly to maintain and market action should be taken to move them to 'star' and 'cash cow' positions.

❑ *Cash cows* earn money in a high market share/low-growth situation. Promotional costs are lower as the market is familiar with the product/service.

❑ *Cash dogs* with a low market share are to the maturity side of the box in a saturated market and have a flat cash flow. 'True dogs' have a low market share towards the saturation side of the box with a negative cash flow.

❑ *War horses* are in a declining market, but still have a relatively high market share, probably as a result of competitors departing from the market. This contributes' to a positive cash-flow.

❑ *Dodos* are in a declining market with a low market share and a negative cash-flow. They should be deleted, but might still remain because management hopes that they will stage a revival.

In concluding this insight into corporate planning through portfolio analysis, we should refer to the planning stages illustrated in Figure 13.1. All planning begins with an analysis of the company's widest environment and proceeds to analyse the company's marketing environment through the marketing information system. The information gathered and resultant analyses are the basis on which strategic corporate objectives can be formulated.

13.5 Operational marketing planning

13.5.1 TOWS matrix

The success of marketing planning depends on careful use of the marketing mix. Before a mix strategy is developed, operational management must consider the company's position in the market, with emphasis on SWOT. A useful tool is TOWS analysis that facilitates the formulation of strategies. Several stages are considered:

1.   Evaluate the influence of environmental factors (PEST/STEEPLE) on the company.

2.   Make a diagnosis about the future.

3.   Assess company strengths and weaknesses in relation to operations management, finance and marketing.

4.   Develop strategic options.

An application of TOWS is best illustrated through the use of an example:

Product: refrigerators

	Strengths 1. Brand name 2. UK sales force 3. Good after sales 4. Competitive price	**Weaknesses** 1. International markets 2. UK specified products 3. Logistics
Opportunities 1. EU market 2. Disposable income 3. Second homes 4. Cheaper transport	Use existing brand name and after sales support to market to EU countries (S1, S3, W1, O1)	Established manufacturing plant in potential EU entrant country to market new low capacity range (W1, W2, W3, O1, O3, O4, T4)
Threats 1. Far East imports 2. Currency variations 3. New low-cost countries entering EU	Establish depots in EU and recruit sales force using UK trainers (S2, S3, S4, W1, W3, O1)	Source components in Far East for new ultra-low cost range of additional home freezers (S1, S3, S4, O3, T1, T3)

Figure 13.10 An example of TOWS analysis in use

13.5.2 Procedure for marketing planning

Figure 13.11 outlines the marketing planning routine including all activity that places marketing in a strategic framework. The strategic planning process should have taken place and an individual plan is required for each SBU.

The marketing plan should include: analysis, setting objectives, forecasting, budgeting, organisation, selecting targets, developing the mix and control. Each is discussed in the context of marketing planning at an operational level:

Analysis

Marketing research provides a picture of the market and profiles of potential consumers. Information is needed on competitive activity, distribution, prices and

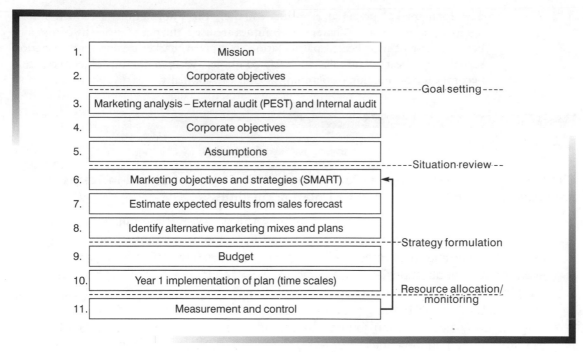

Figure 13.11 A model of marketing planning

products. Potential consumers should be asked where they buy, how they buy and what they consider to be problems with current supplies/suppliers. In particular, we need to know market size. Within a company, costs must be analysed and production and distribution capabilities assessed.

Setting objectives

Based on marketing research/analysis and knowledge of internal capabilities, the company must decide on objectives, i.e. the market position the company will seek. The objectives of a marketing plan must be realistic, attainable and specific so that they can be easily communicated throughout the company. 'To increase sales' or 'to increase brand awareness' are meaningless. More specific (SMART) objectives provide a focus for marketing effort and permit subsequent evaluations of such effort. e.g. a SMART objective would be 'to increase product w sales by x per cent in market y during period z'.

Forecasting

The location of forecasting as a stage in the marketing plan varies according to the type of product (new or existing) and the objectives that have been set (marketing based, e.g. increasing brand awareness, – or financially based, e.g. reducing costs or increasing sales). An existing product can be adapted to a different market, so it is likely here (because of no knowledge of the market) that forecasting will precede the objective-setting stage. If we were considering an existing product and a known market, analysis would have provided sufficient information to permit the setting of objectives. Specific estimates of buyer intentions (i.e. sales forecasting) can then follow.

The total market potential is estimated, then the information is refined into a company sales forecast. Whatever techniques are used, the net result is the company's best estimate of its expected participation in a given market during a given period (usually one year). The sales forecast, combined with marketing objectives, thus becomes the foundation of planning within the company.

CASE 13.3

The New York Times Company forecasts a difficult period ahead in terms of advertising revenue and attempt to plan accordingly.

The New York Times Company, which publishes The New York Times and the Boston Globe newspapers, is facing a difficult period in terms of generating advertising revenues according to its forecasts. A number of factors have affected advertising, even for such publications as these. First, the USA economy was slowing and firms are placing less advertising generally. Second, even before the events in the USA of 11 September 2001, the global advertising market showed signs of weakness. The company has a strong journalistic mission, to which it remains committed despite the fall in revenues. However, forecasts suggest that the advertising environment remains weak and there are many uncertainties which make prediction difficult. The environment is cloudy at present with much uncertainty in the world economy. The company is reacting to the slowdown in advertising by pursuing a systemic cost reduction programme. Overall expenses, including workforce expenses are falling by nearly 5% annually. The group continues to monitor the external environment and tries to produce short, medium and long-term forecasts for advertising spend, though these are difficult under present world conditions.

Budgeting

Once the company has forecast sales, it can allocate resources on anticipated revenue. Marketing objectives can influence resource allocation. Procter & Gamble is known for achieving high market-share through aggressive advertising. The option to inject funds into marketing is important when, for example, the company wishes to transform a 'question mark' SBU into a 'star'. In considering costs of production, distribution and marketing, expenditure should not exceed anticipated revenue. Sometimes finance will not allocate a set amount of money to marketing, but will require a certain level of profit.

How money is then apportioned to individual elements of the marketing mix is the responsibility of marketing. One technique for arriving at the optimum profit level is to forecast the effect of different levels of expenditure on different marketing-mix elements, e.g. operating a high service level will incur high costs, but these may be more than offset by increased sales. There will be a point at which further investment in the level of service is unnecessary and other mix elements assume greater importance. The relationship between marketing and sales is called the 'sales response function'.

Financial resources are always limited and there is pressure on marketing to transform financial resources into profitable results.

Organisation

This is a vital element of the marketing plan. Extra responsibilities are often given to employees without consideration of how this will affect their performance. Similarly, personnel are sometimes 'misplaced' in terms of experience and expertise. The company must consider relationships between departments that might be overstaffed, while others might be under pressure.

Target selection

This involves defining market segments to be approached. It might be that a demographically based segmentation strategy is appropriate, or perhaps behavioural variables such as benefits sought or usage rate might be better.

The marketing mix

When the first five planning stages in Figure 13.10 have been executed, specific marketing strategies can be developed. Each segment should have its own marketing-mix developed within the framework of financial and company resources.

Control

The effectiveness of a marketing mix strategy must be monitored and after a period of time, evaluated and reviewed. This is the control process that considers:

❑ Goals and objectives only have value when translated into action.

❑ Planning is not an end in itself, but a means to an end; the 'end' is the provision of customer satisfaction by a means which provides the company with a profit.

❑ Only if it makes profits, can a company's customers be served and employment maintained.

Figure 13.1 portrayed a simple planning system that can be applied at strategic and operational levels. While we distinguish between these levels, the process is essentially the same for each. Implicit in successful planning is the need to look back with the light of experience so performance can be evaluated and improved. Control systems enable us to find out what has gone wrong and why practice has deviated from the plan.

CASE 13.4

GlaxoSmithKline uses integrated IT systems to control its global operations.

GlaxoSmithKline (GSK) PLC, is a world leading research-based pharmaceutical company with a powerful combination of skills and resources that provides a platform for delivering strong growth in today's rapidly changing healthcare markets. The company has a consumer healthcare portfolio comprising over the counter (OTC) medicines; oral care products and nutritional healthcare drinks, all of which are among the market leaders. GSK has over 100,000 employee's worldwide. Of these 40,000 work in sales and marketing. GSK has 108 manufacturing sites in 41 countries with over 39,000 employees. The sites within the GSK manufacturing network supply products to 140 global markets. The company produces over 1,100 different brands, manufactures 4 billion packs a year and manages about 1,800 new product launches each year. This wide-ranging activity requires sophisticated monitoring and control procedures to keep this global empire running smoothly.

IT is closely integrated with all parts of the company, around the world. It is organised to take best advantage of global scale while supporting GSK people and businesses locally so they have the IT tools they need to succeed. Seven IT departments are integrated within the operating units of GSK. Each ensure that the IT strategy is aligned with operating units. The business units facing integrated IT departments are Consumer, Corporate, Europe Pharmaceuticals, International Pharmaceuticals, Global Manufacture and Supply (GMS), Research and Development, and US Pharmaceuticals. It is through the use of integrated IT systems that GSK is able to run such a sophisticated operation that is truly marketing driven.

Although control procedures are vital to the success of marketing plans, we should not lose sight of the fact that plans are implemented by people. From an organisational point of view, control should be approached with sensitivity. Senior management is ultimately responsible for marketing plans. Managers are also responsible for control procedures. These should be set up with the human factor as a starting point. Managers should attempt to establish a priority of information needs and ascertain minimum rather than maximum requirements. This will mean greater, not less efficiency. At a functional level, marketing personnel often see their role as 'doing' rather than accounting for their activities. The aims of control are often misunderstood. Often, the word is seen as being synonymous with coercion and allocation of blame. Clearly, these are not the objectives. Marketing control is essential as it:

❑   Enables corrections and modifications to be made in response to problems which, if not detected could have serious consequences for the plan.

❑   Provides information that can be used to review at regular intervals (e.g. bi-annually) on how effectively objectives have been implemented. Deviations caused by internal or external forces can be identified and corrected.

❑   Provokes analysis that, in turn, causes opportunities to be identified.

❑   Acts as a motivating force at all levels of operational activity.

Control, therefore, serves to minimise misdirected marketing effort and is concerned with all marketing activity. As well as being a continuous process that permits 'fine tuning' of plans whilst they are being implemented, it involves a review of activity after it has taken place. Usually this is an annual event that allows a company to look objectively at the total value of its efforts.

At an operational level, the company is concerned with the marketing plan. When considering 'what to control', sales, costs and profits are of significance. We must address the reality that marketing costs must not exceed the revenues that sales provide. It is logical to suppose that if each functional activity efficiently achieves its objectives, the net result for the firm would be overall success. However, this is not necessarily true. Often objectives are achieved at cost levels that are disproportionate to the value of the achievement. Annual control of the marketing plan allows the company to consider whether or not its financial resources are being optimised across the marketing mix. In a competitive environment, cost control is usually the key to profitability.

Questions

1. A significant proportion of marketing effort is devoted to satisfying the demands of control systems. How would you justify such a claim on a company's financial and human resources?

2. Differentiate between *corporate goals* and *operational*, or *functional, marketing objectives.* How are these planning activities related?

3. What is the relationship between strategic marketing planning and overall corporate planning?

References

Ansoff, I, (1957) Strategies for diversification, *Harvard Business Review*, September, p.38

Barksdale, HC, and Harris, CE (Jr), (1982) Portfolio analysis and the product life cycle, *Journal of Long Range Planning*, 15, (6)

Hofer, CW, and Schendel, D, *Strategy formulation: analytical concepts*, (West Publishing Company, 1978).

Porter, M, (1980 and 1985), *Competitive Advantage,* (The Free Press, New York).

Further reading

Adcock, D, (2000), *Marketing Strategies for Competitive Advantage*, (John Wiley and Sons ltd.).

Armstrong, G and Kotler, P, (2000), *Marketing an Introduction*, 5th Edition, (Prentice Hall, Inc.).

Bird, D, (1999), *Common Sense Direct Marketing*, (Kogan Page, London).

Blattenberg, RC, Glazer, R, and Little, JDC, eds. (1994), *The Marketing Information Revolution*, (Harvard University Business School Press, Boston).

Blythe, J, (2001), *Essentials of Marketing*, (Pearson Educational Ltd.).

Bolt, GJ, (1981), *Market and Sales Forecasting: a total approach* (Kogan-Page)

Broadbent, S, (1983), *Spending Advertising Money*, (Business Books).

Cateora, PR and Ghauri, PN, (2000), *International Marketing: European Edition*, (McGraw Hill)

Chisnall, PM, (1992), *Marketing Research*, 4th edition, (McGraw-Hill,)

Christopher, M, (1986), *A Strategy of Distribution Management*, (Butterworth-Heinemann, Oxford).

Coulson-Thomas, CJ, (1983), *Marketing Communications*, (Heinemann).

Crimp M, (1992), *The Marketing Research Process*, (Prentice-Hall)

Davies, M, (1998), *Understanding Marketing*, (Prentice Hall)

December, J, and Randall, N, (1996), *The World Wide Web Unleashed*, (Sams Publishing, New York).

Dibb, S, and Simkin, L et al, (1994), *Marketing Concepts and Strategies*, 2nd European edition, (Houghton Mifflin, London).

Hafner, K, and Lyon, M, (1996), *When Wizards Stay Up Late: The Origins of the Internet*, (Simon & Shuster).

Hardaker, G, and Graham, G, (2001), *Wired Marketing: Energising Business for E-Commerce*, (John Wiley and Sons).

Hofer, CW, and Schendel, D, (1978), *Strategy formulation: analytical concepts*, (West Publishing Company).

Hussey, DE, and Langham, MJ, (1979), *Corporate planning - the human factor*, (Pergamon Press).

Keegan, WJ and Green, MS, (2000), *Global Marketing*, 2nd Edition, (Prentice Hall Inc)

Kotler, P, and Andreasen, AR, (1991), *Strategic Marketing for Non-Profit Organisations*, (Prentice-Hall, New Jersey).

Kotler, P, Bowen, J and Makens, J, (1996), *Marketing for Hospitality and Tourism*, (Prentice Hall)

Lancaster, GA, and Lomas, RA, (1985), *Forecasting for Sales and Materials Management*, (Macmillan).

Lancaster, GA and Reynolds, PL, (2002), *Marketing*, (MacMillan Press Ltd)

Lancaster, GA and Reynolds, PL, (1999), *Introduction to Marketing: A Step by Step Guide to All The Tools of Marketing*, (Kogan Page Ltd)

Lancaster G.A, Massingham L.C and Ashford, D, (2002), *Essentials of Marketing: text and cases*, 4th edition, (McGraw-Hill).

MacDonald, M, (1994), *Marketing plans - how to prepare them*, (Heinemann).

Makridakis, S, and Wheelwright, SC, (1978), *Forecasting Methods for Management* (Wiley)

Nickels, W and Burk-Wood, M, (1997), *Marketing, Relationships, Quality, Value*, (Worth Publishers, N.Y.).

O'Malle, L, Paterson, M, and Evans, M, (1999), *Exploring Direct Marketing*, (Thomson, London).

Plamer, A, (2000), *Principles of Marketing*, (Oxford University Press).

Rapp, S, and Collins, T, (1999), *Maximarketing*, (McGraw Hill, New York).

Roberts, ML, and Berger, PD, (1989), *Direct Marketing Management*, (Prentice Hall: Englewood Cliffs, New Jersey, USA).

Rosenbloom, B, (1991) *Marketing Channels: A Management View*, (Dryden Press, Chicago).

Schwartz, EI, (1997), *Webonomics: Nine Essential Principles for Growing Your Business on the World Wide Web*, (Broadway Books, New York).

Soloman, M and Stuart, E, (1997), *Marketing, Real People, Real Choices*, (Prentice Hall, Inc.)

Stapleton, J, (1982), *How to prepare a marketing plan*, (Gower).

Steiner, GA, (1979), *Strategic Planning (what every manager must know)*, (The Free Press).

Stern, LW, and El-Ansary, AI, (2001), *Marketing Channels*, (Prentice Hall, New Jersey).

Index